DATE DUE

AP 16 07			

DEMCO 38-296

The Complete Guide
to Doing Business
in Mexico

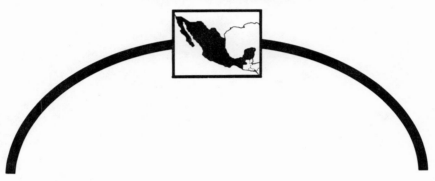

Anita Winsor

The Complete Guide to Doing Business in Mexico

▲ *Business Customs*
▲ *State Profiles*
▲ *The Tax System*
▲ *The Labor Force*
▲ *The Financial System*
▲ *Importing and Exporting Regulations*
▲ *Intellectual Property Protection*
▲ *Establishing a Maquiladora*
▲ *The North American Free Trade Agreement*
▲ *Directory of Resources*

amacom

American Management Association

New York • Atlanta • Boston • Chicago • Kansas City • San Francisco • Washington, D.C.
Brussels • Mexico City • Tokyo • Toronto

This publication is designed to provide accurate and authoritative information in regard to the subject matter covered. It is sold with the understanding that the publisher is not engaged in rendering legal, accounting, or other professional service. If legal advice or other expert assistance is required, the services of a competent professional person should be sought.

Library of Congress Cataloging-in-Publication Data

Winsor, Anita.
   The complete guide to doing business in Mexico / Anita Winsor.
      p.   cm.
   Includes bibliographical references and index.
   ISBN 0-8144-0211-9
      1. United States—Commerce—Mexico.   2. Mexico—Commerce—United States.   3.
Mexico—Commercial policy.   4. Mexico—Economic conditions—1982–   I. Title.
HF3066.W74   1994
658.8'48'0972—dc20   93-30311
                                                                                    CIP

Printing number

10 9 8 7 6 5 4 3 2

Contents

Acknowledgments

The author would like to acknowledge William Edwards; Curtin Winsor, Jr.; Christine Bisho of the J. R. Bisho Co., Inc.; Roger Pardo-Maurer, Judith Rodriguez, Jay Van Heuven, and Brian Marshall of the North American Free Trade Association; and the Embassy of Mexico for their assistance and support.

Foreword

 UNITED STATES-MEXICO CHAMBER OF COMMERCE
1211 CONNECTICUT AVENUE, N.W., SUITE 510
WASHINGTON, D.C. 20036
Telephone (202) 296-5198 — Telefax (202) 822-0075

February 14, 1993

Dear reader:

Since its inception in 1973, the mission of the **United States-Mexico Chamber of Commerce** (USMCOC) has been to cultivate and strengthen the commercial relationship between Mexico and the United States. Established by a group of distinguished Mexican and American businessmen, including Ambassador José Juan de Olloqui, Ambassador from Mexico to the United States during that time, the USMCOC is now in its twentieth year of operation and continues to be a unique **non-profit** business organization 501 (c)(6) which works to promote trade, mutually profitable investment and joint ventures for business interests on both sides of the border. In this regard, the USMCOC assists American and Mexican businesses bridge differences in language, culture, economic and legal systems.

The USMCOC, through our chapters in the Pacific, the Southwest, the Northeast, Washington, D.C. and Mexico City, assists different sectors of industry in each region understand how to do business in Mexico and help them establish contacts that can provide the right channels for their products or services. Presently, the USMCOC is working towards establishing two more chapters in the United States, one in the Mid-West and one in the Southeast, and one in Monterrey, Mexico, as new business opportunities continue to emerge with the rapidly expanding commercial ties between Mexico and the United States, and the potential implementation of a North American Free Trade Agreement (NAFTA).

But perhaps the most fundamental part of doing business in Mexico, is the need for obtaining key information on <u>how</u> to conduct business south of the border. The USMCOC believes this book by Anita Winsor, former Trade Representative of the USMCOC, provides an invaluable resource for understanding not only the economic and cultural peculiarities that American business people will encounter while doing business in the Mexican market, but it provides very practical and pragmatic information for marketing your product in Mexico.

We are sure you will find this book most helpful in developing your business plans in Mexico, and, on behalf of the USMCOC, we wish you success while conducting business across our common borders.

Sincerely,

Albert C. Zapanta
Executive Vice President

Stuart S. Dye
President, D.C. Chapter

Part One
The Mexican Market

The dramatic improvement in the economic climate in Mexico since the crisis of the 1980s has created wide-ranging opportunities for U.S. investors that have not existed since the times of Porfirio Díaz in the latter part of the nineteenth century. The exporter or investor thinking of participating in the modernization of Mexico is looking at a market for 90 million people. Mexico's economy had virtually no economic growth from 1982 to 1988. This was the result of the excesses of extreme state intervention in nearly all areas of production, enormous debt, and a fall in oil prices. Mexico has since endured the pain and risk of transforming its political and economic system into a moderate free-market system. This recovery has led it to a partnership in what will be the world's premier economic alliance, the North American Free Trade Agreement (NAFTA).

The opening of modern Mexico and the creation of NAFTA, as with the formation of the European Economic Community (EEC), have occurred as steps toward the eventual development of an international free trade arrangement, similar to the post–World War II General Agreement on Tariffs and Trade (GATT). Those who would gain from this clear trend in business intercourse would best do so by introducing new ideas and business applications to those countries that will most benefit from the changes. For instance, Mexico shares a 2,000-mile border with the United States; no border on earth separates two more dramatically different economies. Given the nature of free trade, it is therefore probable that no country on earth will expand economically as quickly as post-NAFTA Mexico. The pull of Mexico's growing internal market and the push of U.S. companies that recognize the efficiencies and export advantages accruing from the use of Mexican labor and resources almost guarantee the growth of Mexico and the success of those who attend to it.

Today, as it emerges from years of privation and economic disaster, Mexico is poised for growth. It was the second-largest market for U.S. capital goods in 1992, having just passed Japan in this category, and the United States' third-largest trading partner overall. The growth pattern in this relationship is clear. The United States now enjoys a $5.3 billion trade surplus with Mexico. According to the U.S. Department of Commerce, in 1992 U.S. merchandise exports to Mexico reached a record high $40.6 billion, climbing significantly from 1989, when merchandise exports were valued at $24.9 billion. Banco de México reports a 144 percent increase in U.S. service exports to Mexico since 1986. These exports were valued at $8.3 billion in 1991.

The opportunities created by a receptive Mexican government are epochal. Mexican president Carlos Salinas de Gortari has taken unprecedented steps to deregulate formerly protected and restricted areas of opportunity in the Mexican economy. The laws have been changed particularly to benefit U.S. exporters. The number of products requiring Mexican import licenses has been slashed, as have tariff rates. Nowhere is Mexico's determination to open itself to competitive industry more evident than in the fields of telecommunications, infrastructure, new technologies, and computer capability. Over two thirds of the Mexican gross domestic product (GDP) is now unrestricted to foreign investment. Many such areas, including tourism, manufacturing, and electronics, are open to 100 percent foreign ownership without Mexican government authorization. Many Mexican companies and industries are actively seeking U.S. partners in joint ventures and trade partnerships.

This book is intended as a resource and guide for Americans who recognize today's Mexico as a unique opportunity and wish to become a part of this remarkable situation. This is not to say that Mexico or Mexicans will be exploited by this arrangement. The future demanded by Mexico's leaders and people will feature a free market constrained by sensible regulation and powered by a huge population whose standard of living can only rise—dramatically—well into the twenty-first century.

1

Mexico: An Overview of the Nation

Geography and Climate

Mexico covers 764,000 square miles, making it roughly three times the size of Texas and the thirteenth-largest country in the world. It is the third-largest country in Latin America, after Brazil and Argentina. The majority of its territory is a highland plateau bordered by mountains on all sides except the north.

Nearly half of Mexico, particularly in the north, is semiarid or arid, with rainfall increasing toward the south. The Atlantic coastal region is humid and tropical. The rainy season usually begins in May and lasts through December. The average temperature in Mexico City is 63°F (17°C), occasionally falling as low as 25°F (-4°C) in December and January and rising as high as 90°F (32°C) in May.

Population

Mexico's population in 1992 was estimated at 86 million, with an annual growth rate of 2.3 percent. It is a young country, with 57 percent of the population under age 29. Ethnic breakdowns reveal that 60 percent are Indian-Spanish (mestizo), 30 percent American Indian, 9 percent Caucasian, and one percent from other backgrounds. The infant mortality rate is 32 per 1,000, and the average life expectancy is seventy-two years for women and sixty-eight years for men.

The average population density is 42 inhabitants per square kilometer (110 per square mile). Over 60 percent of the population lives in urban areas, and a steady stream of migration to cities from rural areas continues. Mexico City has the largest population (18.6 million), followed by Guadalajara (3.1 million) and Monterrey (2.7 million). Federal and local government programs are aimed at decentralization to promote increasing growth in other geographical areas.

Government

Mexico is a federal democratic republic divided into thirty-one states and the Federal District (Mexico City). Its constitution separates powers into an executive,

legislative, and judicial branch. The executive branch is represented by a popu-
larly elected president who serves as chief of state for one six-year term and is not
eligible for reelection. There is no vice-president, so in the event of the president's
removal or death, the congress elects a provisional president. The president exe-
cutes the laws of the congress and has very broad additional powers delegated
from the congress to legislate in certain economic and financial fields.

Mexico's bicameral congressional branch legislates on all issues relevant to
the national government. It is composed of an upper house of sixty-four senators
and a lower house of five hundred deputies. Two senators are elected from each
state to serve six-year terms and cannot be reelected. Three hundred deputies
represent single-member districts through direct popular vote. An additional two
hundred deputies are chosen by a modified form of proportional representation
to give the opposition parties a stronger opportunity to participate.

The judiciary consists of the supreme, federal, and state court systems. Supreme court justices are appointed by the president. Most civil cases go to federal
court. Nearly all cases are tried by a judge instead of a jury. Mexico's legal system
is based on the Napoleonic code. Foreign investment regulation, corporate law,
and intellectual property protection are considered federal responsibilities.

The Mexican constitution demands that trial and sentencing be finished
within twelve months after the arrest for all crimes that carry a sentence of at
least two years. Defendants are protected against self-incrimination and have a
right to face their accusers. All defendants are entitled to legal assistance and may
use public defendants.

Political Situation

President Carlos Salinas de Gortari began his six-year term on December 1, 1988.
He is a member of the Institutional Revolutionary Party (PRI) and earned an
advanced degree from Harvard University. Salinas and many members of his cabinet are trained economist-technocrats who, unlike the predecessor adminis-
trations, favor private enterprise and market-oriented economic policies over
socialization and state-controlled industry. The Salinas administration has focused on reducing inflation and lowering foreign debt; it has been successful in
its efforts by executing strict monetary control. Salinas has been a strong sup-
porter of a free trade agreement with the United States and Canada and has
maintained close relations with both countries.

The PRI has controlled the Mexican government for over sixty years. After
the 1988 federal elections, other political parties had an unprecedented victory of
increased congressional representation, but in August 1991, the PRI returned with
a strong victory in the Chamber of Deputies and in five gubernatorial elections.
The PRI remains in power through broad government and party organizational
resources and the extensive use of patronage.

Mexico's other registered political parties are the National Action Party
(PAN), the Authentic Party of the Mexican Revolution (PARM), the People of the
Cardenist Front for National Reconstruction (PFCRN), the People's Socialist Party
(PPS), the Mexican Democratic Party (PDM), the Revolutionary Workers Party

(PRT), the Mexican Ecological Party (PEM), and the Party of the Democratic Revolution (PRD).

Education

Mexico's literacy rate is 88 percent. Free education is provided for six years of primary and three years of secondary school. The level and quality of education vary throughout the country, however, and are usually lower in the rural states, such as Chiapas, Oaxaca, and Zacatecas. Three of the largest universities are also federally funded, and tuition is available at a low price. The National Commission on Foreign Investment assists investors who are considering developing technical training programs.

All companies are legally required to provide some technical or professional training for all their employees. This training can take place at the workplace or at one of Mexico's many technical schools located throughout the country.

Language

Spanish is Mexico's national language, but it is common for Mexicans to also speak English in the larger urban areas and along the U.S. border. It is important that all technical information and catalogs include a Spanish translation.

Religion

Catholicism is the religious affiliation of 97 percent of the population. Several religious holidays are observed by businesses.

Holidays

The following dates are national holidays:

January 1	New Year
February 5	Constitution Day
March 21	Juarez's Birthday
March/April	Holy Thursday and Good Friday
May 1	Labor Day
May 5	Battle of Puebla Anniversary
September 16	Mexican Independence Day
October 12	Columbus Day
November 2	All Saints' Day
November 20	Revolution Day
December 25	Christmas Day

Religious holidays are usually observed by most department stores, banks, and business offices. These holidays are the Thursday and Friday of Easter week, November 1 and 2, and December 12.

Time and Dates

Mexico follows central standard time with the exception of Baja California, Nayarit, Sonora, and Sinaloa. These all follow Pacific standard time. Mexico does not observe daylight saving time. Unlike in the United States, when a date is written, the day is placed before the month, and Roman numerals are sometimes used in writing the month (for example, the 27th of November, 1964, or 27/XI/1964).

Agriculture

U.S. Exports

Since 1987, Mexico has been the most rapidly growing market for U.S. agricultural exports, as exports have nearly tripled. U.S. agricultural exports to Mexico in 1992 were estimated to be valued at $4 billion, rising from their 1991 value of $2.9 billion. Agricultural trade between the two countries is expected to double by the year 2000, with or without a free trade agreement.

Mexico still relies on U.S. exports for traditional bulk products, including corn, wheat, sorghum, soybeans, and animal fats. Other prominent agricultural imports include live animals (including poultry), animal by-products, oilseeds, and dairy products. U.S. high-value exports, including processed foods, frozen foods, and wine, are increasing.

Livestock. Mexico is the third-largest market for U.S. beef exports. In 1991, the United States exported over $360 million in meat and animal fat, $230 million in dairy products, and $110 million in cattle and livestock.

There have been some complaints from U.S. livestock exporters about restrictive regulations in Nuevo León requiring that all beef be graded by the carcass. There have also been U.S. lobbying efforts to stop U.S. beef from being graded "commercial," the lowest quality. Some U.S. exporters also complain that Mexico has excessive import regulations on dairy products.

Another area of dispute has been over U.S. hog exports, which carry the maximum 20 percent tariff; both the United States and Mexico have barred pork exports from each other, citing disease control.

Markets. According to the U.S. Department of Agriculture (USDA), there are four basic "food markets" in Mexico; in order of significance they are Mexico City, Guadalajara, Monterrey, and all of rural Mexico. The majority of food is consumed by Mexico City's enormous population and is purchased from several hundred outlets of seven major supermarkets: Cifra, Superama, Gigante, Almacenes Aurrera, Bodegaurrera, Centro Comercial de Todo, and Comercial Mexicana. These supermarkets are similar to Wal-Mart in the United States and also feature non-food items. Several thousand neighborhood corner food stores (*tiendas*) also offer limited amounts of imported foods.

Mexico's Agricultural Harvest

Mexico's agricultural sector was responsible for roughly 10 percent of the nation's GDP in 1992 and for the employment of approximately 30 percent of the labor force. Its most important crops are dry beans, rice, sorghum, corn, wheat, sesame, cotton, safflower, soybeans, and barley, though a 1990 reduction in subsidies caused a dramatic decrease in rice and soybean production. Mexico is the world's largest avocado producer and the fourth-largest coffee producer. Egg and honey production are important economic activities in many of the states.

Agrarian Reform: Ejidos

Mexico's agricultural production began to increase in 1990 after several years of decline. This improvement was the result of better planning, improved weather, plant health control, technical assistance, and financing. The Mexican government is finally reforming its antiquated agricultural system. Nearly 60 percent of all farmland belongs to the inefficient *ejidos,* semicommunally owned farms that are heavily subsidized and have scant production. A 1991 constitutional amendment allows the peasants to own some of the communal land and to use their titles as collateral. In 1992, the *ejido* system was further reformed so that qualified communal land dwellers could own up to 100 irrigated or 200 nonirrigated acres. Further reforms are also expected to eliminate restrictions on how land is used and to permit corporations to purchase land.

The Secretariat of Agriculture and Hydraulic Resources (SARH) is encouraging joint ventures between multinational companies and the *ejidos,* with the hope that the joint ventures will bring needed funds and incentives for efficiency to the farms. SARH recorded 140 ventures by mid-1992.

Price Control. The Mexican government will probably replace price supports for maize, the largest product produced by the *ejidos,* with income supports. The price is currently fixed above the international standard, and maize imports are restricted to the difference between domestic demand and supply at this fixed price.

Anticipated Effects of the North American Free Trade Agreement on Agriculture

Immediately after the North American Free Trade Agreement (NAFTA) begins, 50 percent of the U.S. agricultural products will enter Mexico duty-free. After ten years, 95 percent of U.S. agricultural products will enter duty-free. Tariffs on corn and beans will be phased out after fifteen years. When NAFTA is fully implemented, officials from the USDA estimate that there will be a $1.5 billion to $2 billion annual increase in U.S. agricultural exports to Mexico.

Inevitably, some segments of the agricultural industry will do better than others. There will be a safeguard to protect U.S. farmers from seasonal import surges. Tariff rate quotas (TRQs) for some Mexican agricultural exports, including orange juice, onions, watermelon, squash, peppers, eggplant, and tomatoes, will be permitted during a ten-year transition phase. The United States will exclude Mexico from Section 22, a regulation that places quotas on peanut, sugar, cotton, and dairy imports during import surges. When the United States drops its sugar import quota for Mexico, it will modify third-country quotas to preserve overall sugar import limits.

Horticulture. Horticultural exports from the United States to Mexico, which quadrupled from 1986 to 1991, rising from $47 million to $209 million, are expected to increase under NAFTA. U.S. exports of peaches, apples, and pears to Mexico are expected to rise 50 percent. On the downside, citrus fruits in the United States will probably be hurt by Mexican imports.

Grain. U.S. grain and oilseed exports to Mexico were valued at $1.3 billion in 1991. Under NAFTA, import-licensing requirements for wheat and corn will be removed immediately, and licensing requirements for oilseeds, oilseed products, rice, and other grains will be removed within ten to fifteen years.

Dairy and Poultry. U.S. poultry exports to Mexico grew from $16 million in 1987 to $110 million in 1991. Licensing requirements for poultry, eggs, cheese, and nonfat dry milk will be eliminated immediately under NAFTA, so exports are expected to increase further. Other trade barriers in these sectors will be removed within ten to fifteen years.

Livestock. NAFTA will maintain the duty-free access that the United States has to the Mexican market for cattle and beef. Remaining Mexican tariffs on U.S. livestock will be eliminated within ten years.

Agricultural Standards. Under NAFTA, the United States will maintain its same high standards for health and safety on all agricultural imports. Individual states will be permitted to set their own standards, which may be even stricter than national standards. All shipments will be tested at the border, and unsuitable products will be prevented from entering. Agricultural imports from regions that carry disease and pests will not be permitted to enter the United States.

Aquaculture

Mexico is a major seafood harvester with an 11,900-mile coastline, but the quality of its marine infrastructure varies greatly in different regions. Mexico's catch is roughly 1.5 million tons per year, with nearly 75 percent coming from harbors in Sonora and Sinaloa on the Pacific coast.

Tuna exportation to the United States continues to be disputed because the United States has placed a ban on all tuna caught without a dolphin-safe net; Mexican tuna does not qualify. The export of shrimp from Mexico to the United

States may soon be disputed because the Mexicans harvest shrimp in a manner that may be harmful to sea turtles.

Aquaculture continues to improve with particularly successful harvests of freshwater bass, carp, and oysters, which accounted for 87 percent of the production in this sector in 1990.

Forestry

Mexico's timber production since 1988 has declined from 90 percent to 60 percent of the lumber consumed domestically. It accounts for 1.4 percent of the GNP. Mexico has abundant timber resources, but it must still improve its infrastructure (road construction and lumber transportation) for a more efficient harvest in unexploited regions. There is currently a large market for forestry and woodworking machinery including saws and sawing machines; planers, jointers, shapers, and lathes; and planning and surfacing machines. The Secretariat of Agriculture and Hydraulic Resources (SARH) and several international development banks are making investments to tap the forestry sector. The World Bank is currently developing the timber industry in Chihuahua and Durango. Among other improvements, the bank is enhancing the states' infrastructure, introducing better technology, and providing increased training. The forestry sector will also be affected by ongoing tariff reductions and changes in the *ejido* laws that will lessen land restrictions.

Energy

Mexico is expected to need investments valued at $20 billion to $30 billion by the year 2000 to upgrade its energy sector.[1] The United States is in a prime position to continue as Mexico's greatest supplier of energy equipment and service, particularly with a free trade agreement, which would open greater public-sector market opportunities. Under NAFTA, Mexico is to follow the General Agreement on Tariffs and Trade (GATT) principles for energy trade.

Electric Power

Mexico has a tremendous market for energy and good resources to generate it. This sector has recently opened significantly to foreign participation, but the Mexican constitution requires that the government maintain exclusive rights to generate, transmit, and distribute energy. Under the Regulations of the Law to Promote Mexican Investment and Regulate Foreign Investment (May 1989), international companies are permitted to own electric facilities and lease them to the Mexican government. International electric companies (including Spain's Mecanica and France's Ahistrom) are constructing power plants and leasing them to the state-owned Federal Electricity Commission (CFE). A new regulation also allows companies to sell excess power to the CFE.

Total installed capacity for electric-power generation in 1990 was 25,299 megawatts. Hydroelectric, steam, and turbogas power account for most of this production.

Under the National Solidarity Program, the government and international development banks brought 3,500 communities into the electric power system between 1988 and 1990, providing electricity to an estimated five million people. These efforts were concentrated in Mexico, Chiapas, Oaxaca, and Guanajuato.

Under NAFTA. Under NAFTA, U.S. and Canadian companies will be permitted to arrange cross-border supply contracts with the CFE and independent Mexican power producers. All sales would have to be on a nondiscriminatory basis and may be arranged directly with the buyers.

U.S. and Canadian investors will be permitted to build, own, and operate cogeneration stations and independent power plants in Mexico.

Petroleum

Mexico has the fourth-largest oil reserves in the world and is the sixth-largest oil producer. The petroleum industry belongs to Petroleos Mexicanos (PEMEX), a huge state entity which has a monopoly protected by the Mexican constitution. It was recently restructured into four subsidiaries: PEMEX Production, PEMEX Refining, PEMEX Gas, and PEMEX Petrochemicals. Approximately 2.5 million to 2.7 million barrels of oil are produced daily, and over 40 percent is exported as crude oil. PEMEX International (PMI) is the entity that promotes investment and trade. Mexico exported petroleum valued at $4 billion in 1991, primarily to Spain, Japan, and the United States, generating 34 percent of its foreign exchange.

According to PEMEX, Mexico still needs approximately $1.7 billion to construct twenty-one petrochemical plants that were planned over a decade ago. Even though PEMEX earned more than $10.5 billion in gross profits for 1991 (56.5 percent revenues), most of this profit is given to the government, leaving very little to reinvest. The Mexican government has also calculated that an additional $20 billion will be needed through 1995 to maintain export levels as the domestic demand rises. PEMEX is hoping to raise $400 million to $500 million annually through factoring contracts based on future oil sales. Those sales will be decided on a nondiscriminatory basis.

PEMEX had contracts with foreign drillers for the first time in 1991. U.S. and Canadian companies were granted contracts for oil exploration and were given a bonus if they struck oil.

Under NAFTA. U.S. suppliers of natural gas would be permitted to have contracts directly with Mexican consumers.

Petrochemicals

Mexico is the largest petrochemical producer in Latin America. Its petrochemical production includes ammonium, ethane, ethylene, and carbonic, anhydrous, and high-density polyethylene. In 1989, Mexico changed its classification system to allow private-sector participation in nearly all petrochemical derivatives. PEMEX exclusively handles the first transformation from hydrocarbons, but the second transformation may now be handled by the private sector, with up to 40 percent foreign participation. These secondary products include ethylene oxide, polypropylene, ethyl benzene, and styrene. A new system of temporary trust funds allows foreigners to participate with majority capital investment in secondary petrochemicals. PEMEX has announced that it will soon open up four fifths of the petrochemical industry to foreign investment.

Under NAFTA. Under NAFTA, all investment restrictions would be immediately abolished for fourteen of the nineteen restricted basic petrochemicals and sixty-six secondary petrochemicals. Import and export licenses would be eliminated immediately on all petrochemicals except five "basic" ones.

Coal

A representative from Mexico's Federal Electricity Commission (CFE) announced at a North American Free Trade Association conference that Mexico plans to become one of the world's largest importers of coal to make the nation less dependent on its limited oil production capacity. Coal is also considered to be nearly 80 percent less polluting than petroleum with the help of new technologies available on the market that offer precombustion, postcombustion, and cleaner power generation and conversion.

The federal government stopped supporting the state mining commission and will soon open the nation's coal industry to private investment. The CFE is encouraging coal importation because Mexico's supply is limited. The government is hoping to quadruple coal consumption by the year 2000 and to rely on twelve new power plants fueled by coal.

Natural Gas

Natural gas exports to Mexico significantly increased in 1991, and this trend is expected to continue. According to one PEMEX official, Mexico's natural gas imports have already grown from a level of 43.4 million cubic feet per day in 1990 to 300 million cubic feet per day during the first half of this year. Plans for the next two years call for further increases with daily imports totaling 600 million cubic feet for the first year and 800 million cubic feet during the second.[2]

The new demand is attributed to an aggressive government environmental program that is encouraging companies to reduce pollution by using natural gas instead of high-sulfur fuel. PEMEX officials reportedly expect that all northern Mexico will be using natural gas by the end of 1994 and that the domestic resources will not be adequate to meet demand. Among projects anticipated are the conversion to gas usage of the Roarito electricity-generating plant in Baja California Norte and the Samalayuca plant in Chihuahua.[3] Since Mexico lacks the efficient infrastructure needed for natural gas, there is also demand for an improved pipeline system.

Minerals

Mexico is one of the world's major producers of raw materials. It is the world's largest supplier of silver, fluorite, and sodium sulfate; the second-largest supplier of graphite and bismuth; the third-largest supplier of arsenic, sulfur, and antimony; and the fourth-largest supplier of zinc, lead, and mercury. Copper deposits produce an estimated 280,000 tons annually.

Many areas are rich in minerals that have not yet been exploited. Mexican mining companies are expected to invest $2.1 billion in exploration and development (more than double the investment of the last five years).

The government's Modernization Program for the Mining Industry (1990–1994) is aiming for a growth figure of 5 percent per year, and the mining sector has been significantly deregulated to attract investment. All production taxes have been abolished, and royalty payments are now regulated. Mining reserves that were previously managed by the government have been released for private investment. In addition, legal, administrative, and concession requirements have been streamlined. Also, foreign investment is now free of heavy restrictions except in the oil and uranium sectors, and foreigners may now have voting rights in ventures.

The Mexican government still does not permit private ownership of subsoil, but renewable concessions for subsoil exploitation are now available for up to fifty years, and the concessions' taxes will be phased out in 1995.

Principal Industrial Centers

The strongest concentrations of industrial activity are in Mexico City, Guadalajara, and Monterrey, but with the encouragement of government incentives, new industrial zones are being developed in medium-size cities, including Hermosillo, Aguascalientes, and San Luis Potosí.

Infrastructure/Transportation

The Mexican government recognizes that the poor condition of its public infrastructure is retarding the country's economic growth. Since public expenditure is being restricted, the Secretariat of Communications and Transportation (SCT) has begun opening up inefficient public property to the private sector for capital investment and services. Private companies may lease the public property for a limited period of time and return it to the government in improved condition. Limited foreign involvement is permitted for leasing and service contracts. Particular focus is placed on building and operating road, sewage, and water systems.

Highways

The condition of Mexico's roads varies widely. According to the Mexican Agenda, published by the Mexican presidency in July 1991, only 35 percent of the roads are paved, and 50 percent are surfaced. Private contractors have been hired to build or rebuild and operate toll roads and four-lane highways and return the concession to the government in less than twenty years. Usually the concession is given to the group that offers to return the road to the public sector in the shortest time.

Trucking is still the predominant method of cargo transport and is responsible for moving 80 percent of the merchandise traded between the United States and Mexico. However, this system is far from efficient. Trucking companies blame the poor quality of the road system for delaying delivery schedules and damaging trucks. Other problems include lack of enforcement of load limits, which contributes to highway deterioration, and improper traffic control, which often leads to delays. Although interest rates are lower and credit is easier to get than during the 1980s, backlogs and high prices still prevent many trucking companies from updating their outmoded fleet. Some U.S. and Mexican trucking companies have arrangements whereby only the tractor is exchanged at the border without having to unload and reload the trailers, significantly reducing delivery time.

The SCT has deregulated surface cargo transportation, but service is still poor. Route requirements, exclusive cargo specifications, and "radius of action" have been eliminated. Over 100,000 new carrier permits have been issued since 1989. These reforms have caused a slight improvement in service and have broken up the trucking "mafia" that set prices and monopolized routes. Although the rate system has been deregulated, many shippers have yet to find lower rates, and in some cases they are actually higher. Freight rates are divided into the following five categories, in decreasing order of price: (1) liquids, chemicals, explosives, (2) glass containers, flasks, bottles, (3) canned products, (4) packages, and (5) bulk goods.

The overland transportation permit and concessions system has been computerized, reducing the required time for official arrangements and responses to inquiries. The road system has been decentralized, and the SCT now has the authority to grant permission for loading and off-loading in federal land zones.

Under NAFTA. Under NAFTA, U.S. haulers will be permitted to carry international cargo to all Mexican states bordering the United States by 1995. U.S. haulers will have access to all of Mexico by 1999. U.S. and Mexican haulers are currently restricted from going into each other's territory. Mexican carriers will also be allowed to use leased vehicles.

NAFTA negotiations have resulted in a six-year compatibility transition to establish mutual technical and safety codes. North American countries would recognize driver's licenses issued by the other countries and have agreed to provide minimum certification and exchange information on license suspensions.

U.S. charter and tour bus services would have full and immediate access to the cross-border market. Regular U.S. bus route companies would have full access to Mexico within five years.

U.S. bus and trucking companies will be permitted to set up new companies, warehouses, intermodal terminals, and international cargo subsidiaries in Mexico and have minority ownership by the end of 1995, majority ownership by the year 2000, and 100 percent ownership by 2003.

Railways

The Mexican railway system is fully operated by the public Ferrocarriles Nacionales de Mexico (National Mexican Railroads) on approximately 7,060 miles of railroad. This system has proved to be inefficient and is used for both cargo and passengers where speed of delivery is not a high priority. The Salinas administration formalized reforms under the title The Concerted Action for the Railroad System's Total Modernization and is committed to updating the system, trimming the operating company's size, and making the railroads more competitive under the free trade agreement. Ferronales (the abbreviated name) is investing $250 million between 1992 and 1995 to double the amount of computer-operated track. The computerized system was sold to the Mexican government by Union Pacific Technologies, a subsidiary of Union Pacific Railroad. Under the new system currently being implemented, computers will control movements between stations and between moving trains and stations. The system will control cargo movements in important distribution points, assign crews, and locate rolling stock. Primary users will be able to access the system directly to locate their cargo. This improvement is expected to expedite transportation between Mexico City, major ports, and the U.S. border. An intermodal system allowing trailers to be moved by railroad and then by truck is growing at a rapid rate.

Major U.S. railroads, including Santa Fe Pacific, Southern Pacific, Texas-Mexican, and Union Pacific, have direct track connections with Ferronales.

The Mexican government is encouraging private investment in railroad-related services. A new company called Ferropuertos S. A. de C. V. will perform loading and unloading services for truck and rail carriers in northern Mexico. The company is constructing four "ferroports" in Torreón, Coahuila, to service General Motors' *maquiladoras* (assembly plants). Union Pacific, GM, and Presidential Lines have constructed a $3.5 million loading facility in Ramos Arizpe, Coahuila, to handle more than fifty containers daily. Other private companies are building grain elevators to service the trains. Eventually, Ferronales will only be responsible for maintaining the locomotives and tracks.

The Pantaco Terminal in Mexico, D. F., is undergoing reconstruction to be used exclusively for double-stack trains. Currently, double-stack trains arrive daily in Mexico, D. F., via the Laredo-Monterrey route and through New Mexico and El Paso on shorter runs.

Other developments include a new fast track between Monterrey in northeast Mexico and Guadalajara on the Pacific coast. Ferronales is receiving a portion of a $2 billion budget for a twenty-year-old government electrification project between Mexico, D. F., and Querétaro, a growing agroindustrial center in northern Mexico.

Piggyback service already serves up to fifty locations throughout Mexico. The railways also serve seven ports of entry where U.S. railways make connections. The American lines linking these ports are the Southern Pacific, Union Pacific, Atchison Topeka & Santa Fe, and the Texas-Mexican railways. Double-loading is offered twice a week from Long Beach, California, to Mexico City and through El Paso-Juarez and Monterrey, reducing delivery time from twenty-four to fourteen days.

Under NAFTA. NAFTA would allow U.S. rail and intermodal companies to own and run their own terminals. It would also enable them to market their services directly to Mexican clients and to run their trains on Mexican tracks.

Air Transportation

Mexico has a sophisticated, comprehensive air transportation system. All communities with populations over 50,000 are served by at least one of Mexico's many airports. Mexico has forty-two international airports, forty national airports, and more than two thousand registered landing fields. Aeropuertos y Servicios Auxiliares, a state-owned enterprise, manages fifty-seven of Mexico's airports. It is possible to fly directly from the United States to many cities in Mexico, including Mexico City, Guadalajara, Monterrey, and Mérida.

At present, Mexico has forty-seven national airlines, including the recently privatized AeroMéxico and Mexicana. There are eleven feeder lines, thirty-four regional lines, and thirty-one foreign airlines with regular flights to Mexico.

There are several national and international air freight services available to U.S. exporters and importers. Major U.S. services include DHL, United Parcel Service, and Federal Express. Less than 5 percent of all goods traded between the United States and Mexico are exchanged via air cargo because of the high price.

Sea Transportation

Maritime transportation moves roughly 375,000 containers annually from one of Mexico's seventeen major seaports. Six of these ports are on the Pacific Ocean: Mazatlán, Puerto Vallarta, Manzanillo, Lázaro Cárdenas, Acapulco, and Salina Cruz. Nine are on the Gulf of Mexico: Tampico, Tuxpan, Veracruz, Coatzacoalcos, Ciudad del Carmen, Altamira, Campeche, Progreso, and Chetumal. La Paz and Topolobampo are on the Gulf of California.

The Mexican government's port development program is significantly improving Mexico's seaports through better infrastructure and equipment and the privatization of port operations. Mexico is realizing this progress through the assistance of the World Bank and private companies. According to Puertos Mexicanos, the national port authority, in 1991 productivity in specialized container terminals increased 100 percent and productivity in the semimechanized handling of bulk agricultural goods increased 50 percent.

Improved infrastructure has enabled Mexico to use a multimodal transport system at most major ports. Container cargo in Mexico's Pacific ports increased 31 percent in 1991. Infrastructure improvements include eight new gantry-type cranes from Azzaldo of Italy and Barelha of Brazil and sixteen backup cranes from Marathon of the United States and Mitsui de España. This equipment will be used at Manzanillo and Lázaro Cárdenas, on the Pacific and Altamira and Veracruz on the Gulf.

Gulf of Mexico Ports

▪ *Veracruz:* In July and August 1991, the government staged a sixty-day takeover, canceling all contracts with the four unions that were running the port. These unions were notoriously inefficient and corrupt and were replaced with three companies. Transportación Maritima Mexicana (TMM), Mexico's largest shipping line, is using its own employees to manage shipping traffic; Astilleros Unidos de Veracruz is installing three new dry docks; and Sokana, a Dutch company, has bought out Mexico's largest shipping yard. Capacity has increased 200 percent with two new container cranes and several pouch cranes.

- *Frontera:* The World Bank is expected to give a $65 million credit to transform a small fishing port on the Tabasco-Campeche border into a large deepwater port for the area's increasing banana exports. This area is attracting European investors for the development of cash crops in a nine-month period. With new technology, box plants have been built in the same zone, eliminating the need for ripening in gas chambers on the receiving end.

- *Tuxpan:* Tuxpan is often used as an alternative to Veracruz, particularly to import car components and parts. It is currently being dredged to eleven meters so larger vessels can enter.

- *Altamira:* A third landing dock, with vertical cranes, is being constructed to keep up with the high level of industrial development. Quimica Hoechst, the Mexican affiliate of the German chemical company, is constructing a $300 million export facility in an adjoining industrial park. Mexinox, a Mexican stainless steel company, is constructing a $100 million plant in this same area. De Acero, a Mexican steel-producing company, is also building a $150 million plant here.

Pacific Ports

- *Topolobampo:* This new port will be receiving more traffic when the Janson Company of Taiwan installs a *maquiladora* in the industrial park that adjoins the port. A U.S. potato-processing company and a Taiwanese fish-processing company have made similar commitments in the same zone. This deepwater port has served as a fuel deposit depot for PEMEX. It is linked to a lagoon that enables merchandise to be transferred from the port docks by water.

- *Lázaro Cárdenas:* This port installed a grain elevator in 1991 with an 80,000-ton capacity and the ability to load 600 tons per hour. Container cargo increased 49.8 percent in one year.

- *Salina Cruz:* PEMEX is being backed by Japanese credits to install a new twelve-inch pipeline linking Salina Cruz with the oil production zones on the Gulf of Mexico. This will allow PEMEX to export liquid gas and ammonia to the Far East and Western markets. It has already built a refinery and compression unit here.

- *Manzanillo:* A covered container patio is being completed, with a new Mitsubishi power plant alongside. The plant is being built on a lease basis to provide electricity to a growing number of seafood- and cirtus-processing plants being constructed nearby.

- *Enseñada:* In 1991, container cargo increased 60.1 percent. TMM (the country's largest shipping line) is transporting approximately 800 containers per month in its all-water ferry service between Long Beach and the *maquiladoras* in Mexico. TMM is using an $838 million credit from the Mexican Foreign Trade Bank (also referred to as BANCOMEXT, or the Mexican Trade Commission) to purchase five new Japanese-made container ships. TMM has also ordered 8,000 new containers on a medium-term basis and is looking for more funding to buy five used grain carriers and three automobile carriers to service Nissan de Mexico. It is also building a warehouse in Manzanillo for bulk shipments of liquids and chemicals.

- *Guaymas:* Cementos Mexicanos (CEMEX) is constructing a cement-loading facility for exports to Japan and Korea.

Communications

The Morelos Satellite System

Mexico launched its Morelos Satellite System (MSS) in 1985, enabling it to reach its entire territory with television broadcasting, data transmission, and telephone signals. MSS is a government project administered by the Secretariat of Communications and Transportation (SCT) and Comsat General, a U.S. consulting company. The system consists of two identical satellites each having twenty-two transponders and using two frequency bands: the Ku ($^{14}/12$ gigahertz) transponders, which produce 44 decibel-watt signals, and the 18 C ($^6/4$ gigahertz) transponders, which produce 35.5 and 38.5 decibel-watt signals. The satellites' total capacity is great enough for 60 million data transmission bits per second, 32,000 telephone channels, or 32 television channels. Morelos II began operation in 1991 and is expected to last until 1999. It was joined by the Solidaridad I satellite system in late 1993.

Private enterprises used 70 percent of the Morelos I satellite system in 1990. The satellite carried 12 international earth stations and 239 local stations, but had a capacity for 573 operated telephone channels, 525 telex channels, and 5 video channels. It provided telephone service for twenty-seven countries. Mexico is a member of the International Telecommunications Satellite Consortium (INTELSAT).

Public Communication Services

Public communication services are provided by the General Office of Telecommunications (DGT), a department in the SCT, and Telefonos de México (TELMEX). All regulations in telecommunications are established at the SCT, which is also responsible for the transmission of TV signals (microwave, cable, and satellite) and the transmission of radio signals for commercial radio stations. SCT also provides international and domestic telegraph services, public and private data transmission networks, and fax, telex, and telephotography services. TELMEX has a monopoly on the telephone system until the end of 1994.

SCT grants concessions for public telephone service, mobile radio telephones, ordinary radio telephones, and radio and television broadcasting. It issues permits for amateur radio, broadcasting network expansion, private radio telephone systems, mobile aeronautic radio, citizens band radio, private data communications services, TV stations, remote mobile radio transmitters, and mobile marine radio.

Telephones

TELMEX was privatized in 1991 and now belongs to a private Mexican investment group, Southwestern Bell, and France Telecom. It was granted a monopoly concession for the national telephone system until the end of 1994. This agreement requires that TELMEX modernize the telephone system, and it has allotted $12.8 billion to do this. In March 1992, Mexico had over 6 million telephone lines. Under the privatization agreement, TELMEX is expected to increase the number of telephone subscribers to 8.3 million lines by 1994. It will also improve the infrastructure to reach a capacity for handling 1,890 million long-distance calls. TELMEX will use a new technology called multiple access radio to extend telephone coverage to all villages with more than 500 residents (a 186 percent increase in the number of villages currently with phone systems). It is also expected to expand telephone density from the ratio of 5 telephone lines per 100 inhabitants in 1988 to 8.6 in 1994. TELMEX has been installing digital lines and is installing 8,388 miles of fiber optic lines. It is installing the Integrated Service Digital Network (ISDN), which offers such services as a triplex function (party line with independent access) for low-income areas, the digital Federal Microwave Network in its Mexico City-Guadalajara and Mexico City-Monterrey trunk lines, facilities for toll-free call service, and value-added features. By the end of 1994, digital infiltration is expected to increase by 64 percent.

Telecommunications exports will be in great demand during this modernization period. U.S. telecommunications exports had an estimated value of $360.4 million in 1992, with an estimated annual growth rate of 10 percent.

Radio and Television

Mexico's television and radio networks cover the entire country. There were more than 1,500 broadcasting companies in 1990, including amateur and citizens band radio, data communications, television, and mobile radio telephone. There were 2,283 radio stations (11 owned by permit holders and 2,272 under concession). There were 580 television channels: 229 under concession, 333 with permits, 115 cable, 25 complimentary, and one controlled by the state.

The government recently deregulated the communications sector, removing authorization requirements to install and operate a private radio communications network. A permit and authorization for frequencies are also no longer required.

International Affiliations

Mexico is an active participant of the General Agreement on Tariffs and Trade (GATT), the Latin American Integration Association (ALADI), the International Monetary Fund (IMF), the United Nations and its affiliate agencies, the World Bank, the Inter-American Development Bank (IDB), the International Civil Aviation Organization (ICAO), the Seabeds Committee, the Inter-American Defense Board (IADB), the Organization of American States, and the Pacific Economic Cooperation Council (PECC).

Notes

1. Anne M. Driscoll, "Key Provisions of the North American Free Trade Agreement," *Business America* (October 19, 1992), p. 9.
2. Brian Marshall, "Conferees Review 'Tremendous' Energy Sector Opportunities Arising From North American FTA," *North American Free Trade Association: Special Report,* Washington, D.C. (November 1992), pp. 4–6.
3. Ibid., pp. 5–6.

2

Business Customs

A U.S. executive planning to do business in Mexico must be aware that when dealing with another culture it is important to be sensitive to local customs and to make the accommodations this may entail.

Business Hierarchies

In most Mexican businesses, the most important official is usually the *director general,* or the *presidente,* in corporations. The *directores* are below this person and are usually in charge of a particular division. They are followed by the *sub-directores* or the *gerentes* (managers). At these levels, staff members usually have the authority to make important decisions pertaining to their division. Below this level, employees have little authority.

In the public sector, the different *secretarías* (ministries) are headed by politically appointed *secretarios,* whose important staff members play an active role in decision making and are usually entitled *sub-secretario, director general,* or *director.*

Titles and Names

Advanced educational degrees are highly respected in Mexico, and Mexicans usually are referred to by the title of the degree they have earned. Americans with advanced degrees should include them on their business cards. A Mexican who has earned a doctorate or a medical degree is referred to as *doctor (Dr.).* An engineer's title is *ingeniero (Ing.),* and attorneys or holders of other advanced degrees are called *licenciados (Lic.).* It is common for Mexican managers and the people working above them to have M.B.A.s or other advanced degrees.

Initially, Mexicans are more formal than Americans and are not accustomed to establishing a first-name basis as quickly. It is recommended to hold off using a first name until it is suggested or used by the Mexican. When a first-name basis is established with an elderly, eminent man, he should be referred to as *Don* and then by his first name (for example, Don José). The feminine equivalent is *Doña* (for instance, Doña María).

A Mexican's given name is usually followed by a double last name that consists of the father's family name followed by the mother's maiden name. For example, for a person named José González-Lopez, the man's father's family name is González, and Lopez is the maiden name of his mother. Sometimes a person will just use his or her father's family name, or the father's family name followed by the first initial of the mother's maiden name.

When a Mexican woman gets married, she usually keeps her father's last name but adds the first part of her husband's last name. For example, if Maria González Lopez married Juan Barrios Gomez, her married name would be Maria González de Barrios. *De* means "of" and is sometimes not used.

Business Hours

Most businesses in Mexico are open five days a week and operate between 9:00 A.M. and 6:00 P.M., closing for a one- to two-hour lunch/*siesta* break (usually two hours outside Mexico City and Monterrey). Retail businesses usually operate from 10:00 A.M. to 8:00 P.M. Senior managers usually begin work around 9:30 A.M. and take a long, late lunch around 2:00 P.M. that can often last two to three hours. In Monterrey, lunch is usually earlier, from 12:00 P.M. to 2:00 P.M. Government agencies are open for a five-day week at 8:30 A.M. and work without a break until 2:30 P.M. Factories operate from 7:00 or 8:00 A.M. to 4:00 P.M. and are often open half the day on Saturday, but without the company's executive officers.

Banks are open between 9:00 A.M. and 1:30 P.M. (except Banamex and Bancomer, which remain open to 4:00 P.M.) and for limited service between 4:00 P.M. and 6:00 P.M. A few branches in Mexico City remain open on Saturdays until 1:30 P.M. There are many automatic teller machines offering twenty-four-hour service in the capital.

Restaurants usually serve lunch from 1:00 P.M. until 4:00 P.M., and this is often the setting for business negotiations. It is appropriate to invite a Mexican businessman to lunch early in the relationship, and it is important to choose a good restaurant. A foreigner unfamiliar with the restaurants should ask the businessman for a recommendation and be prepared for an extensive meal that often will include several alcoholic beverages (only the best brands will be ordered). The bill (*la cuenta*) will include tax and sometimes the tip; a 15 percent tip is the norm.

Socializing

Business acquaintances often meet for a drink around 7:00 P.M. It is an honor for a visitor to be invited into a Mexican home, because this invitation is usually only extended to good friends. The visitor should arrive around twenty minutes late, bearing a gift for the host. A good bottle of wine makes a nice present, or a box of chocolates or flowers for the hostess. Dinner is usually served quite late, between 9:00 and 10:00.

Mexicans are prone to have closer physical interaction with people they consider friends. The distance that friends stand from each other is closer than in the United States. Women often kiss on both cheeks when greeting someone of either sex, and men do the same when greeting women. It is not uncommon for businessmen to hug (*abraza*) after they are well acquainted.

Business Dress

Businessmen dress quite formally and conservatively, particularly in Mexico City. Suits should always be worn with long-sleeved shirts and neckties. Shoes should be conservative and well shined. Women also dress formally, in conservatively cut dresses or skirts, but often wear brighter colors than the men do. Hair should be neatly groomed, and long hair should be pulled up. Panty hose should always be worn.

Office Setup

Nearly every business entity in Mexico has an office in Mexico City. This is usually where the company's executive officers are situated. For prestige and convenience, U.S. companies planning to have offices in Mexico should at least have a shell office there. Secretaries are also important for company image; they can arrange appointments and sometimes act as translators.

Initial Contact With a Mexican Company

Once a U.S. company identifies a suitable Mexican business entity as a potential trading partner, an appropriate contact person within the Mexican company should be identified by name and title. Often this is the *director de negocios internacionales*. This person should be contacted by letter with a brief description of the company and the proposed interest. This letter must be followed up with a telephone call. Mexicans are often slow in responding to this initial contact, so interested U.S. companies must be persistent in following up and further promoting the relationship.

Personal relationships between business partners are necessary before any serious transactions can occur. After the letter and follow-up phone call, a senior officer from the U.S. company should arrange an appointment with a senior officer from the Mexican company. The date should be confirmed by a secretary before the day of the meeting. This appointment will probably be in Mexico City, since nearly all Mexican companies have their headquarters there, with the exception of the industrial groups of Monterrey.

First Appointment

It is very important to be punctual for an appointment with a Mexican senior official, although upon arrival a visitor is commonly kept waiting for as long as thirty minutes. This is especially true for appointments with public officials. Mexican managers and officials (outside Monterrey) often have a more relaxed attitude about time and may treat deadlines and appointment times more casually. However, the visitor should not assume this and do the same or will run the risk of offending. These delays should be kept in mind when scheduling following appointments. The ideal time to set an appointment is between 10:00 A.M. and 2:00 P.M., unless the appointment is for lunch.

For all appointments in Mexico City, ample time for reaching the destination should be allowed. There is always heavy traffic throughout the city, causing short distances to often take more time than expected. It is recommended that foreigners not drive themselves in Mexico City since traffic is heavy and addresses can be hard to find. Taxis are plentiful and a good option, but the price should be agreed to before the trip. A car and driver can be rented at any hotel.

Most managers and executive officers are fluent in English, which is often used during meetings with foreigners. The main purpose of the initial appointment is to establish a personal relationship with a senior officer (often the *director general*) so that transactions can begin. For this reason, negotiation specifics will probably not be discussed at this time, and it is recommended that this subject not be pursued until later. Instead, the visitor may get a general background on the company that sometimes includes a tour or a slide show.

If the *director general* or senior officer approves of starting transactions, often the foreign company from then on will deal in details with a lower-level officer. This should not be considered a snub by the senior officer. It is the lower-level officials who usually deal more with specifics and often make the decisions for the company, for employees in the upper echelons to approve.

When a presentation is made, tools, graphs, flowcharts, and samples are strong ways to make certain a point is clearly understood.

Negotiations

A negotiator should be well rested when negotiations begin; it is not recommended to go directly after a long plane trip.

Before formal negotiations can take place, the representative from the U.S. company should determine whether either party is fluent in a common language. If this is not the case, an interpreter should be hired so there are no misunderstandings. If an interpreter is used, the speaker should look at the person to whom the message is being conveyed, instead of the interpreter. A good way to ensure there are no misunderstandings after the first day of negotiations is to have each side write minutes of the meeting and compare them for any differences.

Nearly every negotiation involves some bargaining and compromise, so it is a good idea for a team of negotiators to decide on "walk away" points prior to the meeting and to also decide on what points can be compromised. It is not wise to first suggest highly inflated prices that are expected to be bargained down, because Mexicans are not used to this and may be offended.

Mexicans place an emphasis on treating visitors with courtesy and good manners, so it is important to be aware that this may sometimes lead them to say what they think the visitor wants to hear, which can be a source of misunder-standing. For this reason and others, all agreements should be in writing that both parties can understand. Official agreements must be under the auspices of the civil code, the commercial code, or the law of commercial companies. Sales contracts are similar to those in the United States and should be written in both languages. They usually require no special procedures.

3

State Profiles

Most of this information was taken from President Salinas's *Mexican Agenda*, published in July 1991. The maps are used with the permission of the Mexican Investment Board. Figure 3-1 lists the Mexican states and shows their location on the map of Mexico. Detailed descriptions of the states, along with individual state maps are also included.

Figure 3-1. Map of Mexico showing state locations.

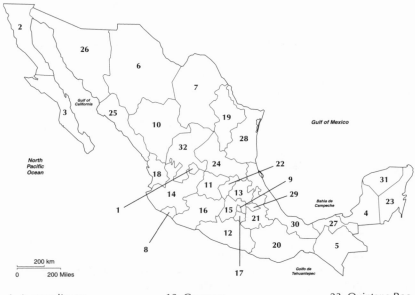

1. Aguascalientes	12. Guerrero	23. Quintana Roo
2. Baja California Norte	13. Hidalgo	24. San Luis Potosí
3. Baja California Sur	14. Jalisco	25. Sinaloa
4. Campeche	15. Mexico	26. Sonora
5. Chiapas	16. Michoacán	27. Tabasco
6. Chihuahua	17. Morelos	28. Tamaulipas
7. Coahuila	18. Nayarit	29. Tlaxcala
8. Colima	19. Nuevo Leon	30. Veracruz
9. Distrito Federal	20. Oaxaca	31. Yucatán
10. Durango	21. Puebla	32. Zacatecas
11. Guanajuato	22. Querétaro	

Aguascalientes

Population 2,719,659
Capital: Aguascalientes
Principal city: Aguascalientes:
   population—506,300
Land area: 2,006 sq. mi.
Airports: international—0; national—1
Highways: main—251 mi.; secondary—
   315 mi.
Railways: 133 mi.
Telephones per 1,000 people: 100
Radio stations: 13
Television stations: 4
Newspapers: 3
Growth Rate: .0353
Industrial parks: 5
Avg. education level: 6 yr.
Cultivated acreage: 229,194 a.; irrigated
   acreage: 77,148a.; irrigation ratio: 34%

Leading Industries

Electronic equipment and surgical
   instruments: $115.7 million

Automotive: $97.9 million
Dairy products: $66.3 million
Soft fibers, excluding knitwear: $61.1
   million
Textile confections, including soft-fiber
   carpets: $40.7 million
Beverages: $37 million

Leading Crops

Alfalfa: 745,537 metric tons
Corn: 47,108 metric tons
Beans: 4,413 metric tons
Sorghum: 3,108 metric tons
Green chilies: 1,451 metric tons
Tomatoes: 729 metric tons

Mining

Silver: 19,501 lb.
Zinc: 4,318 metric tons
Lead: 1,787 metric tons

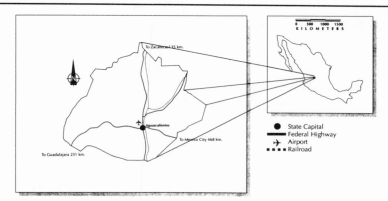

Aguascalientes is located in the center of Mexico and is the most important road and rail link in the country's infrastructure. The federal government is promoting this state as an alternative to overpopulated Mexico City. The National Institute for Statistics, Geography and Information (INEGI) has already transferred to Aguascalientes, and other agencies and businesses are expected to do the same.

Approximately one third of Aguascalientes's territory is used for agriculture. It is Mexico's largest guava producer and its second-greatest grape producer, contributing to a high-quality wine industry.

Roughly 10 percent of investment in Aguascalientes comes from foreign sources, including Nissan, Xerox, Texas Instruments, Sealed Power of Mexico, and General Electric.

Baja California Norte

Population: 1,660,228
Capital: Mexicali
Principal cities: Tijuana: population—
    742,700; Mexicali: population—
    602,300; Ensenada: population—
    260,900
Land area—26,635 sq. mi.
Airports: international—4; national—1
Maritime ports: 17
Highways: main—1,083 mi.; secondary—
    1,027 mi.
Railways: 132 mi.
Telephones per 1,000 people: 102
Radio stations: 45
Television stations: 9
Newspapers: 10
Growth rate: .0330
Industrial parks: 49
Avg. education level: 7.5 yr.
Cultivated acreage: 439,373 a.; irrigated
    acreage: 406,666 a.; irrigation ratio:
    93%

Leading Industries

Beverages: $121.6 million
Food processing: $114.7 million
Metal products, excluding machinery and
    equipment: $106.7 million
Electronics: $78.4 million
Electrical machinery, equipment, and
    accessories, including electricity-
    generating equipment: $54.4 million
Soft fibers, excluding knitwear: $51.9
    million

Leading Crops

Alfalfa: 927,492 metric tons
Wheat: 226,452 metric tons
Tomatoes: 206,831 metric tons
Cottonseed: 99,370 metric tons
Raw cotton 59,622 metric tons
Barley: 25,614 metric tons

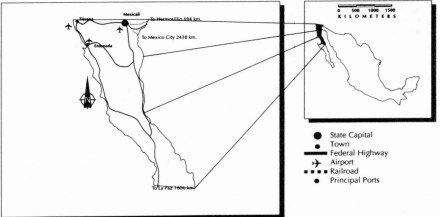

Baja California Norte, located along the Californian border, is in a particularly good position to do business with the United States. Its proximity, efficient infrastructure, sophisticated technology, and skilled labor force are winning combinations for booming *maquiladora* and manufacturing industries.

Baja California Norte is a free trade zone. The state is also a large and varied seafood producer with over 2,000 ships allocated to fishing cooperatives.

Foreign investors include Hughes Aircraft, Fansteel, Beckman Instruments, and Rockwell International.

Baja California Sur

Population: 317,188
Capital: La Paz
Principal city: La Paz: population—
   161,000
Land area: 27,578 sq. mi.
Airports: international—3; national—3
Maritime ports: 22
Highways: main—809 mi.; secondary—
   877 mi.
Railways: 0
Telephones per 1,000 people: 185
Radio stations: 6
Television stations: 24
Newspapers: 3
Growth rate: .0395
Industrial parks: 3
Avg. level of education: 6.8 yr.
Cultivated acreage: 133,271 a.; irrigated
   acreage: 133,271 a.; irrigation ratio:
   100%

Leading Industries

Food preserves, excluding canned meat
   and dairy products: $21.8 million

Cement, lime, plaster, and other
   nonmetallic products: $12.3 million
Beverages: $7.4 million
Soft fibers, excluding knitwear: $4.2
   million
Cereals: $3.3 million
Chemical: $3.2 million

Leading Crops

Alfalfa: 186,607 metric tons
Wheat: 132,881 metric tons
Cottonseed: 15,471 metric tons
Sorghum: 15,062 metric tons
Raw cotton: 9,844 metric tons
Tomatoes: 8,403 metric tons

Mining

Silver: 249 lb.
Gold: 6.39 lb.

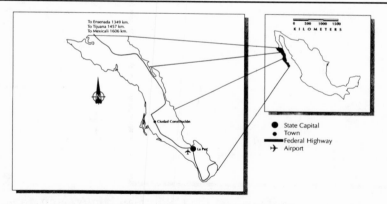

Baja California Sur has Mexico's longest coastline, enabling it to produce 20 percent of the nation's seafood. The state offers many opportunities for development in the seafood industry. It has over 500,000 estuaries and lagoons, making it ideal for aquaculture. Other natural resources include the world's largest salt mines, in Guerrero Negro.

The federal government is investing heavily in Baja California Sur's lucrative tourism industry. There is large growth potential for Puerto Escondido, Loreto, San José del Cabo, and Cabo San Lucas. Baja California Sur is a free trade zone, but its industrial production is still low.

Campeche

Population: 529,081
Capital: Campeche
Principal cities: Campeche: 172,200; Cd.
   del Carmen: 128,200
Land area: 21,930 sq. mi.
Airports: international—1; national—1
Maritime ports: 11
Highways: main—780 mi.; secondary—
   568 mi.
Railways: 247 mi.
Telephones per 1,000 people: 60
Radio stations: 12
Television stations: 6
Newspapers: 5
Growth rate: .0263
Industrial parks: 3
Avg. level of education: 5.8 yr.
Cultivated acreage: 211,731 a.; irrigated
   acreage: 1,477 a.; irrigation ratio: 1%

Leading Industries

Food preserves, excluding canned meat
   and dairy products: $24.4 million
Beverages: $11.3 million
Sugar: $7.3 million
Wood products, excluding furniture: $5.3
   million
Bakery products: $5 million
Corn flour and tortillas: $5 million

Leading Crops

Sugarcane: 260,391 metric tons
Rice: 119,709 metric tons
Corn: 13,519 metric tons
Tomatoes: 4,323 metric tons
Green chilies: 969 metric tons
Avocados: 500 metric tons

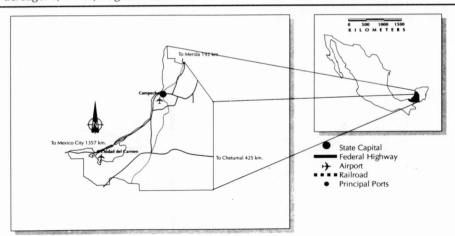

Campeche is in the southeastern tip of Mexico, bordering on Guatemala and the
Gulf of Mexico. It has limited development, but rich natural resources. The Sonda
de Campeche (Campeche Sound) has Mexico's largest oil deposits, and PEMEX
is currently increasing its operations there. Campeche produces approximately
one fourth of Mexico's natural gas supplies.

    Other natural resources include a strong fishing sector with a fleet of over
5,000 ships. Campeche has 56 percent of its territory covered with tropical forests.
The federal government is promoting the tourism industry, and the state has sev-
enty hotels and hosts over 425,000 tourists annually.

Chiapas

Population: 3,205,339
Capital: Tuxtla Gutiérrez
Principal cities: Tuxtla Gutiérrez:
 population—295,600; Tapachula:
 population—222,200
Land area: 28,465 sq. mi.
Airports: international—1; national—2
Maritime ports: 5
Highways: main—1,387 mi.; secondary—
 1,543 mi.
Railways: 338 mi.
Telephones per 1,000 people: 29
Radio stations: 28
Television stations: 21
Newspapers: 12
Growth rate: .0382
Industrial parks: 3
Avg. level of education: 3.7 yr.
Cultivated acreage: 2,436,457 a.; irrigated
 acreage: 92,553 a.; irrigation ratio: 4%

Leading Industries

Basic petrochemicals: $746.7 million
Cereals: $119.4 million
Dairy products: $24.9 million
Meat: $21.7 million
Beverages: $18.6 million
Corn flour and tortillas: $15.5 million

Leading Crops

Corn: 1,053,470 metric tons
Beans: 40,354 metric tons
Soybeans: 40,227 metric tons
Sorghum: 25,055 metric tons
Bananas: 18,511 metric tons
Green coffee: 18,364 metric tons

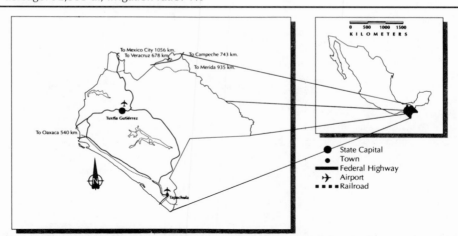

Chiapas is in Mexico's southeast region, bordering on Guatemala. It has an under-developed infrastructure despite its important natural resources. Oil is the state's strongest industry. Its oil fields are located in the north of the state and are part of the national pipeline network.

The state has nearly 23 percent of Mexico's water resources and generates almost 40 percent of its electricity from Mexico's three largest dams. It is responsible for roughly 20–25 percent of the nation's electric power.

Chiapas is Mexico's largest producer of coffee and bananas and a large producer of exotic hardwoods. Nearly 60 percent of the state is covered with pastureland, allowing for significant cattle production.

Chihuahua

Population: 2,439,483
Capital: Chihuahua
Principal cities: Cd. Juarez: population—
797,600; Chihuahua: population—
534,300
Land area: 94,959 sq. mi.
Airports: international—2; national—0
Maritime ports—0
Highways: main—1,756 mi.; secondary—
1,594 mi.
Railways: 1,620 mi.
Telephones per 1,000 people: 124
Radio stations: 56
Television stations: 31
Newspapers: 14
Growth rate: .0198
Industrial parks: 23
Avg. level of education: 6.3 yr.
Cultivated acreage: 1,774,680 a.; irrigated
acreage: 417,363 a.; irrigation ratio:
24%

Leading Industries

Electrical machinery, including electricity-
generating equipment: $521.1 million

Automotive: $362.9 million
Wood products, excluding furniture:
$141.2 million
Electronics: $120.3 million
Dairy products: $98.4 million
Paper and cellulose products: $83.4
million

Leading Crops

Green alfalfa: 3,154,100 metric tons
Apples: 261,885 metric tons
Corn: 250,425 metric tons
Wheat: 220,445 metric tons
Green chilies: 122,800 metric tons
Sorghum: 103,292 metric tons

Mining

Iron: 396,627 metric tons
Silver: 761,017 lb.
Zinc: 96,298 metric tons
Lead: 72,023 metric tons
Gold: 1,135 lb.

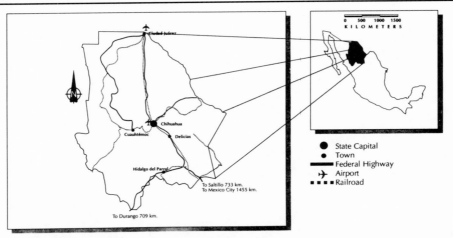

Chihuahua, situated along the Texas border, is one of Mexico's most economically diversified and powerful states. Its proximity to the United States lends to a strong *maquiladora* sector: Chihuahua has 40 percent of Mexico's *maquiladora* employees and accounts for roughly 42 percent of the value-added contributions from all such enterprises.

One of Mexico's leading agricultural states, Chihuahua utilizes modern technology to produce an abundance of traditional and nontraditional crops. Livestock production is also important, with nearly 50 percent of Mexico's livestock exports coming from the state. Chihuahua is Mexico's most important forestry state, producing 32 percent of the nation's timber. In addition, it is the country's largest producer of zinc.

Foreign investors include American Hospital Supply, Toshiba, JVC, General Electric, RCA, Westinghouse, and Sylvania.

Coahuila

Population: 1,972,539
Capital: Saltillo
Principal cities: Torreón: population—
876,400; Saltillo: population—
440,800; Monclova: population—
178,000
Land area: 57,726 sq. mi.
Airports: international—3; national—2
Maritime ports—0
Highways: main—976 mi.; secondary—
1,230 mi.
Telephones per 1,000 people: 119
Radio stations: 49
Television stations: 24
Newspapers: 21
Growth rate: .0255
Industrial parks: 17
Avg. level of education: 6.9 yr.
Cultivated acreage: 319,685 a.; irrigated
acreage: 285,384 a.; irrigation ratio:
89%

Leading Industries

Automotive: $1.19 billion
Iron and steel production: $1.03 billion
Clay construction materials: $129.5
million

Specialized machinery and equipment
with or without an integrated electric
motor, including agricultural machinery:
$100.9 million
Cement, plaster, lime, and other
nonmetallic products: $94.8 million
Soft fibers, excluding knitwear: $79.7
million

Leading Crops

Green alfalfa: 447,979 metric tons
Cottonseed: 77,299 metric tons
Raw cotton: 49,416 metric tons
Corn: 45,822 metric tons
Sorghum: 32,237 metric tons
Wheat: 20,403 metric tons

Mining

Iron: 2,023,743 metric tons
Silver: 100,351 lb.
Coke: 1,775,008 metric tons
Lead: 5,124 metric tons
Zinc: 7,146 metric tons
Baryta: 48,690 metric tons
Fluorite: 192,245 metric tons

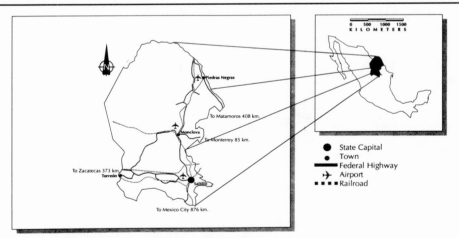

Coahuila borders western Texas and shares its arid, hot climate. Its solid infrastructure, sophisticated technology, skilled workers, and large deposits of iron
and steel make it a big producer for the auto industry. *Maquiladoras* are growing

at a rapid pace in the state, and their production level has risen by approximately 30 percent in each of the past three years.

Coahuila also has a strong agricultural sector. Its large cotton crop uses 39 percent of the state's irrigated land.

Foreign investors include Chrysler and General Motors.

Colima

Population: 428,510
Capital: Colima
Principal city: Colima: population—
  116,000
Land area: 2,098 sq. mi.
Airports: international—1; national—1
Maritime ports: 4
Highways: main—268 mi.; secondary—
  264 mi.
Railways: 124 mi.
Telephones per 1,000 people: 119
Radio stations: 8
Television stations: 4
Newspapers: 9
Growth rate: .0247
Industrial parks: 4
Avg. level of education: 6.1 yr.
Cultivated acreage: 255,494 a.; irrigated
  acreage: 126,699 a.; irrigation ratio:
  50%

Leading Industries

Beverages: $11.9 million
Cereals and other agricultural products:
  $10.2 million
Sugar products: $9.7 million
Corn flour milling and tortilla
  manufacturing: $5.7 million
Chemicals: $4.5 million
Dairy products: $3.7 million

Leading Crops

Sugarcane: 409,379 metric tons
Plantains: 234,666 metric tons
Lemons: 222,796 metric tons
Corn: 68,155 metric tons
Copra: 55,836 metric tons
Rice: 14,885 metric tons

Mining

Iron: 1,882,183 metric tons

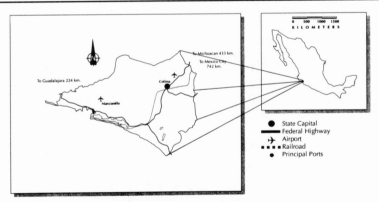

Colima is located in southwestern Mexico on the Pacific coast. It is a state with great potential because of its tremendous natural resources. Its four-lane highway system links it to international airports and Guadalajara. It has a principal seaport (Manzanillo) on the Pacific Ocean with railroad service joining it to the rest of the country.

Tourism is a major industry in Colima. Approximately 700,000 tourists each year are attracted to the beautiful beaches and lush mountains. Popular resorts include Las Hadas, Hotel Playa la Audienca, and Club Med.

Despite its small size, Colima has high agricultural productivity. It also produces large quantities of iron.

Distrito Federal (D.F.)

Capital: Cd. de Mexico (Mexico City)
Principal city: Cd. de Mexico:
   population—15,473,200 including
   metropolitan zone
Land area: 597 sq. mi.
Airports: international—1; national—1
Maritime ports: 4
Highways: main—97 mi.; secondary: 0
Railways: 194 mi.
Telephones per 1,000 people: 311
Radio stations: 72
Television stations: 8
Newspapers: 25
Growth rate: −0.0009
Industrial parks: 0
Avg. level of education: 8.4 yr.
Cultivated acreage: 41,664 a.; irrigation
   ratio: 19%

Leading Industries

Chemical: $1.11 billion
Automotive: $1.04 billion
Pharmaceutical products: $819.7 million
Electrical equipment, machinery, and
   accessories, and electrical energy
   generation: $802.9 million
Printing and editorial production: $746.1
   million
Beverages: $742.3 million

Leading Crops

Corn: 26,152 metric tons
Beans: 413 metric tons
Apples: 239 metric tons
Green alfalfa: 97 metric tons

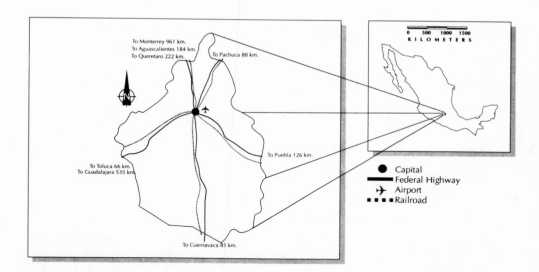

Mexico City is the capital of the nation. It is Mexico's largest consumer market. It continues to grow at a very rapid pace and is already the largest city in the world. Its small geographical size limits agricultural production, but its industrial sector is booming. Tourism also provides significant economic activity.

Durango

Population: 1,348,638
Capital: Durango
Principal city: Durango: population—
 414,000
Land area: 47,018 sq. mi.
Airports: international—0; national—1
Maritime ports: 0
Highways: main—1,267 mi.; secondary:
 871 mi.
Railways: 766 mi.
Telephones per 1,000 people: 68
Radio stations: 14
Television stations: 14
Newspapers: 8
Growth rate: .0161
Industrial parks: 4
Avg. level of education: 5.9 yr.
Cultivated acreage: 1,468,133 a.; irrigated
 acreage: 285,638 a.; irrigation ratio:
 19%

Leading Industries

Wood products, excluding furniture:
 $126.5 million
Dairy products: $90.7 million

Paper and cellulose products: $40.4
 million
Apparel: $39 million
Cooking oil and fats: $31.3 million
Beverages: $31.2 million

Leading Crops

Alfalfa: 843,453 metric tons
Corn: 168,950 metric tons
Beans: 57,193 metric tons
Tomatoes: 40,843 metric tons
Cottonseed: 37,654 metric tons
Wheat: 30,583 metric tons

Minerals

Gold: 3,035 lb.
Silver: 570,546 lb.
Zinc: 10,846 metric tons
Lead: 8,243 metric tons

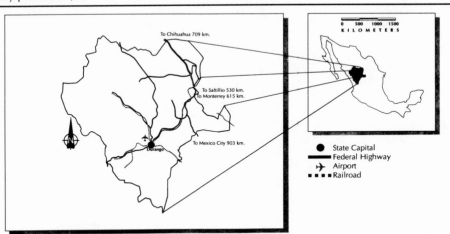

Durango, located in northwestern Mexico, has a strong and diversified economy and a wealth of natural resources. Its advanced infrastructure has fostered a growing *maquila* sector, particularly in the textile and clothing industries.

Durango is Mexico's largest producer of oak and pinewood and the nation's largest supplier of finished sawmill products. It is also a leading agricultural and livestock state, particularly in the cattle industry.

The state's mineral resources are tremendous. Nearly 10 percent of Mexico's nonferrous metals originate here. It is Mexico's second-largest gold producer, providing nearly 25 percent of the nation's gold extraction. Silver production is also high. Durango has numerous iron deposits that have not yet been developed.

Guanajuato

Population: 3,980,326
Capital: Guanajuato
Principal cities: León: population—
956,000; Irapuato: population—
362,500; Celaya: population—315,600;
Salamanca: population—206,300
Land area: 11,887 sq. mi.
Airports: international—0; national—3
Maritime ports: 0
Highways: main—830 mi.; secondary—
1,279 mi.
Railways: 666 mi.
Telephones per 1,000 people: 67
Radio stations: 47
Television stations: 9
Newspapers: 17
Growth rate: .0275
Industrial parks: 10
Avg. level of education: 4.9 yr.
Cultivated acreage: 2,508,329 a.; irrigated
acreage: 1,016,081 a.; irrigation ratio:
41%.

Leading Industries

Petroleum refining: $796.8 million
Footwear, excluding rubber and plastic:
$362.9 million

Leather products and substitute material,
excluding garments and shoes: $175.8
million
Baked goods: $85.2 million
Beverages: $66.5 million
Food preserves, excluding canned meat
and dairy products: $58.4 million

Leading Crops

Green alfalfa: 2,658,192 metric tons
Sorghum: 1,504,970 metric tons
Wheat: 628,703 metric tons
Corn: 411,396 metric tons
Chilies: 61,402 metric tons
Barley: 40,874 metric tons

Mining

Silver: 357,980 lb.
Gold: 5,863 lb.
Copper: 109 metric tons
Fluorite: 93,276 metric tons

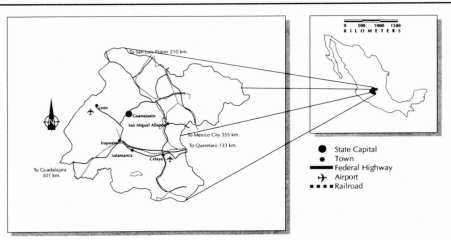

Guanajuato, in central Mexico, is a growing industrial state. It is an ideal place for industrial parks since it is located less than 300 kilometers (186 miles) from Mexico City and Guadalajara, two of Mexico's largest industrial centers. This favorable location is complemented by a four-lane highway system.

Tourism is the state's most profitable industry. Mexico's Old World architecture and culture are still evident here.

Guanajuato has a highly productive agricultural sector. The state will give credit for the development of many high-value-added agroindustrial products. Cattle raising and nontraditional crops also contribute heavily to the economy; however, traditional crops are still predominant.

Guerrero

Population: 2,620,142
Capital: Chilpancingo
Principal cities: Acapulco: population—
   592,200; Chilpancingo: population—
   136,200
Land area: 24,937 sq. mi.
Airports: international—2; national—0
Maritime ports: 6
Highways: main—1,435 mi.; secondary—
   302 mi.
Telephones per 1,000 people: 54
Radio stations: 24
Television stations: 12
Newspapers: 11
Growth rate: .0228
Industrial parks: 2
Avg. level of education: 4.9 yr.
Cultivated acreage: 1,442,112 a.; irrigated
   acreage: 85,865 a.; irrigation ratio: 6%

Leading Industries

Beverages: $53 million
Tortilla making and cornmeal grinding:
   $22.8 million

Dairy products: $16.8 million
Cement, lime, and gypsum processing:
   $12.6 million
Cereal products: $10 million

Leading Crops

Corn: 871,331 metric tons
Plantains: 135,072 metric tons
Lemons: 124,000 metric tons
Copra: 72,842 metric tons
Sugarcane: 64,119 metric tons
Coffee 44,009 metric tons

Minerals

Silver: 138,409 lb.
Gold: 637 lb.
Zinc: 16,241 lb.
Lead: 5,454 lb.
Copper: 638 lb.

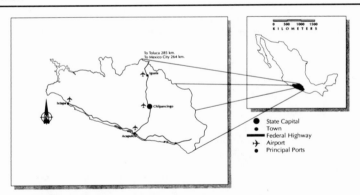

Guerrero, on Mexico's Pacific coast, has one of the country's strongest tourism industries. Its beautiful beaches attract over 5.5 million tourists annually to resorts in Acapulco and the newly developed Ixtapa-Zihuantanejo. Its new four-lane highway system will soon provide easy access to Mexico City and the other states. Guerrero was chosen for the government's tourism megaprojects. A $518 million, 7,000-room hotel development project is under construction in Punta Ixtapa.

   Guerrero is a prosperous seafood producer with more than seventy-five species of fish and shellfish available. The state's industrial sector is less developed than that of most Mexican states.

Hidalgo

Population: 1,877,603
Capital: Pachuca
Principal city: Pachuca: population—
    179,400
Land area: 7,916 sq. mi.
Airports: international—0; national—1
Maritime ports: 0
Highways: main—650 mi.; secondary:—
    1,192 mi.
Railways: 562 mi.
Telephones per 1,000 people: 47
Radio stations: 8
Television stations: 10
Newspapers: 4
Growth rate: .0208
Industrial parks: 11
Avg. education level: 5.1 yr.
Cultivated acreage: 1,037,069 a.; irrigated
    acreage: 247,593 a.; irrigation ratio:
    24%

Leading Industries

Petroleum refining: $730 million
Cement, gypsum, and lime: $260.9
    million
Fiber and yarn production: $150.4 million

Fabrication and assembling of
    transportation equipment and parts,
    including cars and trucks: $132.6
    million
Machinery with or without an integrated
    electric motor, including armaments:
    $74.6 million
Electrical machinery, equipment, and
    accessories, including electric-energy
    generation: $52.7 million

Leading Crops

Alfalfa: 1,804,041 metric tons
Corn: 340,248 metric tons
Sugarcane: 186,211 metric tons
Barley: 65,989 metric tons
Oranges: 39,470 metric tons
Green coffee: 33,082 metric tons

Mining

Silver: 263,053 lb.
Zinc: 14,290 metric tons
Lead: 7,673 metric tons
Gold: 776 lb.

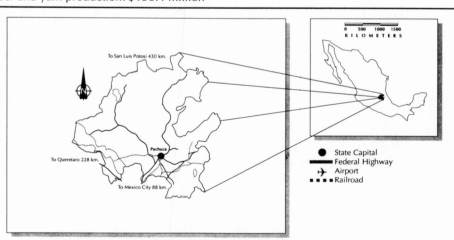

Hidalgo is undergoing an industrial and agricultural transformation. The federal government's ambitious program aimed at decentralizing the nation's commerce (it has been dominated by Mexico City) is responsible for fostering this growth. Hidalgo is close to the nation's capital and enjoys good natural resources.

The state has six industrial parks, defined by the products manufactured: metalwork, crafts, footwear, auto parts, construction materials, and electronics.

Hidalgo has a good irrigation program, particularly in the Valle del Mezquital. It is Mexico's greatest barley producer. Alfalfa, corn, and beans are also predominant crops.

The Miguel Hidalgo oil refinery in Tula de Allende has recently been expanded for greater production. Mining production is also increasing. Hidalgo has large deposits of silver, copper ores, and manganese.

Jalisco

Population: 5,289,816
Capital: Guadalajara
Principal city: Guadalajara: population—
    2,884,000
Land area: 30,266 sq. mi.
Airports: international—2; national—1
Maritime ports: 3
Highways: main—1,504 mi.; secondary—
    1,658 mi.
Railways: 652 mi.
Telephones per 1,000 people: 129
Radio stations: 63
Television stations: 14
Newspapers: 11
Growth rate: .0202
Industrial parks: 3
Avg. level of education: 6.3 yr.
Cultivated acreage: 2,661,549 a.; irrigated
    acreage: 306,769 a.; irrigation ratio:
    12%

Leading Industries

Beverages: $368.9 million
Cooking oil: $274.5 million
Plastics: $239.5 million
Chemicals: $219.1 million
Dairy products: $200.6 million
Food processing: $188.5 million

Leading Crops

Corn: 1,810,245 metric tons
Sorghum: 913,278 metric tons
Wheat: 169,379 metric tons
Tomatoes: 120,019 metric tons

Mining

Iron: 809,127 metric tons
Silver: 110,953 lb.

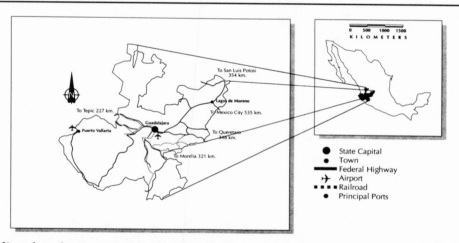

Jalisco has the nation's third-largest economy and is one of Mexico's most techno-
logically advanced states. Its economy continues to grow at a rapid pace with the
help of the government's decentralization plan. Pharmaceuticals, electronics, and
electrical goods are growing fastest. The state is Mexico's Silicon Valley and has
attracted many electronics companies, such as Hewlett-Packard, AT&T, and IBM.
Guadalajara's fast growth during the past decade has strained the city's infrastructure and encouraged the development of other cities in the state, such as Ciudad
Guzmán and Ameca.

    Jalisco's varied climate and plentiful water resources contribute to its strong
agricultural production. It usually harvests nearly 25 percent more than most
Mexican states. It is Mexico's second-largest sugar producer. The forestry industry

is also strong. It is one of Mexico's greatest livestock producers, with an emphasis on cattle (128,600 metric tons) and pigs (143,290 metric tons).

Jalisco is still developing its fishing infrastructure, but it already is a large supplier of seafood, including shellfish, turtles, and sharks.

Tourism is a booming industry, attracting 3.5 million visitors annually. Puerto Vallarta is a popular tourist resort.

Mexico

Population: 9,811,767
Capital: Toluca
Principal cities: Cd. Neza: population—
    1,259,500; Ecatepec: population—
    1,219,200; Toluca: population—
    827,300; Naucalpan: population—
    786,000
Land area: 8,184 sq. mi.
Airports: international: 1; national: 2
Maritime ports: 0
Highways: main—692 mi.; secondary—
    3,521 miles
Railways: 763 mi.
Telephones per 1,000 people: 88
Radio stations: 10
Television stations: 8
Newspapers: 16
Growth rate: .0359
Industrial parks: 31
Avg. level of education: 6.5 yr.
Cultivated acreage: 1,977,097 a.; irrigated
    acreage: 332,479 a.; irrigation ratio:
    17%

Leading Industries

Automotive: $1.29 billion
Plastics: $812.2 million
Paper and cellulose: $744.1 million
Chemicals: $734.2 million
Basic chemicals, including basic
    petrochemicals: $567.2 million
Yarn and fibers: $530.6 million

Leading Crops

Alfalfa: 1,011,698 metric tons
Corn: 710,156 metric tons
Wheat: 50,962 metric tons
Barley: 29,571 metric tons
Avocados: 16,903 metric tons
Beans: 6,038 metric tons

Mining

Silver: 73,113 lb.
Lead: 899 metric tons
Zinc: 858 metric tons
Gold: 126 lb.

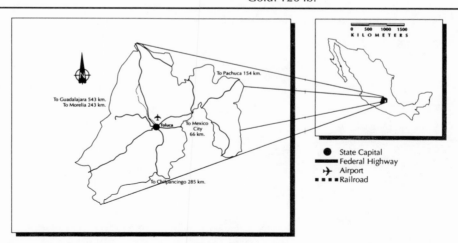

The state of Mexico contributes more to the country's gross national product (GNP) than any other state, generating nearly 20 percent of the nation's industrial production. Its proximity to Mexico City, its strong infrastructure, and its large population encourage this output. Cuautitlán, Naucalpan, and Tlalnepantla are the main industrial areas, but since 1989 the government has been trying to decentralize by fostering industries in other areas, including Toluca and Lerma. After

Mexico City, the state of Mexico is the greatest producer of manufactured goods, representing roughly 65 percent of the nation's transformation industry.

The state also offers significant agricultural production.

Foreign investors include Kimberly Clark, Industrias Bacardi, Ford, Nissan, Chrysler, Motorola, and Celanese Mexicana.

Michoacán

Population: 3,547,680
Capital: Morelia
Principal cities: Morelia: population—
489,700; Uruapan: population—
217,100; Zamora: population—145,000
Land area: 22,470 sq. mi.
Airports: international—0; national—4
Maritime ports: 1
Highways: main—1,583 mi.; secondary—
1,410 mi.
Railways: 713 mi.
Telephones per 1,000 people: 57
Radio stations: 36
Television stations: 20
Newspapers: 23
Growth rate: .0208
Industrial parks: 5
Avg. level of education: 5.1 yr.
Cultivated acreage: 1,970,796 a.; irrigated
acreage: 504,569 a.; irrigation ratio:
26%

Leading Industries

Iron and steel: $346.4 million
Basic chemicals, including basic
petrochemicals: $139.1 million
Paper and cellulose: $50.2 million
Equipment and machinery for general use,
with or without an electric motor: $45.7
million
Wood products, excluding furniture: $44
million
Sugar and sugar products: $41.2 million

Leading Crops

Corn: 839,521 metric tons
Sorghum: 583,521 metric tons
Wheat: 223,492 metric tons

Mining

Steel: 1,508,289 metric tons
Coke: 549,426 metric tons
Silver: 72,933 lb.

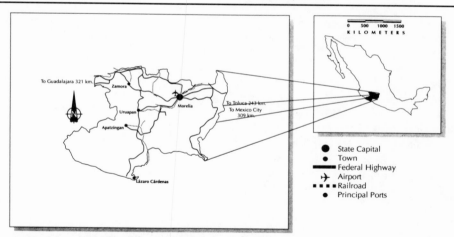

Michoacán has been the focus of commercial development over the past decade. The state's accessibility improved with the construction of the Lázaro Cárdenas seaport and the repair of a highway to Mexico and Guadalajara.

FERTIMEX, the state-owned fertilizer plants, and SICARTSA, Mexico's most modern iron and steel mills, are located in Michoacán. SICARTSA was privatized in 1992. Japan's Kobe Steel is doing a joint venture with Sidermex and NAFIN to produce machinery.

Michoacán is a strong agricultural state; it produces 50 percent of Mexico's strawberries and is the nation's leading producer of melons and avocados. An irrigation project in the Chilatan Reservoir will soon open up an additional 250,000 acres for cultivation. Michoacán is Mexico's second-largest timber producer.

Michoacán also has the potential to be an important seafood producer.

Morelos

Population: 1,195,059
Capital: Cuernavaca
Principal city: Cuernavaca: population—
348,900
Land area: 1,918 sq. mi.
Airports: international—0; national—1
Maritime ports: 0
Highways: main—286 mi.; secondary—
603 mi.
Railways: 169 mi.
Telephones per 1,000 people: 109
Radio stations: 13
Television stations: 2
Newspapers: 5
Growth rate: .0276
Industrial parks: 5
Avg. level of education: 6.5 yr.
Cultivated acreage: 226,309 a.; irrigated
acreage: 38,268 a.; irrigation ratio: 17%

Leading Industries

Automotive: $854.9 million
Basic chemicals, including petrochemicals:
$109.6 million

Other chemicals: $74.1 million
Pharmaceutical products: $51 million
Sugar and sugar products: $49.1 million
Fibers and yarn: $46.3 million

Leading Crops

Sugarcane: 2,083,164 metric tons
Sorghum: 98,177 metric tons
Tomatoes: 73,186 metric tons
Corn: 72,377 metric tons
Rice: 23,285 metric tons
Avocados: 17,320 metric tons

Mining

Silver: 39,266 lb.
Lead: 267 metric tons
Copper: 38 metric tons
Gold: 26 lb.

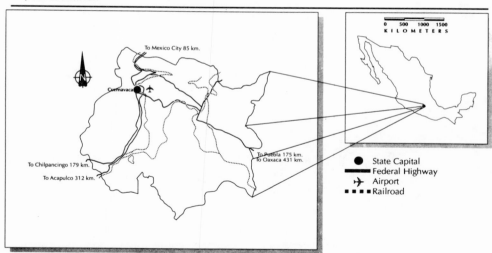

Morelos is one of Mexico's smallest states, but its varied climate and proximity to a large market (Mexico City) have encouraged abundant agricultural productivity. It has strong timber production, primarily featuring evergreen, oak, and pine. The state is a large flower exporter to Europe and the United States.

Industry is growing rapidly. During the past five years, the federal and state governments have been developing a major technology center in Morelos to encourage electric, electronic, cybernetic, and other high-tech industries to open plants. Industrial parks are opening throughout the state to reduce emigration to Mexico City.

Foreign investors include Firestone, Beecham de Mexico, UpJohn, and Nissan Mexicana.

Nayarit

Population: 817,520
Capital: Tepic
Principal city: Tepic: population—238,100
Land area: 10,389 sq. mi.
Airports: international—0; national—1
Maritime ports: 6
Highways: main—520 mi.; secondary—
   492 mi.
Railways: 254 mi.
Telephones per 1,000 people: 92
Radio stations: 13
Television stations: 5
Newspapers: 4
Growth rate: .0146
Industrial parks: 2
Avg. level of education: 5.6 yr.
Cultivated acreage: 486,765 a.; irrigated
   acreage: 98,820 a.; irrigation ratio: 20%

Leading Industries

Tobacco: $40.8 million
Sugar products: $37.2 million
Cereal and other agricultural products:
   $33.6 million
Beverages: $15.7 million

Leading Crops

Corn: 142,871 metric tons
Sorghum: 124,619 metric tons
Beans: 71,067 metric tons
Green chilies: 39,844 metric tons
Tomatoes: 31,580 metric tons

Mining

Silver: 28,163 lb.
Lead: 573 metric tons
Zinc: 342 metric tons
Gold: 300 lb.

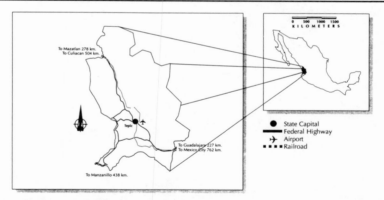

Industrial development in Nayarit is limited, and most of it is related to agriculture. However, the state has potential for diversified commercial development. Nayarit's access to the Pacific Rim is attracting Japan to its *maquiladoras*.

Nayarit's tropical climate has been essential for producing 75 percent of Mexico's tobacco. The country's two leading tobacco companies, La Moderna and Compañía Tabacalera Mexicana, are located here. The government is encouraging high-value fruit products for export.

Nayarit's territorial extension and archipelagos make it very suitable for harvesting shrimp and tilapia. Shellfishing is especially predominant in San Blas, which is also the location of its oyster development center.

There are two processing plants for silver, lead, and gold. Nonmetallic mineral resources have yet to be exploited for the building industry.

Nuevo León

Population: 3,097,860
Capital: Monterrey
Principal city: Monterrey: population—
 2,549,400
Land area: 24,791 sq. mi.
Airports: international—2; national—0
Maritime ports: 0
Highways: main—792 mi.; secondary—
 1,671 mi.
Railways: 690 mi.
Telephones per 1,000 people: 92
Radio stations: 46
Television stations: 9
Newspapers: 9
Growth rate: .0234
Industrial parks: 14
Avg. level of education: 7.6 yr.
Cultivated acreage: 310,420 a.; irrigated
 acreage: 159,004 a.; irrigation ratio:
 51%

Leading Industries

Petroleum refining: $823.6 million
Iron and steel: $693.6 million

Electrical equipment, machinery, and
 accessories, including electric-energy
 generators: $569.5 million
Glass: $395.9 million
Meat: $341.2 million
Transportation equipment: $311.5 million

Leading Crops

Oranges: 249,017 metric tons
Sorghum: 112,069 metric tons
Alfalfa: 74,148 metric tons
Corn: 50,947 metric tons
Wheat: 20,943 metric tons
Apples: 9,857 metric tons

Mining

Baryta: 64,439 metric tons

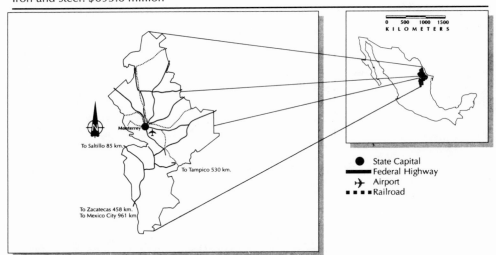

Nuevo León is considered the model city for Mexican industrialization and modernization. It has grown rapidly during the last decade and is in an excellent
position to benefit significantly from a free trade agreement with the United
States. Monterrey's proximity to the United States, its skilled labor force, and its
advanced technology have attracted most of the nation's most important industrial groups, including Alfa, Vitro, CYDSA, and FEMSA. After the reprivatization

of Mexican banks, Monterrey establishments took control of nearly half of the nation's financial system.

Nuevo León's solid infrastructure and strong communications system help make it Mexico's third most important industrial state, after the Federal District and the state of Mexico.

Nuevo León is very hot, and only a small portion of the land is irrigable. However, it is Mexico's second-largest orange producer and second-largest baryta producer.

Oaxaca

Population: 3,019,127
Capital: Oaxaca de Juárez
Principal city: Oaxaca de Juárez:
   population—244,500
Land area: 35,960 sq. mi.
Airports: international—1; national—3
Maritime ports: 4
Highways: main—1,870 mi.; secondary—
   900 mi.
Railways: 425 mi.
Telephones per 1,000 people: 27
Radio stations: 21
Television stations: 19
Newspapers: 7
Growth rate: .0217
Industrial parks: 3
Avg. level of education: 4.2 yr.
Cultivated acreage: 1,683,648 a.; irrigated
   acreage: 118,009 a.; irrigation ratio: 7%

Leading Industries

Petroleum refining: $669.8 million
Beverages: $164.2 million

Paper and cellulose: $74.6 million
Sugar: $47.6 million
Cement, gypsum, and lime production:
   $34.8 million
Cereal and other agricultural products:
   $34.4 million

Leading Crops

Sugarcane: 4,322,845 metric tons
Corn: 522,919 metric tons
Alfalfa: 269,120 metric tons
Lemons: 120,900 metric tons
Coffee: 80,044 metric tons
Plantain: 69,290 metric tons

Mining

Silver: 22,791 lb.
Zinc: 415 metric tons
Gold: 284 lb.

Oaxaca is rich in natural resources. The majority of its economic activity comes from the Salina Cruz oil refineries on the Gulf of Tehuantepec. These refineries are in an excellent location to do business with Japan. The federal government's Pacific Petroleum Project will bring the oil produced on the Gulf of Mexico over to Oaxaca on the Pacific coast.

   Approximately one third of Oaxaca's land is used for agriculture. It is a large coffee and sugarcane producer. It also is one of Mexico's largest producers of fine and semiprecious wood.

Oaxaca's ancient ruins and beautiful beaches attract over one million tourists annually. The government is currently developing the Bay of Huatulco for tourists.

Puebla

Population: 4,125,655
Capital: Puebla
Principal city: Puebla: population—
    1,454,500
Land area: 13,125 sq. mi.
Airports: international—0; national—2
Maritime ports: 0
Highways: main—898 mi.; secondary—
    934 mi.
Railways: 899 mi.
Telephones per 1,000 people: 68
Radio stations: 27
Television stations: 4
Newspapers: 7
Growth rate: .0224
Industrial parks: 16
Avg. level of education: 5.3 yr.
Cultivated acreage: 1,872,458 a.; irrigated
    acreage: 136,379 a.; irrigation ratio:
    7%

Leading Industries

Automotive: $869 million
Yarn and fibers: $441.6 million
Iron and steel: $250.4 million
Beverages: $138.3 million
Basic chemicals and petrochemicals:
    $125.7 million
Cereals and agricultural products: $108.3
    million

Leading Crops

Corn: 572,343 metric tons
Beans: 23,445 metric tons
Sorghum: 23,165 metric tons
Tomatoes: 19,695 metric tons
Barley: 18,469 metric tons
Wheat: 11,061 metric tons

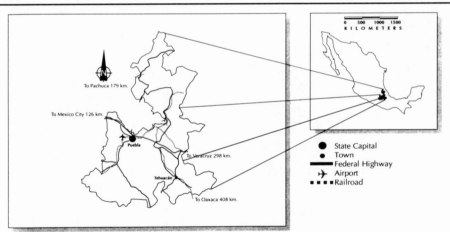

Puebla links the center of Mexico to the southeast. It has a four-lane highway to nearby Mexico City, and the federal government is touting the state as an alternative to the capital for development. Puebla has a large manufacturing sector, and industrial parks throughout the state.

Nearly one third of Puebla's territory is used for agriculture. The state is a major producer of hogs and poultry and has a strong meat-processing industry.

Querétaro

Population: 1,045,203
Capital: Querétaro
Principal city: Querétaro: population—
454,000
Land area: 41,625 sq. mi.
Airports: international—0; national—1
Maritime ports: 0
Highways: main—933 mi.; secondary—
478 mi.
Railways: 276 mi.
Telephones per 1,000 people: 66
Radio stations: 15
Television stations: 3
Newspapers: 6
Growth rate: .0358
Industrial parks: 11
Avg. level of education: 5 yr.
Cultivated acreage: 399,686 a.; irrigated
acreage: 136,603 a.; irrigation ratio:
34%

Leading Industries

Automotive: $218.6 million
Paper and cellulose: $215.8 million

Artificial and synthetic fibers: $145.7
million
Machinery and equipment with or without
an integrated electrical motor: $138.2
million
Electrical machinery, equipment, and
accessories, including electric-energy
generators: $125.2 million
Glass: $90.1 million

Leading Crops

Alfalfa: 257,389 metric tons
Sorghum: 74,606 metric tons
Corn: 44,720 metric tons
Wheat: 11,863 metric tons
Barley: 3,817 metric tons
Beans: 2,915 metric tons

Mining

Silver: 86,687 lb.
Zinc: 3,434 metric tons
Lead: 2,108 metric tons

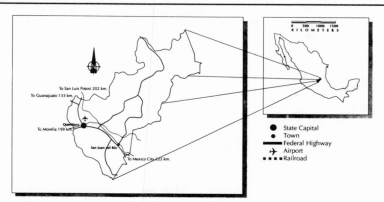

The federal government considers Querétaro an alternative to Mexico City for development. It is conveniently close to the capital and has an efficient highway and communications system making it even more accessible. Querétaro has an industrial corridor nearly forty miles long with a railroad system and a customs station. These factors have attracted a significant number of foreign investors, including Gerber Products, Kellogg's de Mexico, General Electric, Celanese Mexicana, Kimberly Clark, Carnation, Pennwalt, Mitsubishi, and John Deere.

Querétaro is a large mercury producer. It also produces large quantities of alfalfa. Fodder production is important as well.

Quintana Roo

Population: 493,277
Capital: Chetumal
Principal city: Chetumal: population—
111,400
Land area: 15,434 sq. mi.
Airports: international—4; national—0
Maritime ports: 14
Highways: main—566 mi.; secondary—
810 mi.
Railways: 0
Telephones per 1,000 people: 93
Radio stations: 7
Television stations: 26
Newspapers: 3
Growth rate: .0798
Industrial parks: 4
Avg. level of education: 5.4 yr.

Cultivated acreage: 419,989 a.; irrigated
acreage: 35,736 a.; irrigation ratio: 9%

Leading Industries

Cement, gypsum, and lime processing:
$23.7 million
Wood products: $8.5 million
Printing and editorial products: $4.5
million

Leading Crops

Corn: 6,054 metric tons
Rice: 4,253 metric tons
Oranges: 2,600 metric tons
Green chilies: 2,403 metric tons
Copra: 1,560 metric tons

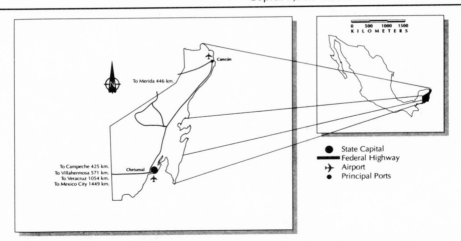

During the past two decades, Quintana Roo has developed into one of the world's most fashionable resort areas. Its famous vacation spots include Puerto Cancun and Puerto San Buenaventura in Cancun and Puerto Bello and Cozumel on Cozumel Island. The federal government is supporting a major tourism development program in the state; Quintana Roo brings in 22 percent of Mexico's foreign income from tourism. Tourism accounts for 66 percent of the state's gross domestic product (GDP) and has strengthened other areas of the economy.

Industrial activity is not very developed.

Seafood production is significant and includes several varieties with high commercial value (lobster, snails, shrimp).

Quintana Roo is Mexico's biggest producer of fine wood, which has fostered many timber-related industries. Since the state is small, agricultural production is limited. It is a free trade zone.

San Luis Potosí

Population: 2,001,284
Capital: San Luis Potosí
Principal city: San Luis Potosí:
    population—658,700
Land area: 24,339 sq. mi.
Airports: international—0; national—2
Maritime ports: 0
Highways: main—1,074 mi.; secondary—
    967 mi.
Railways: 1,074 mi.
Telephones per 1,000 people: 65
Radio stations: 24
Television stations: 11
Newspapers: 4
Growth rate: .0211
Industrial parks: 3
Avg. level of education: 5.3 yr.
Cultivated acreage: 632,500 a.; irrigated
    acreage: 82,903 a.; irrigation ratio: 13%

Leading Industries

Basic nonferrous metal industries,
    including the treatment of nuclear fuel:
    $455.2 million
Iron and steel: $219.2 million

Tobacco: $160.4 million
Electric machinery, equipment, and
    accessories, including electric-energy
    generators: $121.7 million
Transportation equipment and parts,
    excluding cars and trucks: $112.4
    million
Sugar: $73 million

Leading Crops

Alfalfa: 781,928 metric tons
Sugarcane: 385,042 metric tons
Oranges: 250,242 metric tons
Corn: 205,496 metric tons
Tomatoes: 111,821 metric tons
Green coffee: 53,605 metric tons

Mining

Silver: 296,572 lb.
Zinc: 57,874 metric tons
Lead: 8,148 metric tons
Copper: 2,522 metric tons
Gold: 561 lb.

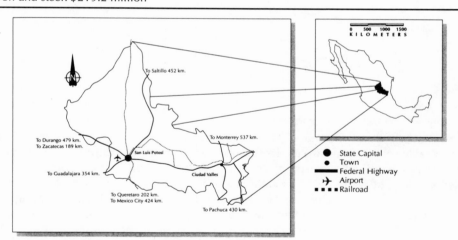

The majority of San Luis Potosí's economic activity is based on its large mineral resources. It is the nation's largest producer of silver, fluorite, antimony, and calcium and the nation's third-largest producer of zinc. Mexico's largest electrolytic foundry is also in the state.

San Luis Potosí has a major cattle industry, with livestock accounting for 37.5 percent of the state's agricultural production. It is Mexico's greatest mutton producer. Approximately 33 percent of the cultivated land is used for beans, basic foodstuffs, and corn, and the government is enlarging this output through a major hydraulic program.

San Luis Potosí is conveniently located near Mexico City, Monterrey, and Aguascalientes. It has a strong highway and railroad system. Foreign investors include Bendix, Sandoz, Crown Cork, Dexter, and Union Carbide.

Sinaloa

Population: 2,193,904
Capital: Culiacán
Principal cities: Culiacán: population—
602,100; Mazatlán: population—
314,200; Los Mochis: population—
305,500
Land area: 21,813 sq. mi.
Airports: international—1; national—2
Maritime ports: 5
Highways: main—530 mi.; secondary—
2,649 mi.
Railways: 772 mi.
Telephones per 1,000 people: 95
Radio stations: 35
Television stations: 8
Newspapers: 15
Growth rate: .0223
Industrial parks: 11
Avg. level of education: 6.1 yr.
Cultivated acreage: 2,407,845 a.; irrigated
acreage: 1,734,733 a.; irrigation ratio:
72%

Cereals and other agricultural products:
$74.7 million
Sugar: $50.7 million
Beverages: $44.1 million
Cooking oil: $43.1 million
Meat: $27.8 million

Leading Crops

Wheat: 1,047,131 metric tons
Tomatoes: 860,484 metric tons
Corn: 214,491 metric tons
Green chilies: 178,244 metric tons
Sorghum: 153,488 metric tons
Sugarcane: 115,875 metric tons

Mining

Silver: 164,148 lb.
Zinc: 5,102 metric tons
Lead: 5,084 metric tons
Gold: 22,458 lb.

Leading Industries

Food processing and preserving: $77
million

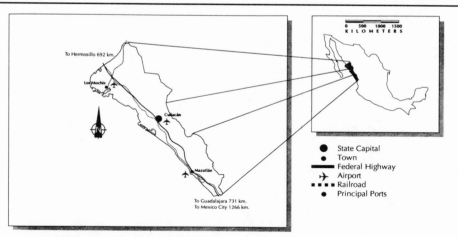

Sinaloa is Mexico's second-greatest producer of grain and vegetables. Approximately 75 percent of its territory is used for agriculture, including orchard and vegetable crops. Irrigation has been a top priority of the state, whose efforts have paid off with an increasingly bounteous harvest.

Mazatlán is an important Pacific seaport for freight and passenger vessels.

Since 1991, a major industrial seaport has been under construction on the Pacific Ocean in Topolobampo. Fishing is Sinaloa's second-greatest economic activity. Its fishing fleet grew 50 percent during the 1980s, bringing in a catch of over 150,000 tons. Flourishing seafood-related industries provide services including canning, freezing, fileting, and flouring.

Sonora

Population: 1,821,602
Capital: Hermosillo
Principal cities: Hermosillo: population—
    449,400; Cd. Obregón: population—
    220,300
Land area: 69,820 sq. mi.
Airports: international—3; national—2
Maritime ports: 12
Highways: main—1,390 mi.; secondary—
    2,077 mi.
Railways: 1,240 mi.
Telephones per 1,000 people: 128
Radio stations: 51
Television stations: 45
Newspapers: 11
Growth rate: .0215
Industrial parks: 17
Avg. level of education: 9 yr.
Cultivated acreage: 1,628,113 a.; irrigated
    acreage: 1,601,553 a.; irrigation ratio:
    98%

Leading Industries

Automotive: $580.8 million
Meat: $81.2 million

Beverages $73.3 million
Cement, lime, and gypsum processing:
    $68.2 million
Cooking oil: $59 million
Electric equipment, machinery, and
    accessories, including electric-energy
    generators: $48.7 million

Leading Crops

Wheat: 1,396,912 metric tons
Alfalfa: 1,097,390 metric tons
Corn: 219,124 metric tons
Oranges: 124,265 metric tons
Cottonseed: 120,429 metric tons
Raw cotton: 76,637 metric tons

Mining

Copper: 269,276 metric tons
Silver: 314,394 lb.
Gold: 1,708 lb.
Zinc: 1,307 metric tons
Lead: 1,231 metric tons

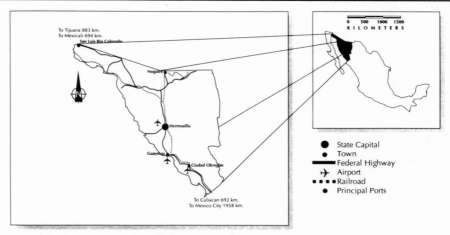

Sonora's sophisticated infrastructure, its proximity to the United States, and its free trade zone have fostered a dynamic *maquiladora* sector specializing in food and beverage processing and electric appliance industries. Ford Motor Company is also located here.

Sonora is Mexico's leading agricultural state. It is the largest wheat producer and the second-largest alfalfa producer. Pigs (110,191 metric tons) and cattle

(67,872 metric tons) also account for significant economic activity, with the latter leading to numerous pasteurization centers throughout the state.

The state has a 620-mile coastline along the Gulf of California. It is the nation's largest seafood producer and processor, handling nearly 450,000 tons of seafood, including sardines, shrimp, tuna, shark, and bass. Major seafood-processing plants are in Yavaros, Puerto Peñasco, and Guaymas.

Sonora is Mexico's largest copper producer.

Tabasco

Population: 1,501,719
Capital: Villahermosa
Principal city: Villahermosa: population—
 390,100
Land area: 9,489 sq. mi.
Airports: international—0; national—1
Maritime ports: 2;
Highways: main—364 mi.; secondary—
 1,632 mi.
Railways: 188 mi.
Telephones per 1,000 people: 52
Radio stations: 15
Television stations: 10
Newspapers: 6
Growth rate: .0335
Industrial parks: 3
Avg. level of education: 5.1 yr.
Cultivated acreage: 355,557 a.; irrigated
 acreage: 0 a.

Leading Industries

Petrochemicals: $1.31 billion
Baked goods: $37.2 million
Beverages: $19.9 million
Cooking oil: $18.3 million
Cement, lime, and gypsum production:
 $16 million
Cocoa, chocolate and other candy: $8
 million

Leading Crops

Sugarcane: 1,436,035 metric tons
Plantains: 188,228 metric tons
Corn: 78,284 metric tons
Copra: 39,394 metric tons
Cacao: 32,500 metric tons
Rice: 38,052 metric tons

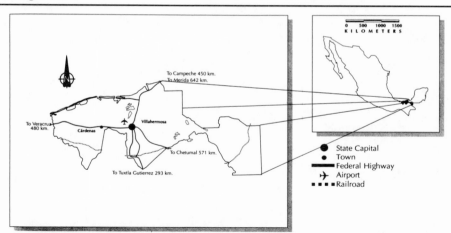

Tabasco is a tropical state bordering the Gulf of Mexico and Guatemala. The state holds the majority of Mexico's oil supplies, fostering advanced petrochemical and oil by-product industries that account for nearly 80 percent of Tobasco's GDP. Tabasco has 409 wells in 49 fields and produces 47.7 percent of Mexico's natural gas and 27.9 percent of its crude oil.

Other industries are not very developed, but Tabasco is working toward overcoming this. A coastal highway is being built that will link it to the other gulf states.

Most of Tabasco's agricultural production is lowland crops. The state is Mexico's largest cacao producer.

Tamaulipas

Population: 2,248,767
Capital: Cd. Victoria
Principal cities: Tampico: population—
559,000; Matamoros: population—
303,400; Cd. Victoria: population—
207,800
Land area: 30,862 sq. mi.
Airports: international—4; national—1
Maritime ports: 4
Highways: main—1,356 mi.; secondary—
1,186 mi.
Railways: 583 mi.
Telephones per 1,000 people: 125
Radio stations: 55
Television stations: 19
Newspapers: 24
Growth rate: .0181
Industrial parks: 26
Avg. level of education: 6.6 yr.
Cultivated acreage: 2,898,436 a.; irrigated
acreage: 985,592 a.; irrigation ratio:
34%

Leading Industries

Petroleum refining: $565 million
Basic chemicals: $347.3 million

Petrochemicals: $161.9 million
Electronic equipment and mechanisms,
including radios, televisions,
communication devices, and medical
equipment: $153.5 million
Automotive: $114.3 million
Beverages: $95.3 million

Leading Crops

Sugarcane: 1,700,513 metric tons
Sorghum: 1,094,025 metric tons
Corn: 546,591 metric tons
Soybeans: 71,201 metric tons
Wheat: 21,389 metric tons
Safflower: 18,004 metric tons

Mining

Silver: 791 lb.

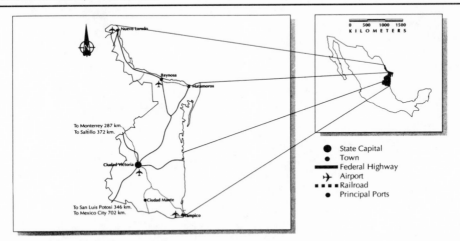

Tamaulipas has a strong diversified economy. It is a big exporter to the United States, which shares part of its border. Tamaulipas has considerable petroleum and petrochemical assets and is responsible for 13.2 percent of Mexico's refining production.

Industries in Tamaulipas are located primarily in the northern region of the state in Matamoros, Reynosa, and Nuevo Laredo. Many involve seafood processing. The state has a good infrastructure and skilled employees for *maquiladoras,* which specialize in toy manufacturing, electronic accessories fabrication, and food processing.

Tamaulipas has a great cattle industry and usually exports 50,000 head annually to the United States. It is Mexico's largest sorghum grower and one of the nation's larger sugarcane growers.

Tamaulipas is located along the Gulf of Mexico, enabling it to harvest shrimp, shark, crawfish, and crabs.

Tlaxcala

Population: 761,259
Capital: Tlaxcala
Principal city: Tlaxcala: population—
    111,800
Land area: 1,558 sq. mi.
Airports: international—0; national—1
Maritime ports: 0
Highways: main—379 mi.; secondary—
    403 mi.
Railways: 224 mi.
Telephones per 1,000 people: 36
Radio stations: 5
Television stations: 1
Newspapers: 1
Growth rate: .0303
Industrial parks: 17
Avg. level of education: 6 yrs.
Cultivated acreage: 609,813 a.; irrigated
    acreage: 73,218 a.; irrigation ratio:
    12%

Leading Industries

Basic chemicals, excluding basic
    petrochemicals: $174.6 million
Yarns and fibers: $90.5 million
Plastics: $52.3 million
Electric machinery, equipment, and
    accessories, including electric-energy
    generators: $46.4 million
Iron and steel: 41.4 million
Cement, lime, and gypsum processing:
    $27.2 million

Leading Crops

Green alfalfa: 289,509 metric tons
Corn: 119,982 metric tons
Wheat: 27,279 metric tons
Barley: 17,328 metric tons
Beans: 1,866 metric tons

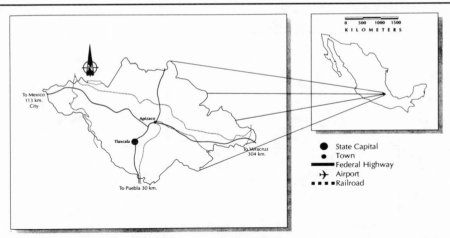

Tlaxcala, located in central Mexico, is Mexico's smallest state. It is an important communications link since it is the only cross-route between the Gulf of Mexico and the center of the country. It has a strong highway and railroad system.

Tlaxcala may become the site for several industries that will be forced to leave Mexico City because of new pollution control laws. Tlaxcala is preparing for the arrival of the industries by completing new industrial parks and upgrading older ones. The state's proximity to Mexico City has already attracted some light industry. It is home to Abbot Laboratories de Mexico and Federal Pacific Electric de Mexico.

Since Tlaxcala is one of Mexico's major barley and malt producers, it also has a thriving beer industry. Agricultural production (especially wheat) has increased significantly during the past decade from improved irrigation systems.

Veracruz

Population: 6,208,995
Capital: Jalapa
Principal cities: Coatzacoalcos:
  population—515,300; Veracruz:
  population—451,300; Jalapa:
  population—349,900; Orizaba:
  population—268,400
Land area: 27,697 sq. mi.
Airports: international—1; national—4
Maritime ports: 8
Highways: main—1,747 mi.; secondary—
  1,963 mi.
Railways: 1,104 mi.
Telephones per 1,000 people: 70
Radio stations: 80
Television stations: 12
Newspapers: 19
Growth rate: .0216
Industrial parks: 11
Avg. level of education: 5.3 yr.
Cultivated acreage: 2,222,555 a.; irrigated
  acreage: 82,236 a.; irrigation ratio: 4%

Leading Industries

Basic petrochemicals: $1.71 billion
Petroleum: $1 billion
Basic chemicals, excluding basic
  petrochemicals: $609.8 million
Iron and steel $378.1 million
Sugar: $284.7 million
Cereals and other agricultural products:
  $246.6 million

Leading Crops

Sugarcane: 800,000 metric tons
Corn: 738,792 metric tons
Rice: 130,629 metric tons
Oranges: 62,109 metric tons
Green chilies: 55,391 metric tons
Beans: 21,826 metric tons

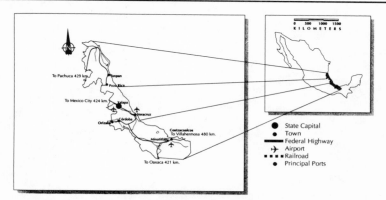

Veracruz is one of Mexico's most important agricultural states. Much of its produce is exported internationally, since it has one of Mexico's largest and busiest ports. Veracruz has Mexico's largest cattle industry, producing 150,000 tons of beef per year. It also is the nation's largest sugarcane grower and the second-largest producer of rice and coffee.

The most important sector of the state's economy is oil. It has 2,500 wells on 112 oil fields and six refining centers. Silica, kaolin and sulfur are also extracted. Manufacturing is concentrated in Coatzacoalcos, Veracruz, Jalapa, and Orizaba.

Veracruz has the largest fishing fleet in Mexico and is its greatest seafood producer, with a harvest including shrimp, clams, oysters, bass, and crabs.

Veracruz has pre-Columbian ruins and a strong local culture that make it a popular tourist site.

Yucatán

Population: 1,362,923
Capital: Mérida
Principal city: Mérida: population—
 595,100
Land area: 16,778 sq. mi.
Airports: international—1; national—0
Maritime ports: 14
Highways: main—762 mi.; secondary—
 1,169 mi.
Railways: 372 mi.
Telephones per 1,000 people: 85
Radio stations: 20
Television stations: 7
Newspapers: 3
Growth rate: .0277
Industrial parks: 6
Avg. level of education: 5.8 yr.
Cultivated acreage: 897,027 a.; irrigated
 acreage: 7,472 a.; irrigation ratio: 1%

Leading Industries

Beverages: $67.5 million
Cooking oil: $61.3 million
Cement, lime, and gypsum processing:
 $57.4 million
Plastics: $40.7 million
Fibers and cords: $40.2 million
Cereals and other agricultural products:
 $40.1 million

Leading Crops

Oranges: 85,093 metric tons
Sisal: 26,217 metric tons
Tomatoes: 19,055 metric tons
Avocados: 10,179 metric tons
Corn: 9,586 metric tons
Lemons: 8,061 metric tons

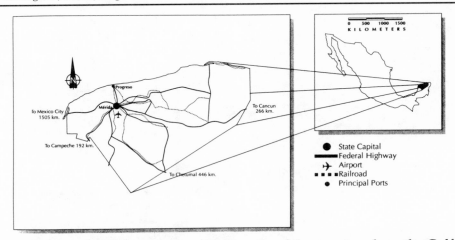

The Yucatán is located on the southeastern tip of the country along the Gulf of Mexico. It has five principal seaports and four shelter ports. Progreso was improved in 1992 and can easily handle high-draft vessels, making the Yucatán more accessible to foreign traders.

Most of the Yucatán's industry is focused on food processing and natural fiber production. The active and rapidly growing *maquiladora* industry is especially concentrated in production of apparel, electronic and electrical mechanisms, and fishing goods.

The Yucatán's location and infrastructure support strong seafood production and processing, particularly of bass, shark, shellfish, and octopus.

The Yucatán is a target for tourism development since it offers beautiful beaches, ancient ruins, and strong local folklore and crafts. There are now direct flights between Mérida and the United States.

Zacatecas

Population: 1,276,088
Capital: Zacatecas
Principal city: Zacatecas: population—
114,800
Land area: 28,225 sq. mi.
Airports: international—0; national—1
Maritime ports: 0
Highways: main—900 mi.; secondary—
1,313 mi.
Railways: 418 mi.
Telephones per 1,000 people: 36
Radio stations: 12
Television stations: 13
Newspapers: 5
Growth rate: .0128
Industrial parks: 3
Avg. level of education: 4.8 yr.
Cultivated acreage: 2,713,962 a.; irrigated
acreage: 185,364 a.; irrigation ratio: 7%

Leading Industries

Beverages: $27.5 million
Meat $8.2 million

Tortillas and cornmeal: $7.5 million
Clay products for construction: $5.6
million
Dairy products: $5 million
Baked goods: $4.4 million

Leading Crops

Beans: 303,267 metric tons
Corn: 279,735 metric tons
Alfalfa: 63,334 metric tons
Tomatoes: 49,931 metric tons
Green chilies: 20,225 metric tons
Wheat: 9,413 metric tons

Mining

Silver: 1,889,353 lb.
Zinc: 90,873 metric tons
Lead: 58,088 metric tons
Gold: 1,145 lb.
Copper 14,179 metric tons

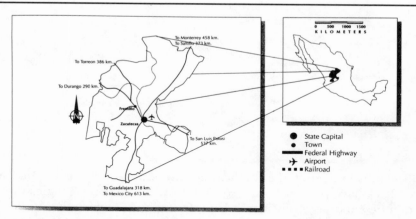

Most of Zacatecas's principal industries relate to the transformation of minerals or food products, such as pasteurization, wheat milling, and meat packing. The level of industrial production is not as developed.

Despite its arid climate, Zacatecas has an impressive level of agricultural production. It is Mexico's largest bean producer and is one of the nation's largest corn and red pepper producers. Cattle (35,329 metric tons) is a principal part of the economy, and sophisticated technology is used for efficient beef and dairy production.

Zacatecas is the largest silver producer in the world. It also has ample supplies of zinc and lead, industrial clays, marble, and nonferrous minerals.

4

The Economy

Mexico has evolved a sound, high-growth economy through the strict monetary discipline and structural transformation that the government has been administering through reforms since December 1988. The basis of these reforms has been a determination to make Mexico's economy competitive through globalization and foreign investment. The government has recognized the importance of deregulating the economy to encourage strong initiative and activity in the private sector. This could only be possible with a stabilized economy that would allow a foundation for economic growth. Today, both foreigners and Mexicans have regained confidence in the Mexican economy, and this is reflected by inflows of foreign investment and retention of former "flight capital."

Stabilization

Mexico's Pact for Economic Solidarity (PACTO), presented in December 1987, had a strong effect on the inflation rate through the voluntary cooperation of both the public and private sector. In twelve months, annualized inflation dropped from 160 percent to 51.7 percent without causing a recession.

The Pact for Stability and Economic Growth (PECE) was adopted in December 1988 as a blueprint to combat inflation during 1989–1994 by combining price stability with a long-term, gradual growth recovery. This agreement stipulates that the peso have a controlled depreciation of roughly 3 percent annually (20 centavos). By the end of 1992, the annualized inflation rate had fallen to an estimated 12 percent, an impressive reduction from the 1988 inflation rate of 51.7 percent. The current goal is to further reduce inflation to the single digits and stick with strict fiscal discipline.

The Mexican government is attempting to reduce price controls wherever it can, but it still controls a number of sensitive commodities, including milk, vegetable fats, oils, butter, corn, rice, beans, fish, and soluble coffee. It must still approve the price of all pharmaceutical products. Price controls based on changes in cost are applied to commodities, including household appliances, paper, tractors, soap, fertilizers, steel, cellulose, and buses.

The Bank of Mexico depends on its foreign reserves for use as a monetary instrument against the downward fall of the peso, the volatile nature of Mexican capital markets, and the high volume of foreign investment. These reserves were an estimated record high of $18.4 billion at the end of 1992. The monetary base is almost completely backed by reserves.

Public-Sector Debt

In 1990, the Salinas administration began a high-priority campaign to reduce public-sector debt through strict fiscal policies, proceeds from the sale of state enterprises, and external debt restructuring. Its efforts have produced remarkable results. The public-sector financial deficit plummeted from 16 percent of the gross domestic product (GDP) in 1987 to 1.5 percent of the GDP in 1991. By 1992, Mexico was among the small minority of world nations to actually generate fiscal surplus (1.7% of the GDP).

The government liquidated or privatized banks and large, inefficient state-held enterprises, bringing in an additional $21.2 billion. In October 1991, Finance Secretary Pedro Aspe stated that $6.56 billion from these sales had been used to pay for 12 percent of the government's internal debt. By the end of March 1992, the government had used another $4.5 million from the sales to lower the debt even further.

The Mexican government's fiscal policies caused the real annual growth rate of the internal debt to fall from an average of 35.9 percent during 1987–1989 to 2.3 percent in 1990. The growth rate turned negative in 1991 (−11.2%) and had fallen to −23.84 percent by June of 1992.

As the public sector's demand for domestic credit has been reduced, interest rates have fallen. The monthly interest rate (which is measured on the twenty-eight-day Mexican Treasury bill) fell from 46.65 percent in March 1990 to 11.84 percent in March 1991. The rate inched up to 18.15 percent by November 1992, but this has been attributed to the necessity to bring capital into Mexico for financing a rising current account deficit in the balance of payments, rather than to an increase in the government's demand for credit.

Rewards. The lowering of interest rates has enabled the government to save approximately $16.1 billion in costs, an amount equivalent to approximately 5 percent of Mexico's 1992 GDP.

Mexico's private sector is also enjoying benefits from the lower interest rates. Mexican commercial bank credit that was being utilized by private entities grew 35.7 percent in real terms between December 1990 and March 1992. Credit from both commercial and development banks to the government fell 18 percent in real terms during this same period.

Foreign Debt Agreement. At the beginning of 1989, Mexico's external debt had reached a height of $105 billion, an amount equivalent to 40 percent of the nation's GNP. Mexico became the first nation to participate in the Brady Plan, established with the United States in March 1989 to restructure and reduce Mexico's debt owed to foreign commercial banks. This plan enabled Mexico to have a cash flow savings of approximately $9.4 billion in 1990 and 1991 and an estimated savings of an additional $11.1 billion between 1992 and 1994.

The Mexican government also began debt swaps for infrastructure, debt swaps for education and social works, and direct buy-back programs in 1990, reducing the external debt by another $7.2 billion. These programs reduced the gross public-sector foreign debt, which fell from $80.75 billion in March 1992 to $73.58 billion in two months. International interest payments for Mexico have been reduced by nearly $400 million annually.

Risk Insurance. Finance Secretary Pedro Aspe stated in June 1992 that Mexico was participating in a risk insurance program that guarantees Mexico will not pay more than 6.25 percent on its public-sector external debt during 1992 and 1993. The purpose of this program is to protect the Mexican economy from external forces and ease the application of the government's economic policies.

Private-Sector Spending in the 1990s

In the 1990s (unlike the two previous decades), the private rather than the public sector has been responsible for the remarkable rise in investment, which has outpaced the rise in consumption. Real private investment now accounts for more than 75 percent of total investment (up 14.1 percent). Real gross fixed-capital spending has increased 8.5 percent. Consumption has risen 4.7 percent, with private-sector consumption growing 5 percent, nearly twice the speed of public-sector consumption; this is partially attributed to the significant growth in Mexico's middle class from 1989 to 1993, during which time the average real wage has grown nearly 20 percent.

Real internal financing has risen 3.5 percent. Financing to the private sector is up 33.2 percent and is responsible for nearly two thirds of total internal borrowing. Real internal financing to the public sector has fallen 26.6 percent.

The trade gap in 1991 had grown by $4.3 billion in one year, to $11.2 billion, which is attributed to both an increase in imports (up 28.1 percent from the previous year) and a reduction in mining exports (down 35.9 percent). Nearly 85 percent of total imports are in capital and intermediate consumer goods; both capital and consumer goods grew more than 38 percent in 1992. The private sector was responsible for 92.5 percent of Mexico's imports.

GDP Growth

The U.S. Department of Commerce estimates that Mexico's GDP real growth rate was 2.8 percent in 1992, equaling $317 billion. GDP per capita was $3,700. During the 1980s, the GDP had fallen from 64,175 pesos in 1980 to 59,778 pesos in 1989, dropping 7 percent. Since there are such sharp differences in Mexico's income distribution, this 7 percent drop caused wage earners to lose as much as 50 percent of their spending money. The Banco de México indicates that the GDP began to pick up in 1990. Imports grew 18.8 percent that year and 16.6 percent in 1991. Exports grew 3.5 percent in 1990 and 5.1 percent in 1991. Government consumption grew 2.3 percent in 1990 and 2.7 percent in 1991 when merchandise exports were valued at $27.1 billion. Private consumption grew 5.7 percent in 1990 and 5 percent in 1991.

The annual GDP growth by sectors fluctuated more widely during these years. The construction sector GDP grew 7.7 percent in 1990, slowing to 2.6 percent in 1991. The manufacturing sector grew 5.2 percent in 1990 and 3.7 percent in 1991. Agriculture boomed in 1990, growing 10.1 percent, only to slow to 1.4 percent in 1991 because of drought. The service sector (including retail, restaurants, and hotels) grew 3.9 percent in 1990 and 4.7 percent in 1991. The transportation, storage and communications sector GDP grew 6.3 percent; the manufacturing industry sector and the electric power, gas, and water sector, 5.2 percent; the mining sector, 3.2 percent; the financial services, insurance, and real estate sector, 2.5 percent; and the community, social, and personal services sector, 1.4 percent.

Privatization

The government has strongly encouraged privatization in many sectors to make them more competitive. From 1989 to January 1993, the government sold 209 state-owned companies (excluding banks) for $9.1 billion to private investors. Ineffective state-owned companies have been liquidated. The number of parastatal enterprises shrank from 1,155 in 1982 to 250 in March 1991. In 1982, the Mexican government was paying parastatal enterprises annual subsidies that amounted to 8 percent of the GDP; in 1991, the subsidies were down to only 4 percent. Mexico's eighteen banks were privatized for $12.1 billion.

Privatized sectors include pharmaceuticals, air transport, financial institutions, petrochemicals, tourism, telecommunications, and steel. Privatized companies include Mexicana de Aviación and Aeromexico (Mexico's two largest airlines); the telephone company, TELMEX; Sidermex and Altos Hornos (Mexico's largest steel mills); Asemex (insurance); and eighteen commercial banks.

Mexico's Exports

As Mexico's economy has diversified, the nation has become less dependent on its petroleum exports. Oil still brings Mexico the most money; however, oil exports to the United States fell to 14 percent in 1991, from 64 percent in 1980.

According to Banco de México, Mexico's international merchandise exports, (excluding *maquiladora* trade,) had an estimated value of $27.5 billion in 1992. When this sector was included, it was valued at $42.948 billion. The U.S. Department of Commerce reports that Mexican exports to the United States had an estimated value of $34 billion in 1992, giving the United States a 2:1 trade balance with Mexico.

Mexico's manufacturing exports grew nearly 14 percent, to more than $16 billion, in 1991, despite a decline in manufacturing employment. Principal Mexican exports to the United States in 1992 included electrical machinery and apparatus ($5.5 billion), crude oil ($4.4 billion), motor vehicles ($2.6 billion), televisions and radios ($1.09 billion), and motor vehicle parts ($2.0 billion). Goods totaling nearly 50 percent of the value of U.S. imports from Mexico in 1991 entered without duty under the Generalized System of Preferences.

Mexico's motor vehicle exports grew 50 percent in 1991. Other export industries with strong growth included chemicals, which grew 25.1 percent, nonmetallic minerals (20.1 percent), electronic products and components (15.3 percent), food and beverages (11 percent), and iron and steel products (8.7 percent).

5

Foreign Investment

Mexico has liberalized regulations for foreign and domestic investment to increase the volume of returning flight capital and to encourage capital investment. Mexico's Law to Promote Mexican Investment and Regulate Foreign Investment was reformed in 1989, opening over two thirds of Mexico's total gross domestic product (GDP) to foreign participation and eliminating or streamlining foreign investment regulations. Now foreigners may have up to 100 percent ownership on ventures under $100 million or located outside Mexico City, Guadalajara, and Monterrey without receiving any government authorization.

Foreign investment reforms have paid off. Banco de México reported that foreign investment in Mexico was valued at a record high of $9.9 billion in 1991, up $3.8 billion in a single year. In 1992, foreign investment declined 16.6 percent and was valued at $8.3 billion. Portfolio investment accounted for 31.5 percent of total foreign investment. The United States continues to be Mexico's largest foreign investor, with U.S. direct foreign investment representing approximately 63 percent of Mexico's total foreign direct investment in 1991. Germany was responsible for 6.5 percent of the total foreign investment and Canada for approximately 2 percent.

By the end of 1991, most U.S. direct investment was in industrial manufacturing, including the *maquiladora* sector (52.4 percent) and the service sector (42 percent). This reflects a significant change in the pattern of foreign investing; total U.S. direct investment in the industrial sector was down almost 78 percent since 1980, while services-sector investments had risen from 8.5 percent in 1980 to about 42 percent.[1] (The services sector includes tourism, financial services and real estate, community and social services, transportation and communication services, electricity and water, hotels and restaurants, professional, technical, and individual services, and construction.)

Foreign investors are varied in size, nationality, and method of investment. For example, Corning has signed a $300 million deal with Vitro, a Mexican glass manufacturer, to sell tableware in Mexico. At the end of 1991, Walmart announced a joint venture with Cifra, Mexico's largest retailer, to open wholesale clubs in Mexico, D. F. Zenith is planning to close its factories in Taiwan and move all its manufacturing plants, employing 600 people, to Mexico. Lotus Development Corporation, Microsoft, and Compaq Computer have opened subsidiaries in Mexico City.

Deregulation

The following sectors have benefited from deregulation reforms:

- *Aquaculture.* Private investors can now own farms for shrimp, oysters, and six other marine species if operations are paid for by private holdings. Permits are no longer necessary, and the only requirements are sanitary standards. Foreign ownership is permitted for up to 49 percent of such enterprises.

- *Automotive.* An automotive decree in November 1990 significantly decreased regulations in this sector. Luxury cars, vans, and sports cars may now be imported into Mexico. Established auto manufacturers (e.g., Nissan, GM, Ford) may now decide which model vehicles they will produce, and the vehicle's local content requirement has been reduced to 36 percent. Companies may also import new vehicles of their brand name, provided they maintain a favorable trade balance and follow specific quantitative conditions.

- *Financial services.* Foreigners may have up to 49 percent ownership of a company or nonbank financial intermediary and up to 30 percent ownership of most banks and stockbrokerage houses by simply registering with the National Commission on Foreign Investment.

- *Mining.* All production taxes have been abolished, and royalty payments are now regulated. Mining reserves that were previously managed by the government have been released for private investment. Legal, administrative, and concession requirements have been streamlined. A foreign investor can own up to 100 percent of a mining company's stock by directly purchasing 49 percent of the stock and owning the other 51 percent through a trust held by a Mexican bank.

- *Passenger transportation.* There are fewer economic and legal obstacles in this sector, so quality has improved. (See Infrastructure/Transportation in Chapter 1.)

- *Petrochemicals.* The Mexican government reclassified basic petrochemicals into a secondary category, thus increasing the number of products that can have foreign investment. Foreign investment is only allowed in secondary petrochemicals and finished products.

Petróleos Mexicanos (PEMEX) has established a program whereby foreign or domestic private investment groups may supply capital funds to construct a plant and be repaid with the petrochemical products that it produces. However, these plants must be constructed under PEMEX supervision and managed by PEMEX. Foreign companies can get contracts with PEMEX for exploration.

There are now specific time periods for processing permits to produce secondary petrochemicals, so there are fewer bureaucratic holdups.

The Mexican government now allows a foreign investor to acquire 100 percent ownership of a secondary petrochemical plant if the foreigner creates a specific trust with a Mexican credit institution. This trust enables the foreign investor to collect the profits from the enterprise, while keeping the direct control of the company with a Mexican trustee.

■ *Technology transfer.* Now companies are solely responsible for the technology that they desire to transfer. All terms for the sale of the technology, the technical assistance, the patents, and the trademarks must be settled completely by the foreign suppliers and the companies. This recent liberation should be particularly helpful in protecting industrial property and determining the conditions for forming franchises. The government's authority to dictate the cost and quality of technology is now very limited.

■ *Telecommunications.* Connection permits for equipment such as telefaxes, telexes, and computer modems have been eliminated. Recent antitrust stipulations have been incorporated, requiring dominant carriers to interconnect with new telephone companies. The new regulations contribute to the development of an aggressive value-added service market.

■ *Trucking.* Regulations first instituted in 1990 have doubled trucking capacity. A $1 billion annual reduction in transportation and production costs is expected. (See Infrastructure/Transportation in Chapter 1.)

Foreign Investment Classifications

The National Foreign Investment Commission (FIC) of the Secretariat of Commerce and Industrial Development (SECOFI) has the authority to approve foreign participation in existing or new companies that do not receive automatic approval. The foreign investment law divides economic activity into four classifications: activities reserved exclusively for the state, activities reserved for Mexican citizens, foreign investment (various classes), and activities subject to general rules. Also listed are industries that have not yet been included in the recent classifications.

Category 1: Activities Considered Strategic and Reserved for the State Exclusively

■ Extraction of petroleum and natural gas, petroleum refining, and basic petrochemical activities
■ Uranium treatment and uses of nuclear fuels
■ Minting of coins
■ Generation, transmission, and supply of electrical energy
■ Railway transportation
■ Telegraphs
■ Extraction or use of uranium and radioactive minerals
■ Ownership and operation of satellites

Category 2: Activities Reserved for Mexicans

■ Forestry and forest nurseries
■ Exploration of woods
■ Retail sales of liquid gas
■ Building materials transportation services
■ Transportation (shipping) services

- Other specialized cargo transportation
- General cargo transportation services
- Passenger bus transportation services
- Urban and suburban passenger bus transportation services
- Taxi transportation services (automobile type)
- Fixed-route taxi transportation services
- Special taxi transportation services (automobile type)
- School and tourism bus transportation services
- Maritime coastal transportation shipping services
- Coastal and sea towing services
- Mexican flag aircraft transportation services
- Air taxi transportation services
- Credit unions
- Private transmission of radio programs
- Transmission and repetition of television programs
- Public notary services
- Customs brokers and representation services
- Administration of sea and river ports

Category 3: Foreign Investment up to 30 Percent

- Commercial banks
- Stockbrokerage houses

Category 4: Foreign Investment up to 34 Percent

- Exploitation or use of carbon and minerals containing iron
- Extraction or use of phosphoric rock and sulfur

Category 5: Foreign Investment up to 40 Percent

- Secondary petrochemicals
- Manufacture and assembly of automotive parts and accessories

Category 6: Foreign Investment up to 49 Percent

- Manufacture of secondary petrochemical products
- Manufacture of parts and accessories for automotive electrical systems
- Manufacture and assembly of automobile and trailer bodies
- Manufacture of motors and parts for automobiles and trucks
- Manufacture of parts for the transmission system of automobiles and trucks
- Manufacture of parts for the suspension system of automobiles and trucks
- Manufacture of parts and accessories for the braking systems of automobiles and trucks
- Ocean fishing
- Coastal fishing
- Freshwater fishing
- Aquaculture

- Extraction or refinement of ores with gold, silver, or other precious metal or mineral content
- Extraction or refinement of mercury and antimony
- Extraction or refinement of industrial ores with lead and zinc content
- Extraction or refinement of copper ores
- Extraction or refinement of nonferrous metallic ores
- Exploitation or refinement of feldspar
- Exploitation of lime
- Extraction or refinement of barite
- Extraction or refinement of fluorite
- Exploitation of ores to obtain chemical products
- Extraction or refinement of salt
- Extraction or refinement of graphite
- Extraction or refinement of other nonmetallic minerals
- Manufacture of explosives and fireworks
- Manufacture of firearms and cartridges
- Retailing of firearms, cartridges, and ammunition
- River and lake transportation services
- Harbor transportation services
- Telephone services
- Other telecommunications services
- Financial leasing
- General deposit warehouses
- Bonding companies
- Factoring companies
- Exchange houses

Category 7: Foreign Investment up to 100 Percent With FIC Authorization

- Agriculture
- Cattle breeding and hunting
- Collection of forestry products
- Felling of trees
- Newspaper and magazine publishing
- Manufacture of coke and other products derived from coal
- Housing construction
- Nonhousing residential construction
- Construction of urban works
- Construction of industrial plants
- Construction of power generation plants
- Construction and erection of electrical transmission networks and lines
- Construction for the transmission of oil and its derivatives
- Mounting and installation of concrete structures
- Mounting and installation of metal structures
- Maritime works
- Construction of traffic works and land transportation facilities
- Construction of railways
- Hydraulic and sanitary installations in buildings

- Telecommunications installations
- Electrical installations in buildings
- Other special installations
- Earth moving
- Foundations
- Underground excavations
- Signals and protection installations
- Demolitions
- Construction of potable water and water treatment plants
- Drilling of oil and gas wells
- Drilling of potable water wells
- Other construction works not mentioned above
- High-seas transportation services
- Leasing of tourism ship services
- Services for companies that manage investment societies
- Private kindergarten services
- Private elementary school services
- Private high school services
- Private college services
- Private university services
- Private education services that combine kindergarten, elementary, high school, college, and university
- Private commercial and language school services
- Private technical, arts and crafts, and labor training school services
- Private music, dance, and other school services
- Private special education school services
- Legal services
- Accounting and auditing services
- Passenger bus central station administration and auxiliary services
- Administration of toll highways, international bridges, and auxiliary services
- Towing services for land vehicles
- Other services related to land transportation not mentioned above
- Air navigation services
- Airport and heliports administration services
- Stock and investment consulting services
- Insurance and bond, agent, and attorney services
- Pension consulting services
- Services for representational offices of foreign financial entities
- Other services related to financial, insurance, and bond institutions not mentioned above

Exceptions to Foreign Participation by Activity

- *Fishing.* Fishing is reserved for Mexicans exclusively whenever the investment society is for fixed income.
- *Coke industry, including coal and oil derivatives.* The Mexican government reserves the exclusive right to produce basic oil.

- *Printing, editorial, and related industries.* These industries may receive foreign investment after it has been authorized by the Foreign Investment Commission. The professional staff, however, must be Mexican.
- *Communications.* Communications services provided by the Mexican government may not have foreign investment participation.
- *Investment societies.* Only Mexicans may invest in fixed-income investment societies.
- *Technical, professional, and specialized services (excluding agricultural services).* Foreigners may invest in these groups with the authorization of the FIC. The professional staff, however, must be Mexican.

Automatic Approval

In sectors open to foreign investment, the Foreign Investment Commission now grants automatic approval without prior authorization to all projects that meet the following six requirements:

1. The investment does not total more than $100 million.
2. The project's financial resources come from outside Mexico and are intermediated by Mexican financial institutions.
3. If the project is an industrial facility, it is located outside Mexico City, Monterrey, and Guadalajara.
4. The project developers expect at least a balance between foreign exchange income and outlays during the first three years.
5. The project is expected to create permanent jobs and to establish worker training and personnel development programs.
6. The project uses appropriate technology and satisfies all environmental requirements.

If a project does not meet all of these requirements, it must apply for authorization from the FIC.

Government Approval

The National Registry of Foreign Investment was set up as part of the Secretariat of Commerce and Industrial Development (SECOFI) to receive information on the following areas: foreign corporations or individuals that are investing in Mexico, Mexican companies with capital stock that are partially or wholly owned by foreign investors, and trusts with foreign participation. Business entities or individuals required to register must file the necessary application within forty business days of the registration date. Registered Mexican corporations either wholly or partially owned by foreign investors must periodically provide information through the appropriate forms on their company's economic, financial, and balance of payment status.

Direct Acquisition

The most common form of direct foreign investment
medium-size Mexican companies are available for p

Purchasing Existing Company Shares

A foreign investor must get authorization from the FIC to acquu.
percent of the shares of an existing company engaged in an unclassified a..

Expansion of Existing Foreign Investments

If existing investors wish to relocate their enterprise or expand or change its focus,
they will not need special authorization if both of the following requirements
are met:

1. The existing investment includes a *maquiladora* or other export operation,
   or the expansion is the consequence of a merger.
2. The owners agree to fund an additional investment equal to 10 percent of
   the net value of the company's fixed assets. The project must also follow
   regulations of foreign investment in unclassified activities.

Foreign Investment in Restricted Mexican Companies

The Neutral Fund Program was established in 1989 to allow foreigners to get
trusts through which they may purchase shares of companies normally reserved
for Mexican nationals (series A shares). These shares are represented by certificates of ordinary participation (CPOs) issued by fiduciary institutions. Foreign
investors may then have shareholder rights but not voting rights.

Foreigners are also permitted to purchase negotiable receipts called ADRs,
which cover the issuer's shares.

Foreign Investment in Mexican Company Stock

The 1989 foreign investment reforms enable foreign investors to purchase the economic rights ("mutual capital") of a publicly traded company's stock. Foreigners
share the company's profit but may not control the company or its administration.

Majority Investment in Classified Activities

It is possible for foreign investors to own more than the maximum limit of capital
shares in a classified activity if they receive the authorization of the FIC. Authori-

may be given if the commission decides that the purchase will have eco-
cally favorable effects by helping domestic investment, enhancing export
ings, assisting the development of less industrialized zones, increasing wages
d employment, or promoting national research and technology.

Foreign Investment in Real Estate

Despite the recent "liberalization" of Mexican laws on real estate, foreign corporations may not own or acquire land in the Republic of Mexico. Instead, they may
become beneficiaries of land trusts that last for thirty-year periods and may then
be renewed automatically for an additional thirty years. Mexican banks act as the
trustees. Beneficiaries are entitled to lease the property (if it is outside certain
restricted zones) for up to ten years and may get real estate participation certificates, allowing them the right to use the property and any proceeds the trustees
may obtain from it. They also have the right to obtain the net proceeds from the
sale of the property. No permit is required for getting a land trust outside the
restricted zones.

The restricted zones are all within 100 kilometers (approximately 62 miles)
of Mexico's land borders and within 50 kilometers (approximately 31 miles) of its
coastline. Unlike before, foreigners are now permitted to invest in restricted zone
property if they establish trusts authorized by the Secretariat of Foreign Relations
within forty-five days after submitting the application.

Guidelines for Land Acquisition

1. Hire an attorney to conduct a title search of the property at the local Public
   Registry of Property. (Such a search may reveal conflicting claims regarding the ownership of property.)
2. Instruct your attorney to obtain from the Agency for Agrarian Reform a
   certificate disclosing the absence of any agrarian restrictions on the land.
   A community or *ejido* settlement may claim rights over property, particularly in the border and coastal areas.
3. When you are negotiating the price of real property, consider the availability of services such as reliable water, electricity, and telephones. If they are
   not available, negotiate with local authorities for provision of such services
   before exercising the purchase option.
4. Instruct your attorney to obtain a reliable survey of your selected land/or
   building and its surrounding boundaries. Quite possibly, the boundaries
   of a lot may be different than appearances would suggest.
5. Instruct your attorney to research the status of land-use permits for the
   land. Despite the existence of facilities, the land may lack the proper permits and legal status.
6. Instruct your attorney to determine whether the land is within an ecological reservation.
7. Instruct your attorney to help you negotiate the closing costs with the
   trustee, including trustee's fees. Trustees compete with each other and
   their fees may vary significantly.

8. Make sure to agree upon the trustee's fees at the beginning, before negotiating a land trust contract with a trustee (Mexican bank).
9. Ask the trustee to expressly identify all closing costs, including taxes, registration fees, notarization fees, permit fees (if applicable), appraisal costs, and so on.[2]

Foreign Exchange

The Mexican government does not limit the inflow of capital or the reinvestment of profits and dividends by foreign investors. The government eliminated currency controls in November 1991 to further encourage the *maquiladora* sector and exports. Brokers are no longer needed for most foreign currency transactions. The government now settles foreign currency obligations in terms of "representative" market rates (previously it used two market rates to indicate the actual cost of the transaction). The peso's value now follows a "fixed slide" that was determined by the 1991 National Stabilization Pact to be an average of 20 centavos per day. This means that while theoretically the peso is free to move at market rates, it actually has a rate managed by Banco de México.

Under NAFTA

NAFTA creates a fairer, more liberated atmosphere for investing, with fewer government regulations and trade barriers. Under NAFTA, U.S. investors in Canada and Mexico are treated the same as domestic companies. They have the right to repatriate capital and profits in hard currency and the right to receive fair compensation in the case of expropriation.

Although most economic activities (construction, petrochemicals, mining, food processing, etc.) are open to foreign investment, Mexico still retains the right to protect "constitutional" activities, including oil, electricity, and railroads. Basic telecommunications, maritime activities, government-funded R&D programs, and technology consortia also are not covered by NAFTA.

U.S. investors may purchase existing Mexican companies or set up their own companies in Mexico with automatic government approval unless their acquisition is greater than $25 million. This figure will be phased up to $150 million (adjusted for inflation and economic growth) over a ten-year period.

U.S. investors no longer need to limit imports to a given percentage of exports and are no longer required to use domestic goods or services. The requirement to export a certain level or percentage of services and the requirement to transfer technology to competitors has also been eliminated.

Notes

1. William J. Gorman, Judith K. Knepper, Bruce L. Kutnick, and Curtis F. Turnbow, *North American Trade Agreement: U.S.-Mexican Trade and Investment Data*, GAO/GGD-92–131 (Washington, D.C.: U.S. General Accounting Office, September 1992), p. 7.
2. Alfredo Andere, "Foreign Acquisition in Mexico," *Twin Plant News* (March 1991), pp. 16–19.

6

Labor

The Work Force

Mexico's large, young work force is one of its strongest resources. It is currently 28 million strong, and, since nearly 30 percent of the population is between the ages of 16 and 30, an additional 12 million workers will enter the force over the next ten years. Although the average Mexican has only a sixth-grade education, and only 3 percent of the people have a college degree, Mexican workers are often as efficient as their U.S. counterparts. Job training is a high priority. There are more than 1,000 technical schools throughout Mexico. All employers are required to establish training programs for their employees, and the results have paid off. Executives at leading U.S. corporations, including Caterpillar, IBM, Ford, and Procter & Gamble, are all very pleased with the productivity and skill of their Mexican employees.

The U.S. embassy estimates that Mexico had an 18 percent (unofficial) unemployment rate in March 1992. The Mexican government continues to place great emphasis on job creation and has strongly encouraged enrollment in one of Mexico's many technical schools. These schools are often funded by the government and international development banks, including the World Bank and the Inter-American Development Bank (IDB). They provide students with technical and other employable skills, such as computer programming, accounting, and marketing.

The Federal Labor Law

Mexico's Federal Labor Law (FLL) is regulated by the Secretariat of Labor and Social Security. It is a very comprehensive law and is applied by the Federal Labor Board, the state labor boards, and the Federal Labor Board of Conciliation and Arbitration. It is designed to protect the worker and, in the event of a dispute with an employer, nearly always gives the worker the benefit of the doubt. U.S. employers of Mexican workers must obey this law.

The FLL requires that at least 90 percent of all employees in a company be Mexican citizens. Executives are not included in the calculation of this percentage. The law guarantees workers the right to earn a minimum daily wage and to form unions and strike, sets a minimum age for children to be eligible to work, prohibits forced labor, and requires employers to have an acceptable workplace with accepted wages, working hours, and health and safety standards.

It is important for foreign investors to understand that under the FLL all employment arrangements are considered permanent, and no written document is needed to validate this point. Therefore, if an employee is hired on a temporary basis, this must be documented in the contract.

Minimum Wage

The FLL requires that workers be paid at least minimum wage in cash, without any deductions or withholdings, on a weekly basis. Mexican labor costs are highly competitive. They are nearly 80 percent lower than in the United States, 70 percent lower than in western Europe, and 60 percent lower than in Southeast Asia. According to the U.S. Department of Commerce and Banco de México, the national minimum wage in 1992 was $0.55 per hour, and the average worker worked 48.4 hours per week. This figure is lower in some rural parts of the country. Only low-skilled workers receive merely minimum wage, but they represent nearly 80 percent of the working population. Minimum wage rates are decided by a board of workers, employers, and representatives from the government and the unions. Wages in unionized businesses are established through collective bargaining. Foreign investors should realize that fringe benefits and additional employee costs are often higher in Mexico than in the United States, so while labor cost is still lower, it is not as low as it appears. An employer should expect to pay 70 to 100 percent of the basic wage in fringe and labor-law benefits.

A survey conducted by the American Chamber of Commerce of Mexico (AmCham) in 1992 found that the average daily wage paid by U.S. companies to their blue-collar workers was more than twice the minimum rate. Most paid $2.08 per hour, or $16.64 per day, which included benefits. This rate fluctuated depending on the sector and size of the company.[1]

The Unions

Approximately eight million workers in 1990 belonged to a union, including nearly 90 percent of all industrial workers. Unions are especially strong in the pharmaceutical, chemical, petrochemical, food and beverage, machinery and electromechanical, and electric-energy industries. The Confederación de Trabajadores de México (CTM; Federation of Mexican Workers) is Mexico's largest union, with over two million affiliates nationwide and strong influence on the government.

According to the Mexican Federal Labor Law, a minimum of twenty employees may form a union and use collective bargaining. Unions are allowed to request that a company recognize and contract with them as the sole bargaining agent for their employees. Unions may ask employers for additional worker rights that fall under the Mexican Federal Labor Law or Social Insurance Law.

Labor disputes and strikes are infrequent in Mexico. Disputes are moderated and controlled by the Secretariat of Labor and Social Security, which may impose sanctions on both unions and employers for labor-law infringements.

An AmCham survey found that 64 percent of U.S. companies operating in Mexico negotiate with a labor union and 43 percent of their labor is unionized. The larger the company, the more likely it will be unionized.[2]

Executives

High-level employees can be found through recruitment services. Mexico suffers from a shortage of highly skilled technicians and executives, resulting in a high level of turnover caused by these employees leaving to get a bigger paycheck. This is particularly true in the *maquiladora* sector. Employers often pay good salaries and offer rapid advancement to keep key personnel from leaving. Managers and skilled laborers can make equal or greater salaries than their U.S. counterparts because the demand for them is great.

Payroll taxes are much higher in Mexico than in the United States. Corporations previously were able to get more tax-free money into the hands of their professionals through loopholes, but those loopholes have been eliminated.

Employee Training

Employers are required by law to train all employees and submit information on their training programs to the government. Training committees of both managers and workers plan the programs. Training classes should be designed to improve workers' skills and welfare. There is no required minimum time period for classes, which may take place outside the business, with the employer receiving a corporate tax deduction for the program's expenses, or within the workplace.

Work Time and Vacations

The Mexican Federal Labor Law allows a maximum forty-eight-hour week with a half-hour break for meals and requires a day of rest. Night shifts last seven hours. Workers are paid for seven days since they must get a paid day of rest. Unlike the United States, overtime rates are not at time and a half; they are double time for one through nine hours, and any overtime after that is triple time. Companies are not allowed more than nine hours of overtime per employee. If an employee does not receive the designated one day of rest, a double wage rate applies. Work on a Sunday entitles an employee to a 25 percent premium, even if the person has another day off during the week.

Children between ages 14 and 16 are not permitted to work in dangerous environments or in the evening. Children cannot be employed if they are under age 14.

Workers are entitled to a week-long vacation after one year of work, with two additional days for each year up to four. After five years, two vacation days are added for each five-year period, with a three-week maximum. Salaries must be paid in full over vacations, including a vacation premium of 25 percent of salary. In addition to this, workers are entitled to eight legal holidays or a workday with a triple wage rate (see Chapter 1).

Work Safety

Businesses must meet the safety and health requirements of the Secretariat of Labor and Social Security. A commission for health and safety must be created from a pool of both managers and workers to investigate work-related accidents and illnesses. The secretariat may issue regulations and inspect workplaces to determine if regulations are being followed. If they are not, penalties may be issued.

Employment Termination

An employee terminated by a company is entitled by law to receive ninety days' severance pay, since there is no unemployment insurance. An employer may discharge an unsatisfactory employee without any compensation other than a seniority premium if the employer can demonstrate to the Secretariat of Labor and Social Security cause to do so. If the employer cannot, the employee may demand to be rehired or offered ninety days' severance compensation and twenty days' wages for each year spent at the company. Usually, employers pay a smaller "bonus" for voluntary resignation.

When a permanent employee dies, the worker's heirs are entitled to receive premiums valued at twelve days' salary for each year of service, provided that the maximum salary is not twice the minimum wage. This same amount is awarded to a permanent employee separated from work, with or without just cause.

Fringe Benefits

Employers should expect to pay 70 to 100 percent of the basic wage in fringe and labor-law benefits. The Mexican social security program covers medical expenses, disability pensions, old age pensions, and workers compensation. This costs the employer 14–16 percent of covered salaries and costs the employee 4.5 percent (unless the employee receives minimum wage, in which case the employer pays the full portion). Workers are entitled to receive a Christmas bonus of at least fifteen days' salary.

Profit Sharing

The Income Tax Law from Mexico's tax code, the Codigo Fiscal de la Federación, requires that employees receive 10 percent of their company's after-tax profit, without any further deductions. Exceptions to this regulation are the following classes of employers, who must instead pay their employees an extra month's salary: companies that have been established for only one year; new companies manufacturing a new product for the first two years; legally approved private and pubic welfare institutions; businesses with capital and gross income below the Secretariat of Labor's minimum; and mining and similar industries during the exploration phase. In businesses that do not have net taxable income figures for income tax purposes, the theoretical profit that corresponds to the tax paid is the taxable income for profit sharing. Profit sharing does not have to be greater than one month's salary for individuals who receive income only by collecting interest, managing rental properties, or participating in professional services, such as consulting, where individuals do not have full employee status.

Profits must be distributed to employees no later than five months past the close of the fiscal year, and copies of the tax return must be distributed to employees. An employee's portion of the distributed profits are measured by the employee's attendance for the year and the employee's salary; it cannot exceed 120 percent of the salary of the highest-paid worker.

Social Security

Employees and their families are entitled to medical and social services through Mexican Social Security (IMSS). There are 11 million workers under this system. Employees who make minimum wage do not have to pay anything to receive coverage. If an employee has a job-related accident and can no longer work, the person is covered for life. Social security also provides nursery care, death benefits, old age pensions, and injury, illness, and maternity pay. Women receive ninety days' maternity leave paid by social security, and their companies must continue to pay their taxes. Employees may even cover their parents if the parents are dependent on them for their well-being; the company pays a large tax on such employees' wages for this coverage, but other insurance coverage is not required.

Mexico's health care has improved significantly over the past twenty years, but medical services are unevenly distributed throughout the different regions. IMSS is active in every state and covers 38 million people. Much of the population, however, live in areas with less than 500 inhabitants, and financial restrictions and administrative obstacles have prevented these groups from getting the proper level of health care. The percentage of gross domestic product (GDP) appropriated to health care has remained at approximately 2.9 percent over the past few years. This money has been used to equip health centers, general hospitals, and a center for drug and alcohol addiction and to start seven new general hospitals.

All nongovernment companies that hire more than one person must register both employers and employees with the IMSS and pay their premiums. Registration protects the employer from liability in connection with job-related illnesses or accidents. Self-employed individuals, domestics, collective-farm workers, and others are covered by different policies. Social security is financed by salary withholdings, federal funds, and employer contributions. Retirement pensions are usually distributed at age 65, but early retirement with reduced rates can be distributed at age 60. Government employees have a separate social security system.

Social security premiums are payable every two months, and the costs are shared by employer and employee. The fee is approximately 14 percent of wages (not including overtime pay) up to a maximum of ten times the Federal District's minimum wage. Employers pay 75 percent of the cost; employees pay the remaining 25 percent through a deduction from their salary. The employer pays all occupational risk premiums as a percentage of the total employee/employer contributions toward old age benefits. Employees must pay an additional premium for day-care centers for children of working mothers; this comes from one percent of covered payrolls. Social security pays for employee medications. From social security, employees receive 60–80 percent of their salary if they are absent from work for more than three days for a non-job-related illness. In the case of permanent disability, a minimum of 50 percent of the covered salary is payable. Heirs receive the benefits if an employee's death is job-related.

Pensions

The Sistema de Ahorro para Retiro (SAR) is a portable pension fund; translated, it means Retirement Savings System. SAR requires that employers contribute the equivalent of 2 percent of each employee's salary to an account that is administered by banks. Pension account statements are sent to the home of the employee, who can decide how the funds should be invested.

Housing

The FLL requires employers to pay 5 percent of all wages to the Federal Workers' Housing Fund Institute (INFONAVIT). This money goes toward INFONAVIT's objective of housing employees by creating a loan fund for them with low interest rates and insurance for the purchase of homes. It also establishes, in the names of the individual employees, deposits from which they repay the loan.

The 5 percent paid to INFONAVIT is deductible from the employer's income tax. Deposits in the names of employees are exempt from all taxation. Employers are also responsible for making deductions, at the rate of up to one percent of earnings and loans, from the salaries of employees to repay the housing loans. Employees who resign or get laid off are given the number of their INFONAVIT account, and the employer no longer needs to maintain this balance record. The 5 percent levy must be paid by businesses for all employees, even those who rent homes from their employer or who have already received a loan from INFONAVIT.

The entire amount of the 5 percent housing contribution is used to create a non-interest-bearing deposit under the individual employee's name. Through this deposit, the employee can receive a 10–20-year, low-interest-rate loan to build, repair, or buy a house. Forty percent of additional employer contributions are used to lower the employee's monthly repayments, and 40 percent of the accumulated deposit in the employee's name is used as the initial loan repayment.

Employees (or their heirs) are paid the entire net balance (after the amount of the loan has been deducted) that has accumulated in their name. In case of death, disability, or retirement, employees (or heirs) also receive an additional equivalent amount. After employees turn age 50, they are paid a net balance if they cease to work twelve consecutive months. In case of disability or death, employees are protected since the loans are insured, so neither they nor their heirs are held liable for any unpaid balance of a housing loan, and the heirs may receive the remaining balance in an employee's name without deduction.

Insurance

In 1990, Mexico's deregulation of the insurance industry took effect, producing sweeping changes in an effort to stimulate the industry's growth. The National Banking and Insurance Commission is the new controlling government agency, but insurance companies may now set their own competitive rates. Foreign companies are now permitted to have a minority ownership.

U.S. companies with subsidiaries in Mexico should be aware that their insurance policies covering U.S. operations will not necessarily cover their Mexican business activities. Mexican law states that U.S. companies with Mexican subsidiaries must buy a policy covering their Mexican operations from an "admitted insurer" licensed in Mexico. There are international carriers that cover domestic operations, Mexican operations, cross-border activity, and *maquiladoras*.

Notes

1. Laura Kelso, "Employment by Numbers," *Business Mexico* (June 1992), p. 32.
2. Ibid.

7

Foreign Personnel

Foreign personnel may occupy up to 10 percent of a company's positions for technicians if the company can demonstrate that workers with the needed skills are not available in Mexico. A company that requires a higher percentage of foreign technicians must have permission from the Secretariat of Foreign Relations.

Foreigners in executive positions may exceed the 10 percent limit, but they must obtain special immigration and work permits. The percentage of resident foreign executives should not be greater than the percentage of foreign capital participation.

Under the General Law for Population and Its Regulation, Mexico's immigration law, foreigners, regardless of their visa status, are permitted to buy real estate in urban areas, open bank accounts, and purchase money-market instruments without a permit from the Secretariat of the Interior.

Entrance Requirements

A *tourist visa* may be used for most business negotiations conducted in Mexico by foreigners, provided that the negotiations do not involve receiving payment from a Mexican company or signing a contract. To enter Mexico as a tourist, foreigners must present proof of nationality, validated by either a passport, birth certificate, naturalization letter, or voter registration certificate. The tourist status is valid for a three- to six-month period. A Mexican consulate may determine whether tourist status is sufficient for the business negotiation.

A *visitor's visa* is required for foreign business executives traveling to Mexico for a specific work assignment. It is granted for a six-month period. There are two types of visitor's visas, depending on whether or not the executive will be receiving compensation from local sources. Visas that allow the receipt of compensation should be applied for well in advance of the trip because they often take a long time to be granted. Foreigners intending to sign contracts or adopt children in Mexico need a visitor's visa, which may also be used by visiting investors who must reside in Mexico for up to a year to establish an investment or by foreign technicians providing services to a Mexican company.

A *consultant visa* is for foreigners traveling to Mexico to advise Mexican companies or to attend meetings of Mexican companies. It is valid for six months and allows multiple entries, provided the visits are for less than thirty consecutive days.

An *immigrant visa* is for foreigners establishing permanent residence in Mexico as investors, specialists, or executives. It is becoming increasingly difficult to get and is not allowed if the applicants are employed at companies less than two years old. Applicants must apply at the Secretariat of the Interior. Foreign professionals must be authorized by the Secretariat of the Government. Approved applicants are initially granted a temporary immigrant visa that must be renewed annually during a five-year period. Permanent status is then granted and the applicants become *imigrados*. During the first two years of immigrant status, immigrants may not be outside Mexico for more than ninety days per year. During the first five years of immigrant status, immigrants may not be outside Mexico for more than eighteen months. After the initial five-year period, immigrants may leave and return as often as they choose. However, immigrants may not stay outside Mexico for a total of five years during a ten-year period or for two consecutive years, or the immigrant status will be revoked.

Once a foreigner's immigrant visa is granted, members of the immigrant's family may also receive immigrant status if the immigrant assumes their complete financial support. The family's immigrant status prevents them from receiving remuneration directly or indirectly until after five years. When they do receive remuneration from within Mexico, they are obligated to pay all Mexican taxes and have the same rights under the Federal Labor Law (FLL) as Mexican citizens. Retired immigrants over age 51 must prove that they receive a certain minimum income from either investments outside Mexico, interest on loans to Mexican banks, or Mexican government securities.

An *executive visa* is for foreigners employed as administrators, controllers, managers, and so forth, by an established company in Mexico until the foreigner's duties can be satisfactorily executed by a Mexican national.

A *specialist visa* has the same conditions as the executive visa, but it is used by specialists offering specific skills, such as engineers or supervisors of technical operations.

Practicing Requirements

Foreign professionals interested in practicing in Mexico are required to register at the Office of Professions at the Secretariat of Public Education.

Foreign contract professionals may only practice their profession under a contract that has been registered at the Mexican Secretariat of Commerce and Industrial Development (SECOFI). If they practice their profession in a joint venture, it must be noted in the contract, and their skills must be highly specialized. No more than 49 percent of the total technical staff can be foreign contract professionals, since the majority of employees must be Mexican.

Under NAFTA

Professional licensing will be based on competence instead of nationality or residency. Within two years of implementation of NAFTA, citizenship requirements will be eliminated.

After-sales service providers, sales representatives, company executives, managerial personnel, and members of sixty-three professional occupations will be able to benefit from uniform, less restrictive regulations for temporary entry into the United States and Mexico.

8

Intellectual Property Protection

Mexico's Law for the Development and Protection of Industrial Property took effect in August 1991. It follows the mainstream of international law for intellectual property protection and reflects the influence of the World Intellectual Property Organization (WIPO) and the General Agreement on Tariffs and Trade (GATT).

For additional information on Mexico's intellectual property laws contact:

U.S. Trade Representative
Office of Investment and Intellectual Property
Tel: (202) 395-7320

U.S. Trade Representative
Office of North American Affairs
Tel: (202) 395-5663

U.S. Department of Commerce
Office of Patent and Trademark Affairs
Tel: (703) 305-9300

Patents and Trademarks

Patents

A patent term lasts twenty years from the filing date and is available for all products and procedures, including alloys, pharmaceutical products, biotechnology, plant varieties, and chemicals. Inventions patented outside Mexico are qualified for a Mexican patent if they have not yet been imported or produced in Mexico. The original applicant of the patent abroad will receive the patent after presenting the evidence in Mexico.

Compulsory licenses for unexploited patents are rare. If the product is imported to Mexico or obtained from the patented process, this is considered patent use and a license is not considered necessary.

Inventions considered by the Mexican government not to be original enough to be patentable may still qualify for legal protection during a nonrenewable ten-year period, after being filed as utility models. Industrial designs may also qualify as utility models and may be protected for a nonrenewable fifteen-year period.

The owner of a patent may grant other parties a license for the patent's use. These licenses must be registered with the Secretariat of Commerce and Industrial Development (SECOFI).

Trademarks

Trademarks, trade names, commercial slogans, and service marks are registered for a ten-year protection term and are renewable indefinitely for ten-year periods. Collective trademarks and tridimensional trademarks may also be registered. Isolated colors, letters, or numbers may not be registered unless accompanied by an additional design making them more distinctive. Three consecutive years of nonuse will lead to registration cancellation unless an acceptable reason is given. It is no longer necessary to submit proof of use. An affidavit of use is satisfactory when renewing the registration within the first three years after the initial filing.

Franchising operations may now be registered without bureaucratic approval and with minimal disclosure requirements. This procedure requires the licensing of trademarks, commercial names, and technical and managerial information.

The owner of a trademark may grant other parties a license to use the trademark. Such licenses must be registered with SECOFI.

Patent and Trademark Application Procedures

SECOFI's Office of Technological Development registers industrial property for protection. Owners of patents and trademarks must submit a written application form in Spanish. This office will execute a novelty examination no later than fifteen months after the filing unless the applicant can skip the novelty examination by providing the results of a novelty examination from a foreign patent office. If SECOFI does not believe that the invention is novel, the applicant is notified and must respond within two months or the idea is considered to be abandoned. To register, contact:

Dirección General de Desarrollo Tecnologico
SECOFI
Tel: (5) 657-3751

Trade Secrets

A trade secret is licensed technical information on the manufacture, testing, and operation of a company's product. Trade and industrial secrets are recognized and protected by a law that prosecutes their usage without proper authorization. A trade secret must be stored on documents, microfilm, electronic or magnetic media, or other similar mechanisms. Enforcement of trade secret rights can be obtained by filing a claim with the Director General de Desarrollo Tecnologico (Office of Technological Development) at SECOFI for a determination of whether the trade secret has been breached. Contact:

Dirección General de Desarrollo Tecnologico
SECOFI
Tel: (5) 657-3751

Transfers of Technology and Licensing

In 1989, the Mexican government significantly softened its Law on the Control and Registration of the Transfer of Technology. A technological transfer no longer requires the approval of SECOFI, and the Mexican government no longer controls the rates for royalty payments between agreeing parties. The confidentiality period between two contracting parties is ten years and can be extended if the technology has improved.

The law requires all incoming technical assistance, technological supplies, licensed names, service marks, and trademarks to be registered with the Director General de Desarrollo Tecnologico in SECOFI and with the National Registry of the Transfer of Technology so that they can be protected against third parties. Failure to register may result in criminal fines. A technological service is often covered by patent, trade secret, or trademark rights. For registration applications, contact:

Dirección General de Desarrollo Tecnologico
SECOFI
Tel: (5) 657-3751

The U.S. seller should also enter into a legal contract with the Mexican buyer that has provisions making it binding and viable even if the trademark or patent rights expire before the end of the confidentiality period.

A transfer of technology can be arranged through a joint venture, direct investment, project work, or a licensing agreement. During the course of a single business project, several of these transfer methods can be used.

It is important that U.S. companies not sell unproven technology. If the technology is still in experimental stages and does not function properly in Mexico, the seller could become involved in a costly lawsuit.

Technological Clearinghouse

The Environmental Protection Agency (EPA), the U.S. Department of Energy (DOE), and the U.S. Agency for International Development (AID) are creating a technology transfer clearinghouse to provide information to other nations and help advance the use and sales of U.S. environmental technologies. The EPA provides Mexico with technical and policy assistance and helps harmonize environmental standards. For more information, call:

EPA, Office of International Activities: or   EPA, Mexico Desk:
(202) 260-2087   (202) 260-4890

Registered Agreements

A registered agreement is treated as a technology transfer, but companies that acquire the technology may continue to use it beyond the agreement's terms. Some agreements do not require registration, including single sales of computer software, technological assistance from visiting repairmen, catalogs, and drawings.

Copyright Protection

Property that requires copyright protection must be registered with the Secretariat of Public Education (SEP). Mexico's copyright law protects computer software, books, videos, and sound recordings against piracy for a fifty-year period or for fifty years after the death of their creator. In the case of the latter, rights will then be transferred to whoever is stipulated in the creator's will. To register for copyright protection, call the Office of Copyright Registration, Dirección de Derechos de Autor, SEP: (5) 250-0380, 250-0291.

Enforcement of Intellectual Property Rights

Upon the request of interested parties, SECOFI will inspect suspected violators of intellectual property protection and will seize all pirated discoveries. The administrative prerequisites to doing this have been greatly reduced. If more than 30 percent of all goods found in an inspected area are pirated or counterfeit, the business will be forced to close. There are criminal penalties of two to six years in prison and fines ranging from 100 to 10,000 days of minimum wage for individuals convicted of infringements.

Violation penalties for copyright protection were increased in July 1991 and now entail a fine of 10 to 500 days of minimum daily wage and a prison term lasting six months to six years. All illegal copies of video and music are to be seized.

Copyright and patent investigations are soaring, with 42 percent of investigations carried out within thirty days after a complaint has been filed.

Under NAFTA

The North American Free Trade Agreement (NAFTA) provides a higher standard of protection for trademarks, patents, trade secrets, and copyrights than has ever been enacted in any other international or bilateral agreement. The United States, Canada, and Mexico have agreed to provide uniform intellectual property protection and conditions for all citizens of NAFTA countries. The high standards and protection will encourage exports in some of the most competitive areas of the

U.S. economy, including high technology, entertainment items, and goods that require significant R&D.

Each North American country will be expected to enforce laws that protect the creator's rights to an original idea or product, including computer programs, motion pictures, sound recordings, pharmaceutical products, agricultural chemicals, and high technology.

9

Finance

Recent reforms have simplified and liberalized Mexico's financial system, enabling commercial banks and private brokerage houses to compete in a free market. The federal government is now financed through the sale of treasury bills and other government paper. Mexican multibanking institutions may invest in equity stock and give direct loans to companies, thereby increasing their overall leverage.

All restrictions on lending to the private sector have been abolished. Financial institutions are now allowed to create financial groups to encourage greater competition among the various intermediaries. The financial system is becoming more specialized and efficient in the face of increasingly tough competition among both domestic and foreign-owned financial institutions.

In addition to standard banks, Mexico has financial institutions that are more specialized in the services they provide. There are private currency exchange corporations (*arrendadoras financieras*) to deal with the dramatic currency fluctuations, as well as factoring houses and financial leasing corporations.

The Banking System

Banco de México is the nation's principal financial regulatory agency. It is the only entity with the authority to issue currency. It oversees the exchange rate policy and holds Mexico's foreign reserves. The bank also regulates the capital market and holds auctions for the buying and selling of government securities.

The National Banking and Insurance Commission is the principal regulatory agency for the operation and auditing of banks.

The Secretariat of Finance and Public Credit (SHCP) is responsible for collecting taxes and monitoring the state of the economy. It also oversees the National Institute of Statistics, Geography and Information (INEGI).

Reprivatization

Mexico privatized eighteen commercial banks between 1990 and 1992. Although Mexican banks have historically been privately owned, President José López Portillo had them nationalized in 1982. The reprivatization is expected to increase the efficiency of the banks' services and brought in approximately $12 billion in bank sales. The average price paid for banks was 3.53 times its book value and 15 times its earnings, reflecting the confidence investors are placing in the banking system. The SHCP arranged the sales, and the proceeds have gone toward repaying the government's debt.

Mexico's banking laws allow a foreign corporation or individual to own up to 10 percent of a bank with special authorization, with total foreign ownership of a bank restricted to 30 percent. Banco de México estimates that 30,000 investors hold shares in the privatized banks.

The Mexican bank system is expected to grow rapidly over the next five years, since there will be a growing demand for loans and underexploited markets for mortgages, leases, and credit cards. Bancomer grew 108 percent and Banamex grew 84 percent, only six months after they were sold.

Mexico's new pension fund, the Retirement Savings System (SAR), should give banks a significant boost, since SAR requires employers to contribute a percentage of each employee's salary to a bank account in the employee's name. This program is expected to bring an additional 10 to 15 million new accounts and a much larger client base to the banking system. Long-term business interests are expected to benefit as well. Not surprisingly, banks are currently competing through elaborate advertising campaigns to lure companies to open accounts. Through mid-1992, nearly 40 percent of SAR accounts were with Bancomer and 30 percent were with Banacci.

Monterrey, Nuevo León, has emerged from the reprivatization as a major financial power. Approximately 44 percent of Mexico's banking assets are controlled by the state of Nuevo León or an investment group located there.

Commercial Banks

In 1989, the SHCP liberalized interest rates, allowing them to be set by the free market instead of Banco de México. The required amount of reserves in banks was reduced from 75 percent to 30 percent, improving the resources available for financing and making the resources cheaper and easier to get. Commercial banks were given greater freedom in choosing where to invest; however, 30 percent of their deposits must still be in federal government development bonds (Bondes), in federal treasury certificates (CETES), or in accounts with Banco de México.

The banks' available credit for the private sector has increased significantly, partially because of growth in the total money supply. The interest paid on savings accounts has also increased. The banks are aggressively seeking to attract funds from companies or individuals interested in other kinds of interest-bearing accounts and securities that offer high interest rates. Interest-bearing deposits are kept in pesos, with the exception of some authorized *maquiladora*-servicing banks that have checking accounts and interest-bearing deposits in U.S. currency. There are no regulatory restrictions on the amount of funding foreign investors are permitted to receive.

Mexico has yet to open its financial system to foreign banks. There are currently 190 foreign financial institutions represented by individual or shared banking offices in Mexico, but only Citibank is allowed to conduct banking operations.

Services. Mexico's eighteen commercial banks provide the usual banking activities and a variety of financial services, including factoring and leasing. They offer many services geared toward international joint ventures. A bank may act as a partner in a joint venture and may provide foreign investors with such services as commercial credit, import financing, commercial references, market identification for international trade, total service for debt-equity swaps, registry and handling for the sale of foreign currency, and counseling and financing for *maquiladoras*. Foreigners may open checking or savings accounts, regardless of their visa status. Short-term credit is also available.

Development Banks

Development banks were set up by the federal government to provide specialized services for promoting industrial development.

The National Financier, Nacional Financiera, S.A. (NAFIN), is Mexico's central development bank, a state-owned entity with a $7 billion budget and forty-eight branches throughout the nation to promote industrial development. NAFIN will finance 25 percent of approved investment projects for a maximum seven-year period. It provides loans to businesses going into underdeveloped regions and industrial sectors. It also offers long-term import financing with CETES (28-day treasury bills) for capital goods and agricultural products backed by the U.S. Export-Import Bank (Eximbank).

NAFIN supports small and medium-size businesses with global credit lines. Environmental protection, infrastructure, and plant improvements are areas often aided. The central bank also acts as intermediary between foreign creditors and the Mexican government. The World Bank and the Inter-American Development Bank provide loans through this bank.

NAFIN maintains joint venture funds to enable domestic businesses to set up new entities with foreign investors for the production of capital goods. Most of its programs operate through trust funds. NAFIN will assist foreign investors with the application process and will also act as a minority partner in international joint ventures.

The National Bank of Foreign Trade, Banco Nacional de Comercio Exterior (Bancomext), is a development bank designed to foster foreign trade and investment. It provides financial services to Mexican exporters similar to those Eximbank offers in the United States. Bancomext promotes foreign investment in Mexico through its eight U.S. offices. The bank offers short-term credit for primary goods (up to 100 percent of their value) backed by the U.S. Commodity Credit Corporation. Capital goods imports backed by Eximbank are eligible to receive long-term credit (up to 85 percent). Bancomext also offers potential U.S. investors opportunities to meet Mexican business representatives and to receive information on Mexican legal requirements and investment opportunities.

The Stock Market

Mexico's stock market (Bolsa Mexicana de Valores) is located in Mexico, D.F., and is run by a private corporation, with participating brokerage companies acting as the shareholders.

Securities

Foreigners may buy and sell in the Mexican stock exchange, but the amount of their involvement depends on the classification of the industry in which they are investing. The public is only permitted to purchase securities that have been approved by the *bolsa*'s regulating agency, the National Securities Commission of the SHCP. Traded brokerage companies are required to follow the Code of Ethics of the Mexican Brokerage Community. Calificadora de Valores, S.A. (CAVAL) is the principal rating agency and functions similarly to rating agencies in the United States. CAVAL appraises the creditworthiness of corporations and measures the performance of securities.

Performance. Most foreign investment comes into Mexico through the securities market. The market's swift improvement in performance over the past three years illustrates the increasing confidence that foreign and domestic investors have in the economy. The 1989 deregulation of foreign investment has also contributed to growth by enabling foreigners to own a larger percentage of Mexican industries with fewer restrictions. There has also been an increase in local capital available for investing in new or growing businesses.

The stock market grew 118 percent in 1991 and another 30 percent during the first half of 1992. The stock market did not react as favorably during the latter half of the year for several reasons, including a sluggish global market, a slight decrease in Mexico's gross national product (GNP), and the upcoming U.S. presidential election, in which two of the three candidates seemed lukewarm toward a North American free trade agreement.

Despite the fluctuations, however, foreign investment remains high. According to the Mexican Investment Board (MIB), in 1992 foreign investment was valued at $8.3 billion and 31 percent of this investment entered through the stock market. According to the Mexican stock exchange, in March 1992, the top five stocks for foreign investors (along with the percentage of shares owned by foreign sources) were Telmex A (56.3 percent), Cemex B (5.5 percent), GFB (4.9 percent), Cifra B (4.2 percent), and Televisa L (3.7 percent).

Shares. There are five forms of shares. Series A shares are reserved for Mexican nationals, but foreigners can still purchase them through the Neutral Fund Program, which was established through 1989 reforms. The Neutral Fund permits foreigners to establish trusts to acquire shares. Shares are represented by certificates of ordinary participation (CPOs) issued by fiduciary institutions. CPOs give foreign investors the economic rights ("mutual capital") to restricted companies but not the voting rights. Foreigners share the company's profit but do not control the company or its administration. These share trusts last for twenty-year periods and may be purchased by Mexican investors at the end of their term. CPOs are not considered when calculating the amount of foreign participation in the capital stock of issuing companies. CPOs may be purchased by foreigners directly from the *bolsa*. Series C shares are similar to CPOs but are administered by NAFIN. In 1991, foreign investment in CPOs and Series C shares was valued at $1.349 billion, compared with $35 million in 1989.

American depository receipts, known as ADRs, are negotiable instruments representing shares of more than two dozen Mexican companies. A foreigner can buy shares of a restricted company through a brokerage, which puts them in a trust at a Mexican bank in an account for the Mexican Securities Depository Institution (S.D. INDEVAL). A U.S. bank then issues ADR certificates representing the shares that were purchased. When ADRs are substituted for Mexican stock shares, they eliminate any differences in the currency exchange. ADRs can be traded on U.S. stock exchanges.

In 1992 more than 70 percent of Mexico's foreign portfolio investment was in ADRs. According to the *bolsa*, sales skyrocketed from $402 million in 1989 to $13.733 billion in 1991. Mexican companies sold through ADRs include Telmex, Vitro, Cifra, and Femsa.

Series B shares may be sold to Mexicans and foreigners in unlimited quantity since they represent unrestricted industries. The *bolsa* had nearly 100 companies offering series B shares. Foreign investment in series B shares was valued at $107 million in 1989, rising to $2.961 billion in 1991.

Money Markets

Money-market operations are carried out by Mexico's twenty-five brokerage companies (*casas de bolsa*). They offer a variety of investment opportunities, including public-sector securities, corporate bonds, and mutual and investment funds.

Public Sector Securities

CETES—certificados de la tesoreria (treasury certificates) are the main medium of the money markets and may be purchased by foreigners. They are similar to T-bills and are auctioned publicly on a weekly basis by Banco de México. CETES are sold at a weekly discount with varying maturities. The active secondary market makes them highly liquid.

Pagafes—pagares de la tesoreria de la federación (promissory notes of the treasury of the federation) are treasury promissory notes denominated in U.S. dollars and have varying maturities. Interest is gathered on the face value of the notes, but the notes are not always interest-paying. *Pagafes* are payable only in pesos.

Tesobonos—bonos de la tesoreria de la federación (bonds of the treasury of the federation) are treasury bonds denominated in U.S. dollars. They have a face value of $1,000 and have varying maturities. They may be purchased by foreigners and are redeemable in free-rate dollars.

Ajustobonos (adjustable bonds) are government-guaranteed debt instruments with inflation indexing.

Bondes—bonos de desarollo del gobierno federal (federal government development bonds) are interest-bearing debt securities denominated in pesos and have varying maturities greater than one year. They may be purchased by foreigners, but their titles must stay in Mexico.

Bondis are bonds for industrial development.

Petropagares are unsecured short-term commercial paper issued by Petroleos Mexicanos (PEMEX).

Private Instruments

Through money markets, the following papers are traded: secured bonds, unsecured bonds, commercial paper, debentures, convertible bonds, and commodity bonds.

Banking Instruments

Banker's acceptances (ABs) are available through money markets.

Metals Markets

CEPLATA (certificados de plata) are silver certificates. Other available markets are the silver troy ounces and the centenario gold coins.

Capital Markets

Mutual and Investment Funds

Mutual and investment funds are available through brokerage houses and banks. There are over 250 available (compared with only 70 in 1987), including the highly successful Mexico Fund. The fast growth of mutual funds available to small investors has created interest in the equity shares traded over the Mexican stock exchange.

Holders of variable-income instruments are authorized to invest a large part of their assets in shares of stocks listed on the stock exchange and in commercial bank shares (CAP).

Investment societies offer regular mutual funds (SIC), fixed-income funds (SIRF), and fixed-income funds for legal entities (SIRFPM). With government approval, foreign investors can own up to 49 percent of the shares in a capital investment fund (SINCAS) for small to medium-size companies.

The following are fixed-income instruments: property participation certificates (CPIs), obligations from private-sector corporations, ordinary participation certificates (CPOs), infrastructure bank bonds (BBIs), development bank bonds (BBDs), bank indemnization bonds (BIBs), and urban reconstruction bonds (BORES).

Insurance Reforms and Regulations

Recent reforms now permit foreign investors to hold minority positions in insurance companies. The SHCP allows foreign insurance companies, individuals, finance companies, and reinsurance companies to make capital investments. Permission is nontransferable. Total foreign investment positions in these entities are limited to 49 percent, and no single investor may hold more than 15 percent.

The Banking and Insurance Commission has authorized the board of directors of insurance companies to decide where to invest their excess technical reserves. They often choose to invest in real property or to provide financing for other entities.

Under NAFTA

U.S. financial service providers may operate wholly owned subsidiaries in Mexico and receive the same treatment as domestic companies. U.S. banking, insurance, and securities companies may provide services without relocating any employees or offices to Mexico. U.S. investors, exporters, and importers would then be able to use the same financial service companies for both domestic and international transactions.

Banks. U.S. companies have a 15 percent limit to their share of the Mexican market until January 1, 2000. An assessment of the market will be made four years later, and if U.S. banks have acquired 25 percent, another three-year cap might be implemented.

Securities Companies. U.S. companies have a 20 percent limit to their share of the Mexican securities market until January 1, 2000. An assessment of the market will be made four years later, and if U.S. security companies have acquired 30 percent of the market, another three-year cap might be implemented.

Insurance Companies. In 1998, U.S. entities may have majority ownership of Mexican insurance companies; by the year 2000, 100 percent ownership. U.S. companies with existing joint ventures in Mexico are permitted to have 100 percent ownership as early as 1996. New, wholly owned entities may be started immediately, but are subject to size limitations lasting until the year 2000.

U.S. insurance companies may sell health, travel, and life insurance to Mexican residents who come to the United States. They may also offer services related to international trade on a cross-border basis, including reinsurance and cargo insurance.

Leasing and Factoring Companies. U.S. companies have a 20 percent limit to their share of the Mexican market until January 1, 2000. Mexicans and Canadians are guaranteed the right to purchase financial services from companies in the United States.

Nonbank Lending. Services in Mexico may be expanded by nonbank lenders to include credit card businesses, mortgage services, and commercial and consumer financing. These operations may be capitalized through domestic money markets.

10

Taxes

Mexican tax rates are established by the federal government annually in the Codego Fiscal de la Federación. Since many of these codes change each year, it is advisable for a foreign company to consult an accounting firm regarding the current regulations. Most major U.S. accounting firms, including Ernst and Young and Price Waterhouse, have subsidiary operations throughout Mexico and have published guides on the tax code.

The government has attempted to repair the complicated and inefficient system through a series of amendments. Changes include lowering the corporate tax rate and streamlining the collection system. The governments of Mexico and the United States are negotiating an accord to protect companies operating in both countries from double taxation. The North American Free Trade Agreement (NAFTA) is expected to harmonize the signatories' tax rules on dividend payments and corporate interest rates.

Main Taxation Categories and Maximum Tax Rates

Corporate income tax:	35 percent
Individual income tax:	35 percent
Dividends:	35 percent
Royalties:	35 percent
Import duties:	20 percent
Value-added tax:	10 percent
Export tax:	0 percent

Taxes provide only 58 percent of the Mexican government's total revenue. Value-added and excise taxes provide 45 percent of the total tax revenue; corporate and personal income provide 42 percent. The federal government levies taxes on income, gross assets, payroll, and value added; the real estate transfer tax is levied as a local tax following federal standards. The fiscal year for taxation purposes is the same as the calendar year.

Income Taxes

The Mexican government considers the effects of inflation when determining the taxable income on capital gains. Adjustments for inflation are based on the National Consumer Price Index (INPC), which is calculated by Banco de México and published in the *Official Gazette*. The monthly adjustment factor is calculated by dividing the INPC for the month under consideration by the INPC of the previous month and subtracting one from their quotient.

Capital gains in real estate are determined by an inflation adjustment based on the original cost of the buildings and land after tax depreciation.

Taxpayers can use the inflation adjustment to their advantage in depreciating fixed assets.

Corporations

The corporation, *sociedad anonima* (S.A.) or *sociedad anonima de capital variable* (S.A. de C.V.), is the most common form of business entity for both foreign and domestic investors. Forming a corporation requires six steps.

1. If the entity is wholly or partially foreign-owned, it must be registered with the National Registry for Foreign Investment, located at the Office of the Undersecretary of Foreign Investment and Industry in the Secretariat of Trade and Industrial Development (SECOFI) (see Government Agencies in the Directories).
2. The articles of incorporation must be validated by a notary public.
3. The notary must give a completed application to the Secretariat of Foreign Affairs (SRE). The application must include

   - The name of the new entity (with a second choice in case it is already registered)
   - A charter (statement of purpose) and bylaws
   - The company's duration
   - Information on a minimum of five or more shareholders (full name, birthplace and date of birth, occupation, address, and federal tax registration number)
   - Equity satisfying the minimum amount
   - Minimum share capital of 25,000 pesos
   - The names of the company officers
   - Shares that show how the equity will be divided among the shareholders
   - Name, address, and occupation of the statutory examiner (*comisario*)

   The application must contain the Calvo Clause, waiving the foreign investor's right to be treated differently from a Mexican citizen and to be free of foreign government intervention.
4. After the SRE authorizes the application, the shareholders must sign the corporation's charter and articles.
5. The notary must distribute copies of the articles of incorporation to the appropriate government agencies, which will take roughly three months.
6. The following offices must be contacted within 154 working days after the articles of incorporation have been delivered by the notary to the government agencies:

- The Social Security Institute
- The treasury of the state (or Federal District) where the corporation is located
- The Secretariat of Finance and Public Credit (SHCP); corporations must file for a federal tax registration number
- The local association or chamber of commerce appropriate to the corporation's activities

To qualify as an S.A. de C.V., the entity must meet the foregoing requirements and be able to change its maximum amount of capital without amending its articles of incorporation or requiring the approval of the SRE.

Income and Profit Sharing. Mexico's corporate income tax is 35 percent. There is no special rate for capital gains. Resident companies in Mexico that were created under Mexican law must pay corporate income tax on their worldwide income, but this is usually counted toward a foreign tax credit. Mexican subsidiaries of foreign corporations are subject to this tax; however, they do not have to pay additional taxes on revenue sent out of Mexico.

Mexican companies with employees must also pay 10 percent of their annual taxable income to an employee profit-sharing account after two years of operation.

Nonresident corporations in Mexico are subject to taxation only on income related to business operations in Mexico, including interest or payments from subsidiaries and dividends.

Capital gains are determined from the difference between the original cost and the sales price, with particular adjustments for inflation. For gains on shares of other corporations, net per share is added to the original cost of the capital and stock contributions. Cash dividends and losses are deducted. This figure is also adjusted for inflation.

Interest Payments. There is a 35 percent withholding tax on all gross interest payments to corporations outside Mexico. All gross interest paid to banks outside Mexico is subject to a 15 percent withholding tax.

Joint Ventures

The joint venture contract is the second most common business entity for foreigners, after the corporation. The joint venture, *asociación en participación,* is an alliance established by a contract between at least two parties and has no independent legal existence. One of the parties (*el asociante*) usually has unlimited liability and manages the operation in his or her own name; however, this is not a legal requirement. The other party (*asociado*) or parties is usually a limited partner with limited liability, depending on that party's contribution to the project. Mexican tax is directed at the parties involved, rather than the entity.

Joint ventures are nearly always in writing. They are not required to be registered with the government.

General Partnerships

Unlike joint ventures, the general partnership, *sociedad en nombre colectivo* (S. en N.C.), has a legal existence independent of the parties to the enterprise. All partners are fully responsible for the partnership's debts and obligations. The entity is classified as a mercantile organization under the General Law of Mercantile Companies but is taxed as a corporation. The general partnership is not often used by foreigners or by Mexicans.

Limited Partnerships

The limited partnership, *sociedad en comandita simple* (S. en C.S.), is one in which the liability of the partners is limited to the degree of their capital contribution. This entity is taxed as a corporation because it is classified as a mercantile organization under the General Law of Mercantile Companies. Like the general partnership, the limited partnership is not often used.

Limited-Liability Companies

The limited-liability company, *sociedad de responsabilidad limitada* (S. de R.L.), is operated like a partnership but has the limited liability of a corporation. Foreign investors seldom use this form of investment. The S. de R.L. is most often used in areas where corporations are not allowed, such as agriculture.

Branch Offices

A foreign corporation may register through a Mexican branch office, *sucursal de sociedad extranjera,* but this format often slows the government's required approval relative to that for other business entities. The Mexican government does not encourage this kind of entity. The approval process may sometimes be accelerated for a foreign company still at the exploration stage and using a branch office because it would like a Mexican presence.

Foreign Affiliates

Shareholders. Foreign shareholders do not have to pay Mexican tax on distributed earnings if the corporate income tax was already paid by the distributing company.

Intellectual Property. There is a 35 percent withholding tax on royalties paid to nonresidents for use of patents, trademarks, and trade names and on interest paid to nonresident affiliates.

Supplier. A foreign supplier does not have to pay Mexican income tax on a sale or change of ownership that happens outside Mexico. A foreign seller is subject to income tax (even if the seller has no agents or employees in Mexico) if the title to products sold changes hands in Mexico.

Trusts

A trust can only be established with credit institutions. All tax on income or profit from the trust's transactions is paid by the trust's beneficiary.

Individual Income

The Mexican government considers a resident individual to be someone who has a home in Mexico and does not stay in another residence outside Mexico for more than 183 days in a single calendar year. Resident individuals are taxed on their worldwide income through a personal, progressive income tax with an upper limit of 35 percent.

Taxes are paid quarterly, with annual taxes due in April. The amount owed is determined by the difference between estimated tax payments and the annual tax. Certain types of income, such as dividends, interest, and capital gains, have a lower schedule of tax liability.

Nonresident individuals must pay taxes on income made from sources in Mexico. A final withholding tax is usually levied on a percentage of the gross income. Nonresidents are also required to pay withholding taxes on interest and dividend income.

Gross Assets Tax

Mexico's 1992 tax amendments added a tax on gross assets. The gross assets tax (*impuesto al activo*) is levied at a rate of 2 percent minus depreciation for fixed assets and at 2 percent for variable assets. The Mexican government allows income or revenue tax payments to be credited against the amount owed for the gross assets tax. However, this is not creditable against the U.S. income tax, making it a disputed topic between the two countries. Businesses with losses that leave no income or revenue tax obligations are still responsible for paying the full amount of the assets tax.

Payroll Tax

The federal government each month charges corporations with a one percent tax based on the gross salaries of their employees. Companies in Mexico City are levied with an additional local tax of 2 percent per month.

Retirement Fund. Companies are required to pay an equivalent of 2 percent of their gross wages to a newly established pension fund called Sistema de Ahorro para Retiro (SAR). This program is run through financial agencies that invest in public debt.

Housing. Employers are required to make bimonthly payments totaling 5 percent of gross wages to the Federal Workers' Housing Fund Institute

(INFONAVIT). This money goes to help employees purchase homes by creating a loan fund for them with low interest rates and insurance. The money is also used to establish deposits in the name of the individual employees through which they repay the loans. The 5 percent an employer pays is a deductible income tax expense. Deposits in the name of employees are exempt from all taxation. A 5 percent levy must be paid by the business for each employee, even if the person rents a home from the employer or has already received a loan from INFONAVIT.

Social Security. The Mexican Institute of Social Security (IMSS) requires employers to share the costs of social security with their employees. Social security premiums are payable every two months. Other insurance coverage is not required. All private-sector companies that hire more than one person must register both employers and employees with the IMSS and pay their premiums. Registration protects the employer from liability in connection with job-related illnesses or accidents.

The employer must pay 75 percent of the cost of social security, the total of which is approximately 14.3 percent of the employee's wages. Employees must pay the remaining 25 percent through a deduction from their salaries. The employer pays all occupational risk premiums as a percentage of the total employee/employer contributions toward old age benefits. Employers are also responsible for the cost of day-care facilities for employees' infants.

Value-Added Tax

A federal value-added tax (VAT) is required on all sales, services, business rentals, and nonbank loan transactions. This tax is also levied on corporations that finance the sale of automobiles and on interest charges on loans from retailers granting credit. The VAT rate is 10 percent of the transaction's value before tax. Transfers of money, sales of securities and shares, medical services, interest-earning transactions with Mexican credit institutions, book sales, school tuition, and sales of personal residences and land are excluded from the tax. The VAT is usually paid by the consumer or patron.

Real Estate Transfer Tax

A real estate transfer tax is levied by the notary public when the title to property is transferred after a sale. The tax rate is set at 2 percent of the property's value, but when it is combined with registration costs, notary fees, and other taxes, the total often amounts to 10–13 percent of the property's value. Tax is not levied on inherited property.

Part Two
Exporting to Mexico

U.S. exports to Mexico have tripled since 1987, growing from $12.4 billion to an estimated $48 billion in 1992. In 1992, the United States had a $5.3 billion trade surplus with Mexico, representing a great improvement from its 1987 trade deficit of $5.7 billion. According to the Office of the U.S. Trade Representative, 70 percent of all Mexico's imports come from the United States and fifteen cents of every additional dollar of Mexican GDP is spent on U.S. goods and services. U.S. exports to Mexico supported more than 600,000 U.S. jobs in 1991 alone.

U.S. merchandise exports in 1992 were valued at more than $40 billion. Mexico has surpassed Japan as a U.S. export market, becoming the second-largest buyer (after Canada) of U.S. capital goods. Trade analysts expect this type of export to grow by an additional $25 billion within five years after the start of the free trade agreement. According to the U.S. Department of Commerce, major U.S. capital goods exported to Mexico in 1992 included electrical machinery and apparatus ($5.3 billion), motor vehicle parts ($3.9 billion), chemicals ($3.2 billion), telecommunications equipment ($1.5 billion), and office machinery and computers ($1.3 billion). Products with the highest growth rates included information-processing equipment (up 54.2 percent), hand tools (up 53.5 percent), measuring instruments (up 47.4 percent), and loading equipment (up 31.7 percent). The *maquiladora* sector generated $4.134 billion in 1991, rising from $1.598 billion in 1987. It accounted for 31.8 percent of all Mexico's imports from the United States in 1991 and consisted mostly of equipment, technology, and various components.

In 1991, U.S. service exports to Mexico were valued at $8.282 billion, representing 5.1 percent of total U.S. service exports. The United States had a $341 million surplus in service trade with Mexico, importing $7.9 billion worth of Mexican services. Travel-related functions dominated U.S. service exports, but the services sector should greatly diversify with the passing of the free trade agreement, because members of the majority of U.S. professions will be able to compete in Mexico's $146 billion services market without discrimination.

11

Export Consulting Services

There is a big demand for information on investing in Mexico's growing markets. The U.S. and Mexican federal governments, chambers of commerce, private consulting companies, and Mexican banks are well prepared to provide information for interested investors and exporters.

U.S. Government Assistance

(For addresses, see the Directories.)

Many U.S. government agencies provide information and assistance to U.S. businesses interested in Mexico. The Trade Promotion Coordinating Committee (TPCC) is a good place to start because it is an interagency reference program to put U.S. exporters in contact with federal programs that could assist them. Contact:

Trade Promotion Coordinating Committee
Tel: (800) USA-TRADE

Following are additional government programs offering information on doing business with Mexico.

U.S. Department of Commerce (DOC)

Several bureaus within DOC provide information and assistance to exporters seeking Mexican markets.

International Trade Administration (ITA)

Flash Facts Hotline
U.S. Department of Commerce
Tel: (202) 482-4464, ext. 0101

Flash Facts is a hot line with information on Mexico that feeds directly into outside fax machines as a free service. It has a comprehensive menu selection that includes North American Free Trade Agreement information; regulations for tariffs, permits, and customs; laboratories authorized by the Mexican government for import testing; and information on marketing, distribution, and finance. For a listing of the complete menu dial the number listed above.

> Office of Mexico
> U.S. Department of Commerce
> Tel: (202) 482-2332

The Office of Mexico will answer any questions on Flash Facts documents. It will not send any Flash Facts information by mail.

> National Trade Data Bank (NTDB)
> Flash Facts Hotline
> U.S. Department of Commerce
> Tel: (202) 482-4464, ext. 0101 and 0103

The NTDB contains documents on export promotion and international trade from fifteen U.S. government agencies. It is on a single CD-ROM disk that is updated monthly and is available at 700 federal depository libraries throughout the United States. Information on Mexico includes USDOC sector analyses and the Foreign Traders Index.

> National Technical Information Service (NTIS)
> Flash Facts Hotline
> U.S. Department of Commerce
> Tel: (202) 482-4464, ext. 0101 or 0102

The NTIS is a self-supporting government agency that reproduces and disseminates government documents, including a state-by-state overview of U.S. exports to Mexico, a directory of Mexican business services providers, and an export promotion services package.

U.S. and Foreign Commercial Services (US&FCS)

> U.S. and Foreign Commercial Service
> U.S. Department of Commerce
> Tel: (202) 482-5013

In Mexico:

> Foreign Commercial Service
> U.S. Department of Commerce
> Tel: (5) 211-0042
> Fax: (5) 511-9980

The US&FCS provides international trade information and counseling for export operations of all sizes. This information can be accessed through the service's forty-seven district offices and twenty-one branch offices located throughout the United States (including Puerto Rico). Trade officers can also contact Foreign Commercial Service officers located throughout Mexico for any information that is not readily available. The services they provide include the following:

▪ *Agent/distributor service.* The FCS will conduct a customized search for interested Mexican agents, distributors, and representatives that could be potential business partners for a U.S. company. The starting fee is $250.

- *Trade aides.* The FCS offices in Mexico can arrange for visiting investors and businesspeople to hire approved interpreters, trade aides, and secretaries. They charge $100 per eight-hour day.

- *Comparison shopper service (CSS).* A U.S. company may commission a customized market study in Mexico for its particular product or service. CSS costs range from $500 to $1,500.

- *Sales quotation mailing.* The FCS will mail a company's sales proposal or quotation to ten potential customers.

- *Display of catalogs/videotapes.* The FCS will exhibit a company's catalogs or videotapes in its widely seen display case. It will keep information on a U.S. company's product or service in the FCS reference material for a renewable fee.

- *Annual report distribution.* The FCS will distribute a company's brochure or annual report throughout twenty Mexican cities.

- *Speakers bureau.* An FCS officer will speak on a variety of trade issues for clubs and other interested groups throughout Mexico and the United States. Only travel expenses must be paid.

- *Advertising in Mexico through a poster display.* For a renewable fee, the FCS will exhibit a company's poster in the much visited U.S. Visa Center.

- *Trade shows.* Trade shows can be a good place to meet potential business partners, competitors, and customers. It can also be a cost-effective way to test a specific marketplace. For more information, contact:

U.S. Trade Center: (5) 591-0155
                       (5) 566-1115 (Fax)

- *U.S. trade show promotion.* The FCS will assist a U.S. company with product promotion by mailing ninety of the company's brochures to appropriate sources, including industry associations, potential show attenders, and the twenty FCS officers throughout Mexico.

- *Trade opportunities program (TOP).* TOP can be transmitted electronically through a personal computer to provide subscribers with names of international companies looking to buy or represent U.S. goods and services. Subscription fees vary.

- *List of key contacts.* FCS officers will provide a list of contacts within a specific industry for a fee of twenty-five cents per name, with a $10 minimum. Names are sent on gummed labels.

- *Business briefing in Mexico.* The FCS provides trade briefings in its Mexico offices for U.S. and Mexican business executives, by appointment only.

- *Custom "repfind," single-company trade missions, special programs.* The FCS Repfind Service will provide a visiting executive with a market study, prearranged appointments with potential Mexican customers or partners, an office for these appointments, a bilingual secretary, and a final debriefing. These services can be arranged in Mexico City, Monterrey, and Guadalajara.

- *Trade missions to Mexico.* The US&FCS will guide small groups of business executives on trade missions to Mexico. It takes participants from a common industrial sector and escorts them to prearranged appointments with people of interest, including Mexican government officials and potential customers. For more information, contact:

Office of International Operations
(Western Hemisphere):   (202) 482-2736
                                          (202) 482-3159 (Fax)

▪ *Business reference service in Mexico.* Business Assistance Offices (BAOs) are located in Mexico and have libraries stocked with trade statistics, commercial and telephone directories, regulatory and customs references, and business publications. Contact:

BAO—Mexico City: (5) 211-0042, ext. 3722 or 3723
BAO—Monterrey: (83) 452-120
BAO—Guadalajara: (36) 252-989

Office of Trade Development

Office of Trade Development
U.S. Department of Commerce
Tel: (202) 482-1461
Fax: (202) 482-5697

The Office of Trade Development coordinates industry representation and associations to provide export marketing plans and regulations within a specific industrial sector. Industries are divided into seven trade development units with specific product specialists for each of them.

Aerospace:	(202) 482-1872
Office of Aerospace Market Development:	(202) 482-1228
Office of Aerospace Policy and Analysis:	(202) 482-4222
Automotive Affairs:	(202) 482-0554
Basic Industries:	(202) 482-0614
Office of Energy:	(202) 482-1466
Office of Forest Products and Domestic Construction:	(202) 482-0384
Office of Metals, Chemicals and Commodities:	(202) 482-0575
Capital Goods and International Construction:	(202) 482-5023

Office of International Major Projects
U.S. Department of Commerce
Tel: (202) 482-5225

The Office of International Major Projects provides U.S. construction, engineering, and architectural companies with information on major overseas projects open to U.S. bidders.

Multilateral Development Bank (MDB) Liaison Team
U.S. Department of Commerce

For Inter-American Development Bank, Tel: (202) 482-1246
For World Bank, Tel: (202) 482-4332

The Multilateral Development Bank Liaison Team maintains information on MDB projects and lending. It provides counseling on project disputes.

Important Telephone Numbers in the Office of Trade Development

Technology and Industry:	(202) 482-3548
Office of Computers and Business Equipment:	(202) 482-0572
Office of Microelectronics and Instrumentation:	(202) 482-2587
Office of Telecommunications:	(202) 482-4466
Service Industries:	(202) 482-5261
Office of Service Industries:	(202) 482-3575
Office of Export Trading Company Affairs:	(202) 482-5131
Textiles and Apparel and Consumer Goods:	(202) 482-3737
Office of Textiles and Apparel:	(202) 482-5078
Office of Consumer Goods:	(202) 482-0337

Trade Information and Analysis
U.S. Department of Commerce
Tel: (202) 482-1316

The Trade Information and Analysis office has information and statistics on such subjects as countertrade, export financing, and state exports.

U.S. Travel and Tourism Administration

U.S. Travel and Tourism Administration
U.S. Department of Commerce
Tel: (202) 482-4752
Fax: (202) 482-2887

In Mexico:

U.S. Travel and Tourism Administration
U.S. Department of Commerce
Tel: (5) 520-1194

The U.S. Travel and Tourism Administration provides information on markets in Mexico's hospitality business. It also promotes joint ventures between U.S. businesses and Mexican regional governments and businesses.

Office of Trade Services

National Marine and Fisheries Service
U.S. Department of Commerce
Tel: (301) 713-2379
Fax: (301) 588-4853

The Office of Trade Services provides information on Mexican markets for fish and fish-related products.

U.S. Trade and Development Program (TDP)

U.S. Trade and Development Program
Tel: (703) 875-4357
Fax: (703) 875-4009
(*Ask for Mexico director*)

The Trade and Development Program funds U.S. private-sector companies producing feasibility studies for a broad range of promising industrial sectors. TDP usually contributes between $150,000 and $750,000 for public-sector projects.

Dairy, Livestock, Poultry:	(202) 720-8031
	(202) 720-0617 (Fax)
Forest Products:	(202) 720-0638
	(202) 720-8461 (Fax)
Grain and Feed:	(202) 720-6219
	(202) 720-0340 (Fax)
Horticulture and Tropical Products:	(202) 720-6590
	(202) 720-3799 (Fax)
Oilseeds and Oilseed Products:	(202) 720-7037
	(202) 720-0965 (Fax)
Tobacco, Cotton and Seeds:	(202) 720-9516
	(202) 690-1171 (Fax)

Agricultural Cooperative Service
U.S. Department of Agriculture
Tel: (202) 720-2556
Fax: (202) 720-4641

The Agricultural Cooperative Service helps U.S. agricultural cooperatives find export opportunities.

Computerized Information Delivery Service (CIDS)
U.S. Department of Agriculture
Tel: (202) 720-5505

CIDS is a news system that offers its subscribers current trade information from the USDA within seconds of its release. It covers the agricultural markets (food and fiber) of many countries, including Mexico. CIDS information includes supplies and demands, trade leads, weather, and information on commodities from the Futures Trading Commission. Nongovernment subscribers are subject to a $75 per month minimum fee.

U.S. Department of Energy (DOE)

Export Assistance Initiative
U.S. Department of Energy
Tel: (202) 586-0153
Fax: (202) 586-3047

The Export Assistance Initiative office provides U.S. exporters with information on trade opportunities and barriers in the energy sector in Mexico.

Coal and Technology Export Program
Office of Fossil Energy
U.S. Department of Energy
Tel: (202) 586-7297
Fax: (202) 586-1188

The Coal and Technology Export Program promotes the global export of U.S. clean coal products and services.

Federal International Energy and Trade Development Opportunities Program
U.S. Department of Energy
Tel: (202) 586-7297
Fax: (202) 586-1188

The International Energy and Trade Development Opportunities Program is an interagency program combining the resources of the DOE, the Agency for International Development (AID), and the Trade and Development Program (TDP) to provide feasibility studies for trade transactions in the energy field.

Small Business Administration (SBA)

According to a study issued by the U.S. General Accounting Office (GAO) in September 1992, SBA's export promotion programs are "unfocused" and not as strong as the export assistance programs offered by the Department of Commerce.[1] However, exporters should examine all their options.

Office of International Trade (OIT)
Small Business Administration
Tel: (202) 205-6720
Fax: (202) 205-7272

U.S. Department of Agriculture (USDA)

Foreign Agricultural Service (FAS). FAS provides market and trade information to U.S. agricultural exporters through several offices.

Trade Assistance and Promoting Office (TAPO)
FAS
U.S. Department of Agriculture
Tel: (202) 720-7420
Fax: (202) 690-4374

TAPO provides information on exporting agricultural products. It can also refer exporters to programs and offices within the USDA that would be relevant to their venture.

AgExport Services
FAS
U.S. Department of Agriculture
Tel: (202) 720-7103
Fax: (202) 690-4374

AgExport Services provides U.S. exporters with names of Mexican agricultural importers for a $15 fee. It also offers AgExport Connections, a free export information kit.

Foreign Agricultural Service
U.S. Department of Agriculture
American Embassy
Mexico, D.F.
Tel: (5) 211-0042
Fax: (5) 533-6194

The FAS counselor in Mexico arranges U.S. national pavilions at many international trade shows. For a modest fee, U.S. exhibitors can receive assistance in getting a booth, advance publicity, product shipment, and custom clearance.

Office of Commodity and Marketing Programs
FAS
U.S. Department of Agriculture
Tel: (202) 720-2705
Fax: (202) 690-3606

The Office of Commodity and Marketing Programs is divided into product sectors that offer export information and evaluations on Mexican markets.

The OIT maintains the SBA's export information system, providing data and market trends for specific products or services in the top twenty-five world markets. Information is organized by product or service rather than country.

Office of Business Development
Small Business Administration
Tel: (202) 205-6665
Fax: (202) 205-7064

The Office of Business Development houses the Small Business Institute (SBI), which assists exporters with managerial consulting information, including strategies for greater operational efficiency and market studies.

Agency for International Development (AID)

Office of Trade and Investment
Tel: (202) 647-9112
Fax: (202) 647-4533

The Office of Trade and Investment assists U.S. companies interested in bidding for procurement contracts for U.S. foreign aid programs in Mexico.

Office of Small and Disadvantaged Business Utility
Agency for International Development
Tel: (703) 875-1551
Fax: (703) 875-1862

The Office of Small and Disadvantaged Business Utility assists minority- or women-owned businesses interested in supplying goods and services to the AID. It maintains the Consultant Registry Information System (ACRIS), which is an automated database of companies and institutions that are able to match AID requirements.

Mexican Government Resources

Secretariat of Commerce and Industrial Development (SECOFI)

SECOFI regulates international trade in Mexico. It has the authority to grant import permits and establish trade regulations. It also investigates dumping charges. It is Mexico's equivalent to the U.S. Department of Commerce.

General Directorate of Foreign Investment (DGIE)

Office of General Directorate of Foreign Investment
Promotion and Coordination
Secretariat of Commerce and Industrial Development
Tel: (5) 540-1426

The DGIE is probably the best starting place for a U.S. investor to approach SECOFI. It provides administrative and legal counseling on all foreign investment and trade. It will refer the investor to the proper division of other Mexican government secretariats for any additional counseling needed.

The DGIE also has profiles of each Mexican state, data about industrial parks and their infrastructures, and a register of other sources of information that an investor may need to know about Mexico.

Mexican Investment Board (MIB)

The Mexican Investment Board is a quasi-government organization designed to provide information to potential foreign investors. Services include publications, market studies, and a twenty-four-hour fax line that offers financial information about Mexico. In the United States, call:

MIB: (800) MIB-2434 or (602) 930-4802

National Institute of Statistics, Geography and Information (INEGI)

INEGI is a great source of information on Mexico, including economic statistics, demographics, and national databases. For more information, call:

INEGI: (5) 709-2538

Business Coordinating Council (COECE)

COECE is Mexico's private-sector negotiating team for the North American Free Trade Agreement. It can provide information on different industrial sectors in Mexico. For more information, call:

COECE: (202) 625-3550

Chambers of Commerce and Associations

Mexico has many chambers and associations that offer information on different sectors of economic activity. The National Chamber of Industrial Transformation (CANACINTRA), the National Chamber of Commerce of Mexico City (CANACO), and the National Association of Importers and Exporters of the Mexican Republic (ANIERM) provide foreign investors with statistical information on different Mexican markets and industry contacts. (For addresses, see Chambers and Associations in the Directories.)

The American Chamber of Commerce of Mexico, A.C. (AmCham) offers its members a variety of useful services and publications. It has information on international trade, including tariff schedules, trade fairs, and legal counseling. AmCham also serves as a business clearinghouse for buyers and sellers of various services and products. For more information, contact:

AmCham: (5) 705-0995

Development and Commercial Banks

(See the section on the banking system in Chapter 9.)

Note

1. Lena Bartoli, David Genser, Henry Jurasek, Stanley Kostyla, Stephen Lord, George Moore, Kevin Murphy, and John Watson, *Export Promotion: Problems in the Small Business Administration's Programs, GAO/GGD-92-77* (Washington, D.C.: U.S. General Accounting Office, September 1992), pp. 1–2.

12

Product Preparation

It is crucial that foreign suppliers adapt their products to Mexico's standards and regulations. A freight forwarder is a reliable source for determining whether a product will be accepted in Mexico. A Mexican customs broker is also a good source for regulation information, although such a broker may sometimes charge a fee.

Product Standards

Electrical System

You should know the basics of the electrical system in Mexico in order to be aware of the standards involved. Mexico has 115-volt, 60-cycle alternating current. Three-phase and single-phase 230-volt currents and higher are available. Most of its electricity comes from hydroelectric and steam-powered plants. Mexico's electrical system is 110 volts with a frequency of 60 hertz.

U.S. and Mexican Government Resources for Product Standards

The Mexican Bureau of Standards and Norms
Dirección General de Normas (DGN)
Secretariat of Commerce and Industrial Development
Tel: (5) 540-2620, 589-9877, ext. 130

The DGN establishes all weight, measurement, and quality standards, including the standards for medical equipment, electronics, chemicals, and construction materials. Mexico uses the metric system, so U.S. exporters should use metric markings on all exports. Mexico uses standards from the Society of Automotive Engineers (SAE), the American Society of Mechanical Engineers (ASME), and the American Society for Testing of Materials (ASTM). For electronics, Mexico follows the standards used in most of Europe, which are set by the International Telegraph and Telephone Consulting Committee (CCITT).

The DGN issues a standards authorization, referred to as the "NOM," that is required for many products including medical equipment, electronics, chemicals, and construction materials before they may enter Mexico. Exporters should consult the U.S. Department of Commerce or a Mexican customs broker to determine if their product requires a NOM.

If a NOM is needed, a completed original application and two copies of it must be presented to SECOFI along with the application fee, product samples, a photograph, a copy of any test results, a copy of the product's instructions, a copy of the product guarantee, an electrical diagram, a description of the availability of spare and replacement parts, specifications, a carbon copy and a photocopy of the customs entrance document, and a copy of the purchase or shipment invoice. Application processing usually takes a minimum of one month.

> National Center for Standards and Certification Information
> National Institute of Standards and Technology (NIST)
> U.S. Department of Commerce
> Tel: (301) 975-4040
> Fax: (301) 963-2871
> GATT Hotline (301) 975-4041

The NIST has standards and certification requirements on all goods, other than food, going into Mexico. It also has a hot line recording on the General Agreement of Tariffs and Trade (GATT) with technical announcements of proposed changes in foreign regulations that influence trade.

> Office of Metric Programs
> NIST
> U.S. Department of Commerce
> Tel: (301) 975-3690
> Fax: (301) 948-1416

U.S. exporters seeking assistance on adapting their exports to the Mexican metric system should contact the Office of Metric Programs.

> Office of Trade Development
> U.S. Department of Commerce
> Tel: (202) 482-1461
> Fax: (202) 482-5697

The Office of Trade Development helps U.S. businesses to compete abroad by providing information and analysis on different industries.

Standards for Agricultural and Food Exports

It is essential for agricultural exporters to consult the U.S. Department of Agriculture (USDA) to confirm that their understanding of Mexican agricultural standards is correct. (See also Chapter 17, Mexico's Importing Regulations.)

U.S. Government Resources

> Office of Food Safety and Technical Requirements
> Foreign Agricultural Service (FAS)
> U.S. Department of Agriculture

Tel: (202) 720-1301
Fax: (202) 690-0677

The Office of Food Safety and Technical Requirements has information on Mexican safety standards and labeling and packaging requirements for U.S. exports.

Livestock and Seed Division
American Marketing Service (AMS)
U.S. Department of Agriculture
Tel: (202) 720-4486
Fax: (202) 720-1112

The Livestock and Seed Division has information on livestock and meat standardization and provides food-quality certification.

Poultry and Eggs Division
AMS, U.S. Department of Agriculture
Tel: (202) 720-3271
Fax: (202) 690-3165

The Poultry and Eggs Division has information on egg and poultry grading and provides quality certification.

Dairy Grading
AMS
U.S. Department of Agriculture
Tel: (202) 720-3171
Fax: (202) 720-6327

The Dairy Grading office has information on dairy exports and provides quality certification.

Export Certification Unit and Plant Protection and Quarantine
Animal & Plant Health Inspection (APHIS)
U.S. Department of Agriculture
Tel: (301) 436-8537
Fax: (301) 436-5786

Office of Trade Services
National Marine and Fisheries Service
U.S. Department of Commerce
Tel: (301) 713-2379
Fax: (301) 588-4853

The Office of Trade Services provides information on Mexican standards for fish and fish-related products.

APHIS has information on Mexican import requirements for agricultural and processed food exports from the United States. This agency will inspect and certify.

Label and Marking Requirements

Products that are exported into Mexico should have a general label and instruction requirements. Labels should follow the metric system and be written in Spanish. The following information must be included: the product's name; the manufacturer's trade name and address; precautionary information; serial number; date of production; electrical specifications; instructions for use, handling, and conservation; and required standards.

Exports Labeled Before They Enter Mexico

In October 1992, Mexico passed some special labeling requirements for specified exports. Exporters are now responsible for placing Spanish-language labels permanently on all leather products, refrigerators, and textiles *before* they enter Mexico. Labeling for all other products may be applied *after* the products enter Mexico, and it is usually considered the responsibility of the distributor or importer. Further specifications for labeling products can be obtained free of charge from:

Flash Facts Hotline, U.S. Department of Commerce: (202) 482-4464, ext.
                                                                                              0101

Products With Trademarks

Products with trademarks are not required to be registered, but it is still important for the exporter to do so to protect against piracy. Products with registered trademarks should be marked "MR" (*marca registrada*) and should include the trademark and the name and location of the manufacturer. For products too small to carry this information, it should be included on their labels.

Special Labeling

Special labeling is required on exports of fertilizers, insecticides, prepared feeds, beverages, packaged foodstuffs, pharmaceutical products, leather and leather goods, apparel, silver, and nickel- and silver-plated items. Detailed information on these labels may be obtained from the importer or from a customs broker. For products requiring special labels, a $225 fee must be paid the Secretariat of Finance and Public Credit (SHCP) for each label registered.

Food Products

Labels for food products must be approved by Mexico's Secretariat of Health. Each product container must bear a label with the product's commercial name, its generic description in Spanish and English, a measurement of its net contents, the importer's name and address, the importer's SHCP taxation number, the product's registration number with the Secretariat of Health, and the words "Producto de E.E.U.U." (made in the U.S.A.). For more information on food product labels, contact:

Dirección General de Regulación Sanitaria de
     Alimentos, Secretaria de Salud: (5) 518-3696

13

Business Environment

Retail

Mexico's retail landscape is undergoing a significant transformation, in which U.S. businesses are playing an active role. The average Mexican's standard of living is rising, so more money is available for middle-class consumer spending. Retailers are gearing up for growing demand by modernizing their stores with technology: price scanners, computerized inventories, and satellite hookups for credit card approval. U.S. companies are major suppliers of this new equipment and the services that it often requires. The demand for U.S. consumer goods is growing, and quality is becoming more important. Mexicans like U.S. merchandise, and they usually associate it with high standards.

Shopping malls are becoming more common and are catering to a broader range of consumers. This is considered the trend for the future. Wal-Mart and Price Club from the United States are joining Mexican retail chains (CIFRA, S.A., and Comercial Mexicana) to create warehouse stores that offer merchandise at lower prices. These stores are usually large, with low overhead and no frills; merchandise is still in cartons, and there often is only one brand per category. It costs an estimated $10 million to begin each store. Many are only open to members, which often are companies rather than individuals and typically buy large quantities of merchandise during a visit. Most stores offer merchandise similar to that of the U.S. Price Club, including food, home and office supplies, and clothing. Merchandise is often priced 20 percent lower than at other stores.

Mexico already has several major department store chains, including Salinas y Rocha, Sanborn Hermanos, Liverpool and El Palacio de Hierro, and Comercial Mexicana, but most of these stores cater to a higher economic class.

The Secretariat of Commerce and Industrial Development (SECOFI) calculates that 90 percent of all Mexican private companies are still small to medium in size. These retail stores are often more specialized, but still look to U.S. exporters to supply a significant amount of their merchandise. U.S. companies interested in finding potential retail partners should consult an appropriate association or chamber or should use one of the many directories available. (For addresses and publications, see Chambers and Associations as well as Publications in the Directories.)

Maquiladoras

A *maquiladora*, also called a *maquila*, a twin plant, or an in-bond operation, is a Mexican corporation partially or fully owned by foreign investors for the purpose of assembling finished or semifinished products to be sold predominantly in the United States. If the goods are exported to the United States, there is no Mexican duty on the imported raw materials, equipment, or components that go into making them. U.S. customs only requires duty on the total value of the imported goods, minus the value of the U.S.-made components. This system enables hundreds of foreign companies to strengthen their competitive standing in domestic and international markets by providing facilities and an effective labor force at lower Mexican labor rates. *Maquiladoras* can also give foreign companies the presence that is sometimes needed to sell goods and services in Mexico and South America.

Many items assembled in Mexico may be imported into the United States without any duty if the items qualify for the Generalized System of Preferences (GSP) and are made with 35 percent Mexican content. Mexican content usually means direct labor costs relevant to the product. The GSP program does not consider administrative expenses, overhead, or selling expenses as counting toward the 35 percent Mexican content minimum. U.S.-origin components may be considered part of this 35 percent if they are substantially transformed in Mexico. This often allows electronics products to qualify for GSP treatment.

Mexico initiated the *maquiladora* program in 1965 to generate foreign capital, create jobs, and promote Mexican exports. This sector has since grown into Mexico's second-largest money-maker, after oil. Since 1985, the *maquiladora* sector has had a 20 percent per year revenue growth. *Maquiladoras* accounted for $4.134 billion in 1991, up from $1.598 billion in 1987. The total value set for exported goods in 1991 was $15.828 billion. *Maquiladora* trade accounted for 36.9 percent of Mexico's total exports and 23.4 percent of its total imports. It also is a major contributor to U.S.-Mexican trade: *Maquiladora* products represented 46.3 percent of Mexico's total exports to the United States and 31.8 percent of U.S. exports to Mexico.

Not surprisingly, plant numbers are growing at a rapid rate and have more than tripled since 1980. There was a 12.8 percent growth rate for *maquilas* in 1991, bringing the total number in operation to 1,925. According to Mexico's Instituto Nacional de Estadistica, Geografia e Informitica—INEGI (National Institute of Statistics, Geography, and Information Systems), *maquila* sectors with particularly strong growth in 1991 included services (23.3 percent), electrical material and accessories and electronics (20.2 percent), food (17.5 percent), and textiles and apparel (16.7 percent).

Most *maquilas* are situated along the U.S.-Mexican border, but nearly 25 percent are now located in interior regions. Approximately 33 percent are wholly U.S.-owned, with particular concentrations in the following sectors: electrical and electronic, furniture and wood and metal, and transportation equipment. More than 50 percent of the *maquiladoras* registered by the end of January 1992 had some U.S. ownership.

Maquiladoras employ approximately 467,000 Mexicans at considerably lower wages than their U.S. counterparts. According to the American Chamber of Commerce of Mexico, the average daily wage for a *maquiladora* worker is $6.22, but this varies, depending on the person's level of skills and the industrial sector. The turnover and absenteeism rate are often better than rates at U.S. plants. Plant managers must be Mexican or foreign nationals. All workers must be Mexican.

Starting a Maquiladora *Operation*

The Mexican government has made it fairly simple to establish *maquiladoras,* but it is very important that the necessary legal steps be reviewed by both Mexican and U.S. legal counsels. It usually takes about two months to complete the administrative work.

There are three ways a foreign investor can participate in the *maquiladora* program: (1) full ownership of the *maquila,* making it a subsidiary company, which allows the most control of the operations; (2) subcontracting with an existing *maquila,* allowing the foreign investor to enjoy the advantages of the *maquiladora* program without having to pay as much capital investment up front; (3) a shelter program where a Mexican company operates the plant while the U.S. company provides the technology and/or raw materials.

Incorporating. A *maquiladora* must be a corporation, so the regular procedures of incorporation must be followed (see the beginning of Chapter 10). The corporate form used is usually the *sociedad de capital variable* (S.A. de C.V.).

The SECOFI Permit. A *maquiladora* must be approved by SECOFI and receive a permit to import raw material and machinery. The permit is not transferable and is specified to a project's particular manufacturing process. This makes it important to have a clear plan of operation before applying to SECOFI for a permit. The application requires identification data for the applying company; the number of jobs that will be created; a list of the equipment, machines, and tools that will be used; a list of the raw materials and components that will be assembled; projections of the operational expenses during the first two years; a description of the manufacturing process and its output; and a breakdown of the proposed investment in fixed assets.

Import Permits and Customs. It is worthwhile to get a customs broker to assist in applying for a variety of routine permits that will be needed for goods to be imported into Mexico (raw goods, tools, and so on). The Mexican government generally dictates that all items not directly involved in the manufacturing process (furniture, office supplies) be purchased in Mexico.

Environmental Permits. Mexico's Secretariat of Social Development (SEDE-SOL) and the U.S. Environmental Protection Agency (EPA) work together in enforcing environmental protection regulations. The following environmental permits are required for a manufacturing facility in Mexico:

- An environmental operating license
- Ecological waybills
- Permits for storing hazardous materials

- An environmental impact statement
- A hazardous waste generator
- Residual water discharge registration
- Any additional reporting requirements

Importing Into Mexico

Capital equipment and materials for a *maquila's* final product may be imported into Mexico without duty. Once SECOFI approves of the *maquila* program, the following may be imported for a period of six months, which is extendable for another six months: raw materials, components, packing materials, labels, related literature, subassemblies, containers, and auxiliary supplies. Blueprints, tools, manuals, security mechanisms, production accessories, machinery, equipment, spare parts, testing and training apparatus, and quality control may remain in Mexico for the duration of the time that the company operates under a *maquiladora* permit. All temporary imports require surety bonds. Records of the storage and nature of all material and equipment imported "in-bond" must be kept until the release of the bond. This is also true for all export documents.

Selling in Mexico

A *maquiladora* that increases the production of an item and maintains a balanced foreign currency position may sell up to 50 percent of its annual export value in Mexico. This requires a special two-year permit from SECOFI. Mexican customs will only subject the item's foreign components to duty. Products not directly involved in production, including transportation equipment and computers, may be imported without either duty or an import license.

Payment of Operational Expenses

Mexico's Exchange Control Decree requires operational expenses to be paid with foreign currency that has been brought into Mexico and exchanged for pesos by a Mexican bank. Records of these transactions must be maintained by the *maquiladora* and filed monthly with Banco de México and SECOFI. The purchase of fixed assets is excluded from these payment requirements.

Taxes and Production Costs

Maquiladoras have the same taxes as other Mexican businesses. The 35 percent corporate tax rate is based on income recovered in Mexico. Since most companies use *maquiladoras* as service centers instead of profit centers, profit margins tend to be only 3–4 percent, so employees can receive the required profit sharing. *Maquiladoras* also pay a 2 percent assets tax. Foreign employees do not pay Mexican income tax unless they spend more than 183 days per year in Mexico. If they do qualify as taxpayers but their earnings derived from Mexico are less than $10,001, they do not have to pay any income tax. They have a 15 percent rate if they make from $10,001 to $80,001 in Mexico and are subject to a 30 percent rate if they make over $80,001.

Production costs are still substantially lower than in the United States. Production cost is based on imported primary materials that must be covered by import taxes, labor, and other inherent expenses. The production cost does not include the cost of the machinery if it has been lent free of charge by the *maquiladora's* parent company. The corporate income tax law prohibits any depreciation on machinery. *Maquiladoras* may be subject to a rental income tax on equipment lent under a free-loan agreement if it is used in production for sales to Mexico. It is possible to lease equipment.

Franchising

Franchises have more than quadrupled in Mexico since 1991, and this rate is expected to continue. The International Franchise Association reports more than 140 franchises in 1992. Nearly two thirds of them are owned by foreigners. According to the U.S. Embassy in Mexico, the estimated market size for franchises in 1992 was $5.350 billion, and the projected average annual growth rate of this market from 1992 to 1994 is 20 percent. The estimated value of franchise-related imports from the United States into Mexico is $3.5 billion, with an average annual growth rate of 25 percent. Fast-food restaurants and supplier services franchises have the greatest markets within this sector and are expected to bring in $2.82 billion and $1.65 billion respectively in 1993.

Much of this growth is attributed to recent Mexican law reforms that have created a favorable climate for foreign franchises. Franchise agreements for the first time are represented as a separate topic in the law, giving the franchisor more control over the franchisee. The Law for the Promotion and Protection of Industrial Property (IPL) defines a franchise as an agreement where (1) a license is needed to use a trademark, (2) either technical assistance or knowledge is shared to allow the licensee to produce or sell products or provide services in a uniform manner, and (3) the commercial, operating, and managing methods are decided by the holder of the trademark and are used to maintain the standard and image of the product or service that this trademark represents. Competition from local and Third World suppliers is limited by this law. The franchisor can intervene in the management of the franchisee's business and restrict the franchisee's development activity.

Mexican investors are receptive to U.S. franchises because they offer an easier, safer opportunity to enter business. The franchisee receives help in choosing a location, training personnel, advertising, and selecting products.

A franchise does not need government approval, but its agreements must be registered. Franchise registration is denied very rarely, since to do so the government must prove that the franchise agreement violates public policy or has a condition that disclaims its applicability.

Franchisors may now receive both initial franchise fees and continuing royalties. The parties to a franchise agreement determine the percentage of royalties and the length of the agreement. Agreement renewals are allowed.

The reformed Law for the Protection of Intellectual Property has eased the process of transferring technology. Technology is required to be registered for protection, but is not required to be approved by the government.

Working Out an Agreement With a Mexican Business Representative

It is very important for a U.S. company working with a foreign sales representative to draw up the contract in both Spanish and English so that there are no misunderstandings. It is recommended to include the following terms in the contract:

    i. The representative may not conduct business with competitive companies.
   ii. The representative may not reveal any confidential information in a way that would prove injurious, detrimental, or competitive to the U.S. company.
  iii. The representative may not enter into agreements that would bind the U.S. company without its permission.
  iv. The representative must refer to all inquiries received from outside the designated sales territory to the U.S. company.
   v. The representative must demonstrate performance requirements regarding a minimum sales volume and an expected rate of increase.

14

Selling to the Mexican Public Sector

Mexico's public sector purchased 17 percent of Mexico's imports in 1991. The Mexican government tries to buy domestic products whenever it can, but sometimes these products are not available.

Application Procedures

The Mexican government will do business only with foreign companies registered at the Departamento de Registro de Proveedores de la Administración Pública, Secretaria de Programación y Presupuesto (Programming and Budget) and with the government agency that will be purchasing their product. For more information, contact:

> Departmento de la Administración Pública: (5) 740-7840, ext. 519 or
> 532, or 740-2431

The Secretariat de Hacienda must be paid a registration fee of approximately $150, but this fee is subject to change every three months. This fee will cover registration for one year. To renew registration, a smaller fee must be sent before February 28 of each year or the company will be penalized with a surcharge. The company must also submit an HD-1 form (Declaración General de Pago de Derechos).

The Secretariat de Proveedores de la Administración Pública must receive all six of the following documents from the applicant:

1. A written application (Form X-90) with the name, address, and telephone number of both the company's local Mexican representative and the foreign applicant.

2. A letter from either the U.S. Department of Commerce, the U.S. Treasury, or a chamber of commerce verifying the firm's legality in the United States. This letter must be sent within six months after being signed and certified by a Mexican consul in the United States. The letter must be translated into Spanish by an

official translator employed by the official entity certifying the letter. The date, the applicant's full name, and the legal status of the individual representing the company in Mexico must be highlighted.

3. A photostatic copy of the public document issued to the Mexican representative. The document should record the country and place where the power of representation was granted, the full name of the local company or individual, and the date. This information must be highlighted.

4. The company's most recent financial statements, including the balance sheet and the profit and loss statement, notarized by a Mexican consul. This data must not be more than two months older than the date on the application form.

5. A photostatic copy of all agreements and contracts between the foreign and local company, including copies of purchase orders, translated into Spanish by an official translator. The complete name of the contracted company or receiver of the purchase order and the dates should be highlighted.

6. A proof of payment for the initial registration fee to the SH.

All documents must be typed or printed in block letters and translated into Spanish. All documents must be notarized by a Mexican consul, and no corrections or deletions are acceptable. Each page of the application form must be signed by the company's owner or legal representative. If the requested information is not highlighted, it will be rejected by the computerized system.

The National Association of Mexican Importers and Exporters (ANIERM) will register foreign companies for a payment of roughly $300. For more information, call:

Departmento de Comercio y Servicios
(Commerce and Services)
ANIERM: (5) 584-9522

Companies wanting to do business with Petroleos Mexicanos (PEMEX) require a separate process and should register with that entity. PEMEX has an office in Houston, Texas, that can provide further information also. Call:

PEMEX International: (5) 250-2611
                             (713) 978-7974

Under NAFTA

NAFTA will give U.S. exporters greater access to Mexico's public-sector markets, which include government-owned enterprises such as PEMEX (national petroleum company) and CFE (national electric company) that actually purchase more than the secretariats. U.S. companies will be able to compete in Mexico and Canada in an open, explained bidding process without discrimination on account of their nationality. Companies will have the right to an independent review of the process if they would like to challenge the outcome of the bidding. U.S. sectors that should especially benefit from increased public-sector access include construction services and equipment, steel products, electronics, pharmaceutical products, communication systems, environmental services and products, computer systems, hardware, heavy electrical equipment, and petroleum-related products and services.

15

Financing an Export Transaction

The success of an exporter's sale is shaped by how favorably the exporter can obtain financing. It is important to explore all viable options. Since the export market is so competitive, the advantage of being able to offer good payment terms is often essential to making a sale. The following methods for receiving payment are ranked in order from most secure to least secure:

1. Cash in advance
2. Letter of credit
3. Documentary drafts for collection
4. Open account
5. Consignment sales

U.S. Commercial Banks

There are approximately 300 U.S. commercial banks that provide financing for international sales transactions. Usually they are the larger banks. A good place for exporters to start in finding financing for their projects is by going to their own banks. If they don't do it themselves, these banks can refer the exporters to correspondent banks that do. Other possible sources for this information are organizations that work with exporters doing business with Mexico, such as the American Chamber of Commerce in Mexico or an international freight forwarder. The Export-Import Bank (Eximbank) has credit lines with commercial banks available for international sales transactions, and its marketing division can also provide names of potential financiers.

Banks can offer the same type of commercial loans for international exports that they use to finance domestic transactions. Banks often seek assistance from state and federal small business export finance programs to alleviate the problem of tying up potential collateral and using up limited credit lines.

Many U.S. banks have offices in Mexico. Under Mexican law, they are allowed to participate in preliminary and auxiliary banking activities related to the administration of U.S. bank loans. Only Citibank, however, is permitted to directly extend credit in Mexico to U.S. and Mexican companies. The following banks have offices in Mexico:

American Express Bank, Ltd.	Manufacturers Hanover Trust Co.
Bank of America, NT	Mercantile National/Mellon
Bank of Boston	Bank, N.A.
Bank One	Midland Bank, Ltd.
Bankers Trust Co.	Morgan Guaranty Trust Co. of
Barclay's Bank of California	New York
California Commerce Bank	Nations Bank
Chase Manhattan Bank, N.A.	Northwest Bank Minnesota, N.A.
Chemical Bank	Pittsburgh National Bank
Citibank, N.A.	Provident National Bank
Continental Illinois Bank	Republic National Bank of Dallas
First Fidelity Bank, N.A. New Jersey	Republic National Bank of New
First Interstate Bank of California	York
First National Bank of Chicago	Security Pacific National Bank
First National City Bank	Texas Commerce Bank
Greyhound Financial Corp.	Texas National Bank
Intercontinental Credit Corp.	Wells Fargo Bank, N.A.

U.S. Federal Government Financial Assistance

Several financial programs of the U.S. government provide financial assistance to exporters of various sizes and experience. An exporter should consider public-sector financing programs for transactions considered too risky for private-sector financing. The Overseas Private Investment Corporation (OPIC) is not on this list, because it does not yet have a program for transactions involving Mexico.

Export-Import Bank

The Export-Import Bank of the United States (Eximbank) is an independent corporate agency of the U.S. government. Founded in 1934, its purpose is to facilitate the financing of U.S. exporters of goods and services by covering credit risks that are too great for the private sector to consider. Eximbank neutralizes the influence of export credit subsidies provided from foreign governments. Qualifying transactions must involve goods and services that have at least 50 percent U.S. content.

Eximbank strongly promotes trade with Mexico. Its programs in 1991 issued over $3 billion in guarantees, over $4 million in loans, and $417 million in medium-term insurance for business transactions involving Mexico. Eximbank places Mexico in its category 2 for risk, considering it an intermediate country for risk.

Important Telephone Numbers

Eximbank's Export Financing Hotline: (800) 424-5201
Eximbank's Washington, D.C., office: (202) 566-4490
Eximbank's Los Angeles office: (213) 575-7425

Small Business Administration

The Small Business Administration (SBA) provides financial export assistance to independently owned and operated U.S. businesses that are not dominant in their fields. Most accepted applicants have businesses that are at least one year old. SBA will not fund joint ventures and will not make loans to businesses if they are able to get funds from private financial institutions or banks.

Office of International Trade (OIT)
SBA
Tel: (202) 205-6720

The OIT is a good starting point for exporters who do not know which of the SBA programs would be most appropriate for their transaction.

Export Revolving Line of Credit (ERLC)
SBA
Tel: (202) 205-7516

The Export Revolving Line of Credit Program guarantees loans up to $750,000, and its proceeds can assist with the financing of foreign market formation or operational expenses. The maximum maturity is three years. ERLC guaranteed approximately $26 million in loans in 1991.

International Trade Loan Guarantee Program
SBA
Tel: (202) 205-6720

The International Trade Loan Guarantee Program offers small businesses import-competition loan guarantees of up to $1 million for equipment and facilities and up to $250,000 for working capital. Loan maturities can be extended up to twenty-five years.

Small Business Investment Companies
SBA
Tel: (202) 205-6512

The Small Business Investment Companies program provides venture capital and equity to small U.S. companies whose investment design includes exporting. Amounts range from $10,000 to $10 million.

Business Loan Guarantee Program
SBA
Tel: (202) 205-6490

The Business Loan Guarantee Program assists private lenders in making loans (maximum of $750,000) to companies that could not borrow without government aid. It provides financing for general working capital or fixed-asset acquisition.

Agency for International Development

The Agency for International Development (AID) provides financial assistance for U.S. companies doing projects in Mexico that will have a developmental impact on the community. Projects must generate employment opportunities that earn net foreign exchange, develop employees' managerial and technical skills, or transfer technology and sustain environmental development.

Private Sector Revolving Fund
AID
Tel: (800) 872-4348

The AID's Bureau for Private Enterprise has loans or guarantees that finance up to 25 percent of a project's total cost (usually from $250,000 to $1 million).

Forfait Guarantee Program
AID
Tel: (800) 872-4348

The Forfait Guarantee Program has nonrecourse financing guarantees that help U.S. companies procure financing to export manufactured goods (spare parts, tools, automotive parts, and so forth) to Mexico. Financing guarantees are provided for up to five years, with a maximum value of $1 million.

U.S. Department of Agriculture

The Market Promotion Program of the U.S. Department of Agriculture (USDA) supports U.S. agricultural exports by reimbursing agricultural businesses conducting foreign market development projects for specific products. For more information, contact:

Office of Marketing Operations, USDA: (202) 720-4327

Commodity Credit Corporation (CCC)
USDA
Tel: (202) 720-3224

The CCC's Export Credit Guarantee Program and Blended Credit Program offer short-term financial assistance to U.S. exporters, insuring most of the value of the exported product plus a portion of any interest that might be owed. The Export Credit Guarantee Program (GSM-102) covers credits with terms up to three years. The Intermediate Export Credit Guarantee Program (GSM-103) covers credits with terms up to ten years. Mexico was the second-largest recipient of GSM-102/103 loans in 1992, receiving $1.313 billion.

Export Credit Program
USDA
Tel: (202) 720-5173

The USDA's Foreign Agricultural Service (FAS) provides financial assistance for U.S. agricultural commodity exports through the Commodity Credit Corporation and the Food for Peace Program.

U.S. State Government Financial Assistance

Twenty-seven state governments have export finance offices for small to medium-size exporters. Services and applicant qualifications vary. Services may include export insurance, working capital loans and guarantees, and receivables financing. Some states work with Eximbank, and some provide financing only after the exporter has been turned down by the private sector.

Mexican Commercial Banks

Mexico's major commercial banks provide international trade financing. (For more information, see the first part of Chapter 9.)

Mexican Government Financial Assistance

Banco Nacional de Comercio Exterior

Banco Nacional de Comercio Exterior (BANCOMEXT) is Mexico's national foreign trade bank. Its Import Financial Support Program provides short-term loans (up to 360 days for 100 percent of the value) to support the import of primary goods that are guaranteed by the Commodity Credit Corporation of the USDA. The minimum amount financed is $100,000. The bank also extends long-term credits (up to five years for 85 percent of the value) for imported capital goods that are guaranteed by Eximbank's credit insurance programs. The minimum amount financed is $200,000. The Import Financial Support Program is open only to enterprises that are established in Mexico. BANCOMEXT also provides services to Mexican exporters. For more information, call BANCOMEXT:

New York office:	(212) 826-2916
California office:	(213) 655-6421
Texas office:	(214) 688-4097
Illinois office:	(312) 856-0316
Georgia office:	(404) 522-5373
Mexico office:	(5) 568-2122

Nacional Financiera, S.N.C.

Nacional Financiera (NAFIN) is Mexico's national development bank. It was created to encourage growth in high-priority areas, which are usually rural and not very developed.

Approximately 90,000 medium, small, and microsize Mexican businesses received credit from NAFIN in 1992 through financial intermediaries, including commercial banks, leasing companies, factoring companies, and credit unions. NAFIN offers lines of credit, letters of credit, and guarantees to Mexican businesses buying U.S. raw materials, capital goods, and services that will increase production in underdeveloped areas. For more information, call NAFIN:

U.S. office:	(202) 338-9010
Mexico City office:	(5) 521-8099 or 518-1680

Bonds

Mexican bonding companies (*afianzadoras*) sell bonds that can be used by a Mexican importer to guarantee payment to a foreign exporter. If the Mexican importer fails to pay what is owed the exporter, the bonding company will make the payment and then attempt to collect from the importer. Some bonding companies offer bonds that are less costly than letters of credit.

Leasing

Financial leasing companies (*arrendadoras*) are often quicker and more flexible than banks in providing lines of credit to industries and individuals for the purchase of specific goods. As the demand for credit has grown, so has the leasing industry, increasing from only twenty-five companies in 1989 to fifty-seven by mid-1992. According to Francisco Padilla of Consultants Macro Asesoria Economica, "The growth in leasing is tied in large part to the growth of investment in Mexico. Investment has increased at a rate of between 14 and 15 percent a year. There has been a big demand for leasing companies to finance that investment."[1] Businesses generally approach banks for short-term loans to purchase items such as raw materials or product components, but use leasing companies for credit to purchase fixed assets such as plant machinery and equipment.

Most leases are financial and must be approved by the Secretariat of Finance and Public Credit (SHCP). Financial leases require the product to be sold to the customer for a low price at the end of the leasing period. Under Mexican law, financial leases are treated as a long-term sale, with the customer buying the product at the end of the leasing period for a nominal sum. "Pure" leases do not have a nominal buyout plan. They are used for transactions such as car rentals and often are tax-deductible. They do not require SHCP authorization. The client must pay market value for the product at the end of the leasing period.

According to the Mexican Association of Financial Leasing Companies (AMAF), the portfolio value for the top six leasing companies in April 1992 was $4.2 billion. Arrendadora Bancomer (of Grupo Financiero Bancomer) is Mexico's biggest leasing company and is worth more than $800 million. Second in value is Internacional (of Grupo Financiero Prime), which is valued at approximately $660 million. Banamex (of Banacci) is third, and Monterrey (also of Grupo Financiero Bancomer) is fourth. For more information on these banks, call:

Arrendadora Bancomer:	(5) 553-9788
Arrendadora Internacional:	(5) 531-6734
Arrendadora Banamex:	(5) 664-1904
Arrendadora Monterrey:	(5) 395-2494

Credit Checks and Collection Problems

It is crucial for a U.S. exporter to investigate a foreign buyer beforehand if the company is to be paid through one of the riskier methods of payment. A good way to get a credit check is to ask the foreign buyer for three references that can be contacted directly. Several credit-checking services are listed in the Directories.

U.S. international banks often will provide their customers with credit checks on foreign buyers; however, these checks usually are not very detailed. For a nominal fee, a Foreign Commercial Service officer at the American embassy in Mexico City will investigate the reputation of a potential Mexican trading partner. Their reports will include the company's financial status, business lines, location, and local reputation.

An exporter who is owed money and is having trouble collecting should make every attempt to negotiate directly with the customer. If this fails, the International Chamber of Commerce (ICC) can be contacted for assistance. Since this entity is not affiliated with a single country, it is often accepted as an unbiased arbitrator. The Foreign Commercial office at the U.S. embassy may also be of assistance. For more information, call:

Foreign Commercial Service:	(5) 211-0042
U.S. Council for the ICC:	(212) 354-4480

Note

1. Patrick McCurry, "Alternative Financing," *Business Mexico* (August 1992), p. 39.

16

U.S. Government Export Regulations

It is essential that exporters have accurate and current information on U.S. export regulations since their violation can entail both criminal and civil penalties.

U.S. Department of Commerce Controls

Export Licenses

Export licenses enable the U.S. government to supervise the flow of all U.S. exports. They are issued for specific transactions rather than for the exporter. Mexico is placed in Country Group T, with other countries considered part of North America. There are two kinds of licenses, the general license and the individually validated license (IVL). Approximately 10 percent of all U.S. exports require individually validated licenses and must follow U.S. export control procedures. An IVL is an authorization from the U.S. government for a specific export transaction or time period for exporting certain goods.

Questions pertaining to licensing should be directed to:

Bureau of Export   or   Office of Export Counseling,
   Administration (BXA), U.S.   BXA:
   Department of Commerce: (202) 482-4811
(202) 482-8536

BXA's Export License Application and Information Network (ELAIN) can accept and process export licenses through its computer. For more information, call:

ELAIN: (202) 482-4811

BXA's System for Tracking Export License Applications (STELA) dispenses instant license application updating from a touch-tone telephone. License processing usually takes fifteen days. For more information, call:

STELA: (202) 482-2752

The Export Licensing Listening Voice Information System. The Export Licensing Listening Voice Information System (ELVIS) provides automated licensing information and emergency handling procedures. ELVIS also transfers the caller to a human consultant if that is needed. It is possible to order by phone publications, forms, or subscriptions to the Office of Export Licensing (OEL) newsletter, the *Insider,* which provides regulatory updates. For more information, call:

ELVIS: (202) 482-4811

Applying for an Individually Validated License. An exporter who wishes to receive an IVL for a transaction must submit form BXA-622P, Application for Export License.

U.S. companies using a representative in Mexico to sell goods and services that require IVLs should include a "kickout clause" in their contract. This ensures that the representative agrees to abide by the regulations of the BXA.

General Licenses. A general license is a broad grant of permission from the U.S. government for exporters of particular categories. Exporters do not have to apply for general licenses. It is important to mark packages with the proper symbols to indicate general license status, including packages sent by the postal service.

U.S. Department of State Controls

The Office of Munitions Control (OMC) oversees the export of arms, munitions, and police/military equipment through licensing and registration. The Munitions Control List itemizes the products that fall under the OMC's auspices and is available upon request. A minimum fee is required for the exports that it covers. Companies planning to export military products and technology should contact:

Office of Munitions Control,
    U.S. Department of State: (703) 875-6652

Food and Drug Administration Controls

The Food and Drug Administration (FDA) enforces U.S. laws pertaining to the quality and safety of foods, drugs and medical devices, cosmetics, and biologics. Exporters must follow guidelines from Section 801, "The Importing and Exporting Products Act." Under this act, drugs for human or animal use that have not been approved by the FDA may not be exported to Mexico, unless they are requested by the Secretariat of Health for limited investigative use. They are not allowed to be sold in Mexico commercially. This regulation also applies to medical devices, ranging from dental plates to X-ray machines, and biologics (which include blood products). If the exported product falls under the auspices of the FDA, contact:

Office of International Affairs, FDA: (301) 443-4480

Environmental Protection Agency Controls

The Internal Activities office of the Environmental Protection Agency (EPA) is required to be notified by all exporters planning to ship hazardous wastes to Mexico. Under the Resource Conservation and Recovery Act (RCRA), the EPA must notify the importer's government about the transaction. The export transaction cannot take place until a written approval has been received from the importer's government. For more information, contact:

Office of International Activities, EPA: or   EPA, Mexico Desk:
(202) 382-4880   (202) 260-4890

17

Mexico's Importing Regulations

Mexico passed reforms in May 1987 that open many of its markets toward greater foreign participation. The Secretariat of Commerce and Industrial Development (SECOFI) now only requires a prior import permit on 330 items, instead of the previous 12,000.

Product Inspection

Laboratories Authorized by SECOFI to Test Imported Products

Apparel and textiles, chemicals, construction products, electric and electronic goods, metal-mechanical items, and food and foodstuffs must first be approved for import by an authorized Mexican laboratory before they are granted a permit by SECOFI. For listings of authorized laboratories, exporters should contact:

Dirección General de Normalización (Office
of Standardization), SECOFI: (5) 540-1619, 540-3842
                                     (5) 540-5153 (Fax)

Import Licensing and Permits

Approximately 200 product categories (mostly agricultural, food, chemical, pharmaceutical, and automotive products) still require importing permits. For information on whether a particular product falls into these categories, exporters should contact a Mexican customs broker, a freight forwarder, or the appropriate government agency. Exporters should be careful about allowing enough time for these permits to be issued.

Prior import permits are still needed for the following: new and used automobiles, buses, trucks, and spare parts (SECOFI); explosives, firearms, and other weapons (Defense); radioactive materials (Energy, Mines and Parastatal Industry);

sixty agricultural product categories (Agriculture and Hydraulic Resources); computer equipment (SECOFI); some pharmaceutical products (Health); some heavy machinery for agriculture and construction (SECOFI); and apparel made of leather or fur (SECOFI).

Import Permits From SECOFI

There is a SECOFI office at the Mexican embassy in Washington, D.C. Its representatives are available to answer any questions on permit requirements:

Commercial Section, SECOFI: (202) 728-1700

The correct office to call for information on import permits at SECOFI in Mexico is:

Dirección General de Asurtos Fronterizos: (5) 683-4394, 683-7055, ext.
                                                                          2706

Import Permits From the Secretariat of Agriculture and Hydraulic Resources and the Secretariat of Health

The Secretariat of Agriculture and Hydraulic Resources (SARH) sets quotas for nearly all major agricultural commodities. Import permits are needed for sixty agricultural categories, including oilseeds, dairy products, grains, and certain horticultural products. The U.S. Department of Agriculture (USDA) cautions exporters to be aware of the expiration date on their Mexican import permits since there is usually little or no flexibility on extensions. Other import clearances from other government agencies may also be needed. For more information, contact:

Agricultural Attaché of the Mexican Embassy: (202) 728-1720

Health Import License for Livestock and Plants. SARH has three branches responsible for granting authorizations of compliance with sanitary standards for agricultural exports entering Mexico. Authorizations of compliance with sanitary standards for livestock and livestock products, except for processed meat, animal feed, and feed ingredients, are issued by:

Directorate General for Animal Health
  (Dirección General de Salud Animal),
  SARH: Tel: (5) 534-1131
                                                             Fax: (5) 534-3985

Authorizations of compliance with sanitary standards for fresh fruits, vegetables, live plants, tobacco leaves, planting seeds, and certain grains are issued by:

Directorate General for Plant Protection and
   Quarantine (Dirección General de Sanidad
   Vegetal), SARH: Tel: (5) 554-0512
                                                 Fax: (5) 554-0529

Authorizations of compliance with sanitary standards for forest products including lumber, logs, and panel items are issued by:

Directorate General for Forestry Protection
   (Dirección General de Protección Forestal),
   SARH: (5) 658-8974

Authorization of compliance with sanitary standards for dairy products, seafood, alcoholic beverages, vegetable oil, animal fat, and other processed food products are issued by:

Directorate General for Sanitary Control of
   Goods and Services (Dirección General de
   Control Sanitario de Bienes y Servicios),
   Secretariat de Salud (SS):   Tel: (5) 521-3050
                                                 Fax: (5) 510-3999

Seeds, plants, plant products, live animals, and animal products that are imported into Mexico must also be accompanied by four copies of a certificate of sanitary compliance from the Animal and Plant Health Inspection Service (APHIS) of the USDA, an accredited veterinarian, or local authorities from the export's origin. The original certificate must be notarized by a Mexican consulate.

U.S. Government Inspection Agencies

The U.S. government agencies listed below can provide certificates of sanitary compliance for marine and agricultural products.

Animals, Plants, and Animal By-Products. For inspection and certification of animals, animal by-products, and plants, contact:

Office of Import-Export Products, Animal
   and Plant Health Inspection (APHIS),
   USDA: (301) 436-7885

Grains. For inspection and certification of grains, contact:

Field Management Division, USDA-FGIS: (202) 720-0228

Meat and Poultry Products. For inspection and certification of meat and poultry products, contact:

Export Coordination Division, USDA-FSIS: (202) 790-9051

Seafood and Fishery Commodities. For inspection and certification of seafood and fishery commodities, contact:

National Seafood Inspection Program,
    National Oceanic and Atmospheric
    Administration (NOAA), U.S. Department
    of Commerce: (301) 713-2363

Product Registration

Some products must be registered with the Mexican government. Exporters should check with their Mexican importer or a Mexican customs broker to see if their product requires registration.

Processed Food Products and Beverages

Processed food products and beverages must be registered. This can occur only with the assistance of a representative who is registered for import and export operations at the Secretariat of Finance and Public Credit (SHCP). This representative registers the product with the Secretariat of Health (SS) after it has been approved by the agency for following Mexican safety standards. The registration is valid for five years.

To register with the SS and receive a permit number, the representative must supply the agency with three copies of the product's U.S. label and three copies of the product's labels that have been approved by the Mexican government, three color photographs of the product with the U.S. label and three color photographs with the Mexican label, a certified copy of the Mexican articles of incorporation, a photocopy of the importer's sanitary license, and a photocopy of the importer's license to warehouse products.

For temporary imports to be distributed on a trial basis, the SS must also receive the name of the importing company and the product, a product description, the amount of the product (number and weight) to be imported, the invoice value, the origin, examples of the product's use, and the proposed port of entry.

Product registration is authorized by:

Directorate of Sanitary Control of Goods and
    Services (Dirección General de Control
    Sanitario de Bienes y Servicios), SS: Tel: (5) 581-9717
                                              Fax: (5) 510-3999

Pharmaceutical Products and Cosmetics

Laboratory Testing. Pharmaceutical products for industrial usage only do not have to be registered. Exporters of pharmaceutical products and cosmetics that will be sold to consumers must submit product samples, dosage instructions, and other product literature to the Secretary of the National Laboratory of Public Health. For more information, contact:

Laboratorio Nacional de Salud Publica, SS: (5) 573-3720

After the laboratory inspection, completed test results, an official application form, company documents, and a 450,000-peso remittance fee must be submitted to:

Dirección General Control Insumos para la
    Salud, SS: (5) 254-2525, 250-6962

Certificates of Quality

Since August 1992, the Mexican government has required certain products to have certificates of quality to be imported into Mexico. The Mexican importer must import no more than three samples of the product to be tested at authorized Mexican laboratories. Test results are then sent from the labs to the Secretariat of Commerce and Industrial Development, which will issue a certificate if the product satisfies the standards. SECOFI regulations stipulate that the Mexican importer is responsible for getting the certificate of quality, but U.S. exporters may also arrange for tests from authorized Mexican labs. If the results are positive and accepted by SECOFI, all Mexican importers of the product may use this certificate.

Only the products listed below require certificates of quality:

- *Ceramic and glass products.* Kitchen sinks, lavatories, and bathtubs
- *Containers.* Portable liquefied petroleum (LP) gas containers and nonportable pressurized L.P. gas containers used as fuel in motor vehicles
- *Electric household appliances.* Refrigerators and freezers, garbage grinders, food processors, juicers, meat grinders, can openers, potato peelers, microwave ovens, food heaters, pans, and shavers
- *Electronic products.* Cash registers and registers connected to computer terminals and automatic data processors, analog and hybrid type; recorders with automatic record changer; record players except cassette and sound type, without recording capability, for domestic use or for automobiles, with a weight of less than 3.5 kilograms (7.7 pounds) and with specific wattage levels, except those classified under Harmonized Tariff System (HTS) no. 8519.91.01; other record and sound players not elsewhere classified; and cassette players operating magnetic tapes of up to 13 millimeters wide
- *Industrial instruments.* Industrial glass thermometers; liquid gas and anhydrous ammonia level indicators; LP gas low-pressure regulators; positive displacement measurers (diaphragm type) for natural or LP gas with a maximum capacity of 12 cubic meter per H and pressure fall of 125 pascals (12.70 millimeters of water column)
- *Medical appliances and instruments.* Plastic or glass disposable syringe cylin-

ders or emboli of up to 30 millimeters; Foley model urinal catheters; blood pressure mercurial or barometric sphygmomanometers for human use; and electrical massage apparatus

- *Other products.* Electronic taximeters and tricycles
- *Plastic products.* Safety triangles for motor vehicles and other latex products not classified elsewhere
- *Photocopying equipment.* Direct reproduction type; indirect type; blueprinters; other optical photocopiers not elsewhere classified, operated by direct contact; and thermocopying machines
- *Plumbing products.* Domestic-use water heaters (storage type) operated with natural or LP gas distillates, submersible portable water heaters, shower heads, and tubular-type electric heaters
- *Pumps and valves.* Pumps for diesel injection; gasoline pumps; bottle-type hydraulic jacks, with an integrated pump and weighing up to 20 kilograms (44 pounds), with a maximum loading capacity of up to 20 tons; inner tubes for tires; safety valves for gas (domestic-use type) except those classified under Harmonized System no. 8481.40.04; safety valves for nonelectric heaters; valves for portable LP gas containers, cylinder weights precision square meter class of 1 to 10 kilograms, precision weights class E1, E2, F1, F2, and MW of 1 milligram to 50 kilograms; and valves for water closets (domestic-use type)
- *Radio and television products.* Radio receptors except those classified under HTS nos. 8527.21.02 and 8527.29.02; television receptors except those classified under HTS nos. 8528.10.02 and 8528.20.02; coaxial cable television receptors without frequency selector
- *Rubber products.* Motor vehicle tires; rubber gloves and other rubber-made surgical clothing; animal skin chest protectors, aprons, sleeves, or leggings
- *Safety/security products.* Military and fire fighter helmets; fire extinguishers with a capacity of up to 24 kilograms (53 pounds) operated with pressurized dried chemical dust, pressurized water, or chemical foam; fire extinguishers with a capacity of more than 24 kilograms operated with pressurized dried chemical dust, pressurized water or chemical foam
- *Silver objects (carved)*
- *Stoves and ovens operated through gassed fuels*
- *Wines and liquors.* Charanda and tequila

Tariffs and Other Import Charges

Mexico's tariff schedule is on the Harmonized Tariff System (HTS), which the United States also uses. U.S. exporters may determine the tariff rate for their specific product by contacting:

U.S. Department of   or   SECOFI, Mexican Embassy:
  Commerce, Mexico Office: (202) 728-1700
(202) 482-2332
(202) 482-5865 (Fax)

For duty rates on agricultural products and information on trade barriers, contact:

> Trade Assistance and Promoting
> Office (TAPO), FAS, U.S.
> Department of Agriculture: (202) 720-7420
>   (202) 690-4374 (Fax)

The Mexican importer is usually responsible for paying the import duties to Mexican customs when the products cross the border. The products will not be released to the importer until the tariff and other charges are paid and the importer is given an import declaration (*pedimento de importación*) as proof of payment. Usually there are three import charges:

1. *Tariff.* Levied on the cost, insurance, and freight (c.i.f. value) of the shipment at the port of entry. Tariffs are either 10, 15, or 20 percent, depending on their HTS classification number.
2. *Customs-processing fee.* Equal to 0.8 percent of the c.i.f. value.
3. *Value-added tax (IVA).* A 10% levy on the tariff, the customs-processing fee, and the c.i.f. value. Particular imports that the Mexican government considers essential are exempt from the IVA or subject to a lower tax. This is also true for imports entering through free trade zones.

Mexican payments to foreign technological suppliers are subject to a Mexican withholding tax of 15 to 35 percent.

When Tariffs Become Barriers

Some trade restrictions take the form of a high tariff. U.S. exporters should consult the Office of the U.S. Trade Representative (USTR) if they find a tariff that seems discriminatory or difficult to overcome. For more information, contact:

> Office of the U.S. Trade Representative
>   (USTR), Office of Mexico: (202) 395-4866
> Agriculture: (202) 395-5006
> Industry: (202) 395-5656
> Investment and Intellectual Property: (202) 395-7320
> Science and Technology: (202) 395-6864
> Services: (202) 395-3606
> Textiles: (202) 395-3026

Importing Used Machinery

The Mexican government will usually permit a piece of used machinery to be imported if it is in good condition and is less than ten years old. The duty on used equipment is determined by the value of the machine's current replacement cost, minus a discount based on the equipment's years of use. A machine that is one to four years old gets a 10 percent discount; four to eight years, 20 percent; eight to 12 years, 30 percent; 12 to 15 years, 40 percent; and fifteen years or older, 50 percent.

The exporter of used equipment must also provide the manufacturer's certification documenting the year the equipment was built, a copy of the equipment's original sales invoice, and a certification of the price of a new piece of equipment of the same kind. These documents must be notarized by a Mexican Consul and should be with the product when it is shipped. The exporter must also provide the usual shipping documentation.

Temporary Imports

Temporary Imports for Export Manufacturing

Mexican businesses that export over $1 million annually or export 10 percent of their production may request government approval for the temporary importation of machinery, raw materials, and components to use in fabricating their export products. This allows for the suspension of license requirements and duties for the equipment and materials used in the exports. These goods may be converted into permanent imports if the duties are paid.

Mexican indirect exporters (who supply direct exporters) are also qualified for this program. The goods may remain in Mexico only for the time granted on the authorization, and the importer must give a fiscal deposit amounting to the item's import duty.

Commercial Samples and Demonstration Equipment

All samples and demonstration equipment imported into Mexico on temporary terms must have a bond. The bond must be obtained in advance through a customs broker, or the equipment will be seized by Mexican customs until a bond is produced. The samples and equipment are usually permitted to stay for six months. Items imported into Mexico for exhibition are subject to a monthly tax of 2 percent of the customs duty. They are exempt, however, if they are to be exhibited at a trade fair or convention, and are usually permitted to stay for a six-month term. For information on customs procedures for trade fairs, contact:

Director of the U.S. Trade Center: (5) 591-1055

Cross-Border Leasing

Cross-border leasing to Mexican companies is a logical maneuver in certain circumstances. Leasing is widely used in the *maquiladora* sector and on projects where a Mexican company cannot afford to buy the expensive equipment it needs. Mexican customs generally requires the lessee to post a bond for the import duties and an additional 10 percent. The equipment is imported without duty, under a temporary import permit. The import documents require the parties involved to predetermine the length of time the equipment will be in Mexico and the manner in which it will be removed. Rental payments to foreign suppliers are subject to a Mexican withholding tax of 35 percent.

Mexican Customs Procedures

The Mexican Customs Service is a branch of the Secretariat of Finance and Public Credit (SHCP). All merchandise going into Mexico must be cleared through customs. There are customs offices at all points of entry, including seaports, airports, inland ports, and along the U.S.-Mexico border.

The Mexican Customs Service was greatly reformed under the Salinas administration. Nearly 3,000 customs agents were dismissed in December 1992, after gaining a reputation over the years for accepting bribes from shippers to supplement their low salaries. Their replacements have proved to be more efficient and better trained. The new officials have also been given a much higher salary and are rotated regularly to different customs posts.

Customs Brokers

Customs brokers are licensed individuals or organizations that may enter and clear goods through customs. They give exporters and importers the option of not having to do all the shipping legwork themselves. They are familiar with tariff schedules and Mexican customs requirements. They can arrange all the necessary shipping documentation and can recommend a good freighter. Many customs brokers have warehouses on the border where products can be stored before being exported. It is not necessary to use a customs broker, but for first-time exporters, it is recommended. Mexican customs brokers are located at all border entrances. Mexican customs brokers' fees are set by the government and are based on a percentage of the value of the import.

Customs Warehouses

Exported products entering Mexico must be kept in a customs warehouse until the required documents have been presented and the duties and other charges have been paid. Storage charges begin fifteen days after the arrival of the merchandise. Merchandise that has not been claimed after ninety days is considered legally abandoned and becomes the property of Mexican customs.

Exports stored in Mexican customs warehouses are under Mexican custody and may be reexported without any duty, if they are permitted for Mexican trade. Once exports have cleared customs, however, they are considered nationalized, which means that Mexican import duties on them will not be refunded if they are reexported and they will be subject to Mexican export regulations. Products that require import licenses usually need a customs permit if they are to be reexported.

Under NAFTA

Customs procedures between the North American countries would be standardized under NAFTA. Mexico and the United States would end customs processing fees by June 30, 1999, and no new customs user fees may be adopted. Exporters would be required to have a certificate of origin for their products to be eligible for NAFTA's tariff benefits. Certificates of origin have a twelve-month duration for single or multiple importations of identical products.

Programs With Customs Benefits

Free Trade Zones

Free trade zones offer for import or reimport transactions an exemption from the duties or federal excise taxes that would normally be charged on foreign goods (unless the goods or products created from them are then transported into customs territory).

All territory within Baja California Norte and Baja California Sur is free of customs duties unless the products are shipped to other parts of Mexico. This also is true for the city of Agua Prieta and parts of Sonora. The Mexican government offers special incentives for companies that establish manufacturing plants in free trade zones to produce items that are not manufactured elsewhere in Mexico. For more information, contact:

SECOFI, Mexican Embassy: (202) 728-1700

Foreign Sales Corporations

The Foreign Sales Corporation (FSC) Act was established in 1984 as a tax incentive for U.S. exports and as a substitute for the domestic international sales corporation (DISC). An FSC qualifies for a permanent federal income tax exemption of up to 15 percent, if income is generated by the sale or lease of exported property or services. FSCs must still pay Mexican taxes without receiving U.S. tax credit.

If the FSC purchases from contracts or independent suppliers, offering a price equal to a price paid by an unrelated buyer to an unrelated seller, then 32 percent of the FSC's gross income from exporting is exempt from corporate tax.

A business entity that qualifies as an FSC must be incorporated and have its principal office in a qualified country (such as Mexico) or U.S. possession. FSCs may be created by manufacturers, nonmanufacturers, and export groups. An FSC may be an independent dealer or a subsidiary of a manufacturing business. At least one director cannot be a U.S. resident. The FSC may act as a commission agent or purchase and sell for its own account. Goods are exported from the United States. For more information, contact:

Office for the Chief Counsel for International
   Commerce, U.S. Dept. of Commerce: (202) 482-0937

18

Shipping and Its Requirements

An inexperienced exporter should consult with a freight forwarder when deciding the best method of shipping to Mexico. Sending goods by mail to Mexico requires the recipient to pay a duty and an import surcharge of 10 percent of the general import duty before receiving the goods.

Freight Forwarders

An international freight forwarder is an independent business that handles the shipment of exports. Freight forwarders are familiar with Mexico's import regulations and U.S. export regulations and can advise exporters on what documents are necessary. Many are licensed customs brokers. They can assist exporters in price quotations and advise them of necessary costs, including port charges, freight costs, consular fees, and insurance costs. They can also recommend appropriate packaging and arrange for the product to be packed at the port or containerized. They can work with customs brokers to deliver to a designated vessel the products that will be exported.

A freight forwarder operates on a fee basis and collects payment from the exporter. Payment may also include a percentage of the carrier's freight charge. Fees vary and consist of an agreed amount plus documentation charges. An exporter must provide the freight forwarder with a packing list, a commercial invoice, and a bill of lading or an airway bill. Exporters should ensure that these documents are accurate, because Mexican customs officials are very strict about their correctness and may fine exporters if there are any inconsistencies in their documents.

Multicompany shipments of commodities with similar handling requirements and headed for the same destination can be combined to lower the shipping rate. Interested exporters should inquire with their freight forwarder about this possibility.

Cargo Insurance

Most exports are protected by cargo insurance for damage or loss during transit. Either the supplier or the purchaser arranges for the coverage, depending on the sales terms. If the buyer agrees to do this, the exporter should make sure that it has been done before shipment and that the coverage amount is suitable. The International Trade Administration advises exporters to consult international insurance carriers or freight forwarders for more information. A freight forwarder can arrange to obtain an open policy to cover foreign shipments, or the exporter can use his freight forwarder's open policy. Cargo insurance is used for shipments by U.S. sea freight, airlines, and mail.

U.S. Government Assistance

U.S. Department of Transportation

Different branches of the U.S. Department of Transportation (DOT) provide technical information and assistance to U.S. exporters on Mexico's transportation policy and infrastructure, including information on ports, aviation, and highways. For more information, contact:

Office of the Secretary of Transportation:	(202) 366-9515
Federal Aviation Administration (FAA), DOT:	(817) 624-5005
Federal Highway Administration (FHA), DOT:	(202) 366-0111

U.S. Department of Agriculture

The Transportation and Marketing office of the U.S. Department of Agriculture (USDA) provides information and publications to assist U.S. agricultural exporters to best use transportation resources. The USDA also publishes *Traveler's Tips* providing information on transportation regulations for moving plants and animals across the U.S.-Mexico border.

For more information, contact:

Office of Animal and Plant Transportation Requirements, Documents Management Branch, USDA:	(301) 436-8413

19

Border Infrastructure

The United States and Mexico have taken measures to accelerate border crossings, but congestion and delays still occur regularly. The U.S. Customs Service now uses an automated and simplified procedure to process goods. Its "line release" program eases the entry of certain commodities by using personal computers and bar code technologies. However, the program is still hampered by an insufficient number of clerical workers. Mexico has tested a new program referred to as *despacho previo* and requires rail and truck traffic to pay their applications and submit their documents before actually crossing the border. The program has yet to be tested at the majority of border crossings.

Mexican and U.S. customs adopted a *maquiladora* sealing program in 1989 to expedite low-risk shipments through customs procedures. Most of the plants, however, have stayed with the line release system and have been reluctant to use the new program because it requires a strict security system.

Truck traffic across the border has increased dramatically in the past several years, and Mexico's infrastructure is still inadequate. Most roads are in very poor condition. According to a 1990 study by Laredo State University entitled "U.S. Trucking in Mexico: A Free Trade Issue," only 8.5 percent of Mexico's primary roads are four-lane highways, and very little has changed since then.[1] Another major impediment is Mexico's prohibition on nearly all U.S.-registered commercial trucks, restricting them from entering Mexican territory. Mexican trucks are also restricted from entering the United States. This subject is currently under binational negotiation.

Note

1. Gregorio T. Druehl, Juan R. Gobel, Patrick F. Gormley, Grace K. Sakoda, Larry S. Thomas, and Curtis F. Turnbow, *U.S.-Mexico Trade: Concerns About the Adequacy of Border Infrastructure, GAO/NSIAD-991-228* (Washington, D.C.: U.S. General Accounting Office, May 1991), pp. 8–11.

20

The North American Free Trade Agreement

The North American Free Trade Agreement is a 2,000-page legal treaty document-ing a staged elimination of all trade and investment barriers between the United States, Mexico, and Canada. The agreement is the result of extensive negotiations between the three countries and includes a tariff phaseout schedule for 27,000 items and the harmonization of standards. NAFTA negotiations were concluded on August 12, 1992.

The objective of NAFTA is to create the world's largest market, with over 360 million people and a combined GNP of $6 trillion. Canada and Mexico are al-ready the first- and third-largest trading partners of the United States, with U.S. exports to these countries growing 56 percent faster than U.S. exports to the rest of the world. According to the U.S. Department of Commerce (DOC), U.S. mer-chandise exports to Mexico and Canada in 1992 were valued at $131.2 billion and accounted for 30 percent of total U.S. exports. U.S. merchandise imports from Canada and Mexico were valued at $133.7 billion for 1992 and accounted for 25 percent of total U.S. imports.

Under NAFTA, there will be increasing integration of North American mar-kets and far fewer trade barriers, so trade is expected to reach far greater volume. U.S. goods will be more competitively priced in Mexico and will have a great advantage over non-North American exports to Mexico and Canada, which will still have to pay an external tariff. NAFTA will be an impetus for the three nations' economic growth and advancement. Mexico's abundant natural resources and labor combined with Canadian and U.S. capital and technology will enable North America to stay competitive with Asian and European producers.

Tariffs

NAFTA phases out all tariffs on goods traded between the United States, Mexico, and Canada within fifteen years. When the agreement is implemented, tariffs will immediately be removed on 50 percent of all U.S. industrial exports to Mexico, including medical equipment, electronic equipment, and machine tools. Within five years, tariffs will be eliminated on 65 percent of all U.S. industrial exports, including semiconductors, computers and parts, most auto parts, paper products, light trucks, aerospace equipment, and telecommunications equipment. All other tariffs on U.S. exports will be removed within ten years after the implementation of NAFTA except for those on beans and corn, which will be phased out over fifteen years. Mexican tariffs averaged 10 percent in 1992, 2.5 times the average of U.S. tariffs.

Eliminating a local-content requirement will create greater demand for U.S. goods in Mexico. Other border restrictions will also be reduced over a fifteen-year period. Customs duties cannot be adopted or increased. Drawback programs will cease on January 1, 2001. Quotas, import licenses, performance-based duty waivers, and duties on temporarily imported tools and equipment will be eliminated.

The governments are harmonizing tariff standards wherever possible. Mexico is cutting over 3,000 classifications and revising its code so it will be similar to the codes of the United States and Canada.

Rules of Origin

NAFTA's benefits are available only for goods and services produced in North America. Since many of these goods are made up of imported components, the trade agreement establishes certain rules of origin to ensure that North American producers are the recipients of the benefits. Specific guidelines have not yet been issued. However, if any one of the following qualifications is met, the merchandise should be eligible for NAFTA's benefits:

- The merchandise has totally originated in North America.
- The merchandise contains some nonregional components but has been sufficiently transformed in North America so as to change its Harmonized Tariff System (HTS) classification.
- The merchandise has minimal North American content but has been sufficiently transformed there so as to change its HTS classification.
- The finished merchandise falls under the same HTS subheading as its parts and satisfies the minimum requirement for North American content.
- The merchandise is composed of non-North American materials that add up to no more than 7 percent of the merchandise's value.

Regional Value

North American businesses are permitted to choose between two systems when calculating the value of their product's content from the region (regional value):

1. *Transaction value.* The price paid for the product
2. *Net cost.* The total cost of the product minus some handling, financial, and promotional charges

The following equation is used in determining regional value:

$$RVC = \frac{V - VNO}{V} \times 100$$

RVC is the percentage of regional value content. *V* is either the transaction value of the product or the net cost of the product, depending on the system chosen by the business. *VNO* is the value of the non-North American material used in the production.

Standards

NAFTA will not let standards and technical regulations become trade barriers. Standards will be implemented in a nondiscriminatory way for imported and domestic products. Standards will be developed openly in a process that will involve all three countries. Industries that will be affected will be given enough time to adapt and, in some cases, participate in the development process. U.S. testing laboratories will become accredited in Mexico and Canada under the same terms as the domestic laboratories. Approved laboratories can then test products domestically for all three nations' markets.

The United States will not lower its current health and safety regulations. Countries will decide their own level of risk with scientific reasons to back their judgment. The goal will be to make products increasingly harmonized so that trade will be further encouraged. Merchandise will still bear a label stating the country of origin.

Dispute Resolution

NAFTA is establishing a trilateral trade commission that will review the three nations' trade situation on a regular basis. Commission members, who will rank at the cabinet level, will meet at least once a year. The commission may create independent panels of private- and public-sector experts to resolve disagreements in interpreting NAFTA's regulations and to arbitrate dumping, countervailing duty, and other commercial disputes. Disagreements will be resolved within eight months. Countries must follow the panel's recommendations or offer acceptable compensation. Otherwise, the country that is adversely affected may reciprocate by removing "equivalent" trade concessions.

Health and Environmental Disputes

Health and environmental disputes that arise will be settled by a NAFTA panel of experts in the particular field. The burden of proof is on the complainant party.

Investment and Commercial Disputes

Investment disputes that deal with monetary damages will be handled through international arbitration following NAFTA's investment regulations.

North American countries will each have an approved legal system that will enforce NAFTA's commercial regulations.

Dumping and Countervailing Duty Cases

NAFTA will not alter U.S. laws that protect U.S. markets against subsidized imports or unfair dumping. However, Mexico will be required to abide by legal reforms that will guarantee U.S. exporters a complete judicial review of any Mexican allegations involving dumping or subsidized sales in the Mexican market. Complaints may be addressed to a binational review panel.

The Job Market

The U.S. International Trade Commission (ITC) issued a report in May 1992 analyzing the conclusions of a series of academic studies on NAFTA's impact on the U.S. job market.[1] The report noted "a surprising degree of unanimity" in the studies' conclusions that there would be a net gain in U.S. jobs and wages would rise. Exports to Mexico currently sustain over 600,000 U.S. jobs in all sectors. The U.S. Department of Commerce predicts that NAFTA would support over one million U.S. jobs by 1995.[2] Jobs related to exports were generally found to pay 17 percent more per hour than the average U.S. wage in both the service and manufacturing sectors.

Safeguards

NAFTA has a bilateral safeguard allowing a country to "snap back" tariffs on certain items to their pre-NAFTA rate. This may be done only if the country's industry is suffering heavily from a surge in North American imports or if many jobs in a particular industry are being lost.

NAFTA's global safeguard will allow the United States to keep the right to impose quotas or tariffs on Mexico and Canada if imports are seriously threatening a particular market.

The Service Market

NAFTA will open Mexico's $146 billion services market to U.S. and Canadian businesses. Nearly all services are covered by NAFTA except basic telecommunications, maritime activities, and aviation. U.S. companies will be able to offer services in Mexico without having to move an office and employees from the United States. Citizenship requirements for licensing professionals will be eliminated within two years.

The Environment

NAFTA signatories are committed to the proposition that economic growth will improve the environment. Throughout the world, it has become evident that sustainable economic growth is the key to stronger environmental policies. Today, the poorest environmental conditions are found in impoverished areas.

NAFTA is expected to create enough economic growth to give the Mexican government the financial resources to monitor and enforce environmental regulations. Mexican companies will get wider access to international capital and new, environmentally sensitive technology.

The Mexican government's 1988 General Law for Ecological Equilibrium and Protection of the Environment, largely based on U.S. legislation, has raised the nation's environmental standards and increased use of criminal penalties for violations. Since the law was passed, Mexico has closed hundreds of plants, including one of its largest oil refineries, despite the huge loss of revenue this caused. The law was reinforced by creation of the Secretariat of Social Development (SEDESOL), which has taken over the responsibility of environmental affairs from the overburdened Secretariat of Urban Development and the Environment.

The United States-Mexico Border Environment Plan

The Border Environment Plan is a ten-year binational plan to protect the ecosystem and human health conditions along the border. Mexico has allocated $466 million for the first phase. Plan objectives include improved education about the environment and tougher enforcement of existing laws. There are already wastewater treatment centers, and joint air pollution monitoring programs and emergency response efforts have been started.

Notes

1. U.S. International Trade Commission, "Economy-Wide Modeling of the Economic Implications of an FTA With Mexico and a NAFTA With Canada and Mexico" (Investigation No. 332-317), USITC publication 2516, May 1992, and addendum, USITC publication 2508 (May 1992).
2. Jay Camillo, U.S. Department of Commerce, "Growth Through North American Trade: The Economic Facts," *Business America* 113, no. 21 (October 19, 1992), p. 14.

21

Economic Sectors With Strong Growth for U.S. Exporters

The Top Ten Sectors for U.S. Exporters

There are numerous markets in Mexico that will be very receptive to U.S. exports during the next few years. The U.S. Embassy assembled a Best Prospects List for 1993, listing the top forty sectors in Mexico with the biggest market growth for U.S. exporters. The top ten sectors are listed below in the order in which they are ranked. Textiles and apparel, also highly ranked, are also included.

Franchising

See Chapter 13.

Automotive Parts and Services

The automotive sector is the second-largest area of U.S.-Mexican trade, after oil. The estimated market size for parts and services in this sector in 1992 was $13 billion. The estimated average annual growth rate of the market between 1992 and 1994 is 10 percent. Mexico is expected to be the only rapid-growth market in the Western Hemisphere for this sector.

Sector-related exports from the United States to Mexico in 1992 had an estimated value of $5.7 billion, with a 10 percent growth rate from 1992 to 1994. The estimated sizes of the most promising subsectors are

Engines and parts:	$2 billion
Electrical:	$2.1 billion
Transmission, suspension, steering, and clutch:	$1.5 billion
Stamped parts:	$1.1 billion
Accessories:	$710 million

Upholstery, seats, etc.:	$480 million
Glass components:	$480 million
Braking systems:	$360 million
Cooling systems:	$120 million
Gas analyzers:	$21.7 million
Hoists and jacks, tire removing systems, and wheel alignment and balancing systems:	$10.1 million

Under NAFTA. The automotive industry is expected to thrive under NAFTA. It is predicted the agreement will increase North American competitiveness, provide jobs, and lower prices for North American consumers. Mexican tariffs on auto and auto-part imports currently average 20 percent. Immediately after NAFTA takes effect, the 20 percent tariff on auto and light truck imports will be reduced to 10 percent and then eliminated over ten years. The 13.2 percent on most auto parts will be reduced by half immediately, then phased out over five years. Mexican import restrictions on buses and medium and heavy trucks will be eliminated within five years.

Mexico's Automotive Industry Decree is to be eliminated over a ten-year period. This would end Mexico's condition that the Mexican automotive sector maintain a positive trade balance. Foreign automotive manufacturing plants in Mexico will no longer have mandatory export quotas or previous-performance requirements.

Other NAFTA benefits include a reduction in the local-content requirement to 62.5 percent for passenger vehicles and light trucks and 60 percent for other automotive products over a ten-year phaseout period. The Mexican demand for U.S. auto parts and vehicles should rise significantly because current regulations are so strict that it is nearly impossible for Mexican dealers to supply anything but Mexican autos and parts. A ban on North American used car imports will be phased out over a ten-year period.

A North American automotive standards council will be created to guarantee that safety and pollution standards are harmonized. The United States will not lower its standards on safety or fuel efficiency.

Chemical Production Machinery

The Mexican government is applying more flexible investment restrictions to encourage foreign participation in chemical production. Mexico will need investment programs of $500 million to $600 million annually to improve and expand its chemical production if it is to keep pace with the growing domestic market for chemicals. The estimated market size for chemical production machinery in 1992 was $799 million, with an estimated average annual growth rate of 20 percent from 1992 to 1994. Exports from the United States to Mexico in 1992 were estimated at $558.8 million, with an expected average annual growth rate of 15 percent. The estimated market sizes for the most promising subsectors are

MBD technology and equipment:	$200 million
Vacuum distillation units:	$194.2 million
Evaporative coolers:	$129.4 million

Centrifugal dryers: $109.1 million
Filtration units: $92.5 million
Environmental control equipment for the
    chemical industry: $73.8 million

Plastic Materials and Resins

Mexico has a strong plastic resins industry, but it must still import large quantities to satisfy demand and, sometimes, to get higher quality. The import market for plastic resins is approximately 350,000 tons per year.

The estimated market size for this sector in 1992 was $2 billion, with a 10 percent estimated average annual growth rate for 1992 to 1994. U.S. exports to Mexico in 1992 had an estimated value of $445.4 million, with an estimated average annual growth rate of 10 percent. The estimated market sizes for the most promising subsectors are

Polypropylene: $600.5 million
High-density polyethylene: $450 million
Low-density polyethylene: $450 million
Polyurethane resins: $370 million
Plastic resins: $202 million

Industrial Chemicals

In 1989, Mexico reclassified many chemicals from primary to secondary, thereby opening up the market to increased foreign participation and to privatization. Petroleos Mexicanos (PEMEX) was previously the sole supplier of all of Mexico's petrochemical products, but it is now entitled to exclusive production rights for only seventeen chemicals.

The estimated market size for industrial chemicals in 1992 was $1 billion, with an estimated average annual growth rate of 14 percent from 1992 to 1994. Estimated U.S. exports to Mexico in 1992 were valued at $393 million, with an expected average annual growth rate of 10 percent. The estimated market sizes for the most promising subsectors are

Inorganic chemicals for food processing: $310.3 million
Chemicals for basic foods: $183.5 million
Amides and thioamides: $164.2 million
Aromatic acids and salts: $142.4 million
Fluorine-containing compounds: $132.8 million
Amino acids and peptides: $124 million

Under NAFTA. NAFTA would prevent Mexico from raising tariffs beyond the 50 percent limit set by the General Agreement on Tariffs and Trade (GATT). It also would prevent Mexico from unilaterally raising tariff rates, which are currently at 10–20 percent.

Machine Tools and Metalworking Equipment

Mexico must import large quantities of machine tools and metalworking equipment to develop many of its industrial sectors. The steel and automotive sectors are advancing at a rapid pace and will have a large demand for this equipment during the next few years. Japan and Germany are currently giving U.S. exporters tough competition, since they have better credit conditions for the expensive machinery.

The estimated market size for this sector was $1.35 billion in 1992. The estimated average annual growth rate for 1992 through 1994 is 42 percent. The estimated worth of U.S. exports to Mexico in 1992 was $338.6 million, with an estimated average annual growth rate of 15 percent. The estimated market sizes for the most promising subsectors are

Drills, dies, and punches:	$215.8 million
Hydraulic and mechanical presses, guillotines, and shears:	$115.9 million
Parts and accessories for machine tools:	$108.7 million
Machining centers:	$89.2 million
Multiprocess welding equipment:	$64.1 million
Thermoplastic welding equipment:	$53.7 million
Numerically controlled lathes:	$47.6 million
Numerically controlled presses:	$46.3 million
Grinding, honing, and threading machines:	$40.9 million
Milling, boring, and copying machines:	$36.5 million
Other lathes:	$30.3 million
Wire-drawing machines:	$28.8 million
Planers, drawers, and sharpening, broaching, and other cutting machines:	$25.6 million
Boring and threadmaking attachments:	$23.7 million
Stainless steel welding wire:	$22.6 million
Rasps, files, pliers, shears, punches, and cutters:	$20.9 million
Numerically controlled grinding and honing machines:	$18.6 million
Numerically controlled milling, boring, and copying machines:	$16.4 million
Aluminum welding wire:	$15.4 million
Saws and accessories:	$14.8 million
Laser-operated machine tools:	$14.3 million
Vises and grinders:	$13.7 million
Drilling tools:	$9 million
Parts for arc-welding apparatus:	$8.9 million

Under NAFTA. Mexican tariffs on most machine tools will be eliminated immediately when NAFTA is implemented. Remaining tariffs on this sector will be phased out within five years.

Laboratory and Scientific Equipment

Imports of scientific and laboratory equipment by Mexico are expected to increase significantly as the public sector, the private sector, and learning institutions place greater emphasis on upgrading their equipment and modernizing the country to keep up with global competition.

The estimated market size of this sector in 1992 was $487.2 million, with an estimated average annual growth rate of 20–30 percent between 1992 and 1994. U.S. exports to Mexico had an estimated value of $290 million in 1992 and are expected to have an average annual growth rate of 20 percent. The estimated market size for the most promising subsectors are

Quality control equipment:	$220 million
Biotechnology equipment:	$25.8 million

Computers and Peripherals

Mexico relies on foreign imports for its advanced computer systems. The government encourages related direct investments and joint ventures, but requires a prior import permit from the Secretariat of Commerce and Industrial Development (SECOFI) for used computer and peripherals equipment. This market is growing because private companies, government agencies, and newly privatized banks are increasing their computer capability.

The estimated market size in 1992 was $798.1 million, with a 12 percent estimated average annual growth rate for 1992 through 1994. U.S. exports to Mexico in 1992 were estimated to be valued at $272 million, with an expected average annual growth rate of 10 percent. The estimated market sizes for the most promising subsectors are

Personal computers:	$51.5 million
Connectivity peripherals:	$27.3 million
Laptop computers:	$20 million

Under NAFTA. U.S. exports of computer parts and modems will be duty-free when NAFTA is implemented. The current required import license forused computers will be phased out within ten years after implementation ofNAFTA.

Telecommunications Equipment

Mexico is modernizing its telecommunications system and will be relying on numerous services and equipment from the United States. The estimated market size in 1992 for telecommunications equipment was $407.7 million, with a 10 percent estimated average annual growth rate for 1992 through 1994. The estimated worth of U.S. exports to Mexico in 1992 was $266.5 million, with an estimated average annual growth rate of 10 percent. The estimated market sizes of the most promising subsectors are

Satellite communications equipment:	$94.7 million
Local area network (LAN) and wide area network (WAN) equipment:	$63.5 million

Under NAFTA. Under NAFTA, all discriminatory sales and investment restrictions in the $6 billion telecommunications sales and service market are to be eliminated for U.S. and Canadian companies. U.S. companies will be permitted to operate corporate communications networks (computers, faxes, telephones) across the border with their own purchased or leased equipment. A company's private network can be interconnected to the public phone system or other networks.

Investment restrictions on most enhanced services will be eliminated immediately. In 1995, all restrictions on packet-switched services are to be eliminated. Product standards will no longer be used as a barrier to trade, since test data will be mutually recognized among the three NAFTA nations. Standards, registration, licensing, and permits will be applied indiscriminately.

Oil and Gas Field Machinery and Services

PEMEX is trying to attract foreign investment to expand its capacity. The tariffs for U.S. equipment and petrotechnology have been reduced.

In 1992, the estimated market size for oil and gas field machinery and services was $1.55 billion. Its estimated average annual growth rate from 1992 through 1994 is 15 percent. U.S. exports to Mexico in 1992 were valued at $236 million and are expected to have an average annual growth rate of 15 percent. The estimated market sizes for the most promising subsectors are

Pipes for oil and gas extraction:	$400.6 million
Cooling towers:	$260 million
Pumps:	$211.9 million
Underground gas tanks:	$200.5 million
Seamless steel tubes:	$120 million
Boring machines:	$116.4 million
State-of-the-art geological analytical equipment:	$110 million
Valves:	$106.6 million

Under NAFTA. During the first eight years of NAFTA implementation, Mexican companies are to be sheltered by a 50 percent limit for U.S. and Canadian companies' share in the Mexican market for oil field equipment. After eight years, the limit to the market share will be reduced to 30 percent and then eliminated after ten years.

Apparel and Textiles

The estimated market size for apparel in 1992 was $2.72 billion, with U.S. exports to Mexico having an estimated value of $156.5 million. The estimated annual growth rate for U.S. apparel exports is 8 percent. The Mexican middle and upper economic classes have traditionally bought apparel abroad, but the market is opening and U.S. apparel exports are more available to a greater number of people. All major Mexican department stores have been carrying U.S. apparel since 1990. Quality design and price are key factors.

The estimated market size for textile fabrics was $1.20 billion, with U.S. exports to Mexico having an estimated value of $152.6 million. The estimated annual growth rate for U.S. exports is 10 percent. The textile fabrics market has just opened recently to foreign exports. Import permits or quotas are not required. The Mexican government is supporting this industry through a development plan.

The textile-labeling decree of October 1990 was amended in March 1991, and all textiles must be labeled following its specific requirements. Prior to importation, all textiles must be labeled with durable material that should last for the duration of the product's use. These labels should carry the required information in Spanish and should be permanently stuck or sewn in a visible location, depending on the type of product. A lined garment should have the information on the lining as well. For pieces or coordinates made of the same material and marketed as an ensemble, a label needs to be sewn to only one of the pieces. A product packed in such a way that the labels are not visible must have a label on the package. After importation, Mexico allows the importers to apply a label with their name and tax identification number. For more information, call:

National Technical Information Service: (703) 487-4650

Under NAFTA. The current tariff on U.S. garment exports is 20 percent. Ratification of NAFTA would eliminate the tariffs on 97 percent of U.S. apparel exports after five years. Tariffs on some items, including T-shirts, sweatshirts, swimwear, underwear, and jogging suits of man-made fiber, are to be eliminated immediately.

The current tariff on U.S. textile fabric exports is 15 percent. These exports will have 89 percent of all tariffs removed after five years. Some fabrics, including twills, blue denim, thread, and textured polyester filament would have tariffs removed immediately.

The rule of origin would require garments and fabrics to be manufactured in North America, beginning at the yarn-spinning stage ("yarn forward").

If Mexican imports prove to damage the U.S. apparel industry, tariffs or quotas may be applied as safeguards.

Part Three
Directories

Accountants *(Contadores)*

Arthur D. Little Mexicana, S.A. de C.V.
Sinaloa 149-10
Col. Roma
06700, Mexico, DF
(5) 525-1026

Coopers and Lybrand
State National Bank Plaza, Ste. 1600
El Paso, TX 79902
(915) 545-5800

Coopers and Lybrand
Matamoros 1441 Pte.
Monterrey, NL
(83) 449-871

Coopers and Lybrand
Av. Universidad 3300-301
Chihuahua, CHIH
(14) 140-770

Coopers and Lybrand
Durango 81
06700 Mexico, DF
(5) 533-5580

Deloitte & Touche
One World Trade Center, Ste. 2200
Long Beach, CA 90831-2200
(310) 499-8330

Deloitte & Touche
Av. Universidad 3300-201
31170 Chihuahua, CHIH
(14) 142-133

Deloitte & Touche
Jaime Balmes II Edo. B
Pisos 1–3
Mexico, DF
(5) 395-0455

Deloitte & Touche
Av. López Mateos Sur 2220
Piso 10
45040 Guadalajara, JAL
(36) 228-068

Ernst & Young
2121 San Jacinto St., Ste. 400
Dallas TX 75201
(214) 969-8478

Ernst & Young
Plaza Jaime Balmes II Torre D
Piso 4
11510 Mexico, DF
(5) 557-9322

Ernst & Young
Río de la Plata 449 Ote.
Piso 4
66220 Garza García, NL
(83) 563-076

KPMG Peat Marwick
The Cortez, Ste. 1000
El Paso, TX 79901
(915) 532-3665

KPMG Peat Marwick
Bosque de Duraznos 55
11700 Mexico, DF
(5) 251-6299

KPMG Peat Marwick
Roble 701
Piso 10
Garza García, NL
(83) 359-777

Price Waterhouse
Río de la Plata No. 48
Col. Cuauhtémoc
06500 Mexico, DF
(5) 211-7883

Price Waterhouse
Calle 3ra. 803
Piso 1
31000 Chihuahua, CHIH
(14) 161-950

Price Waterhouse
Río Nilo 4049-6, Planta Baja
32310 Juárez, CHIH
(16) 165-077

Price Waterhouse
Prol. Americas 1592
Piso 4
44620 Guadalajara, JAL
(36) 401-080

Price Waterhouse
Condominio Los Soles D-21
Av. Lázaro Cárdenas Pte. 2400
66270 Garza García, NL
(83) 633-500

Price Waterhouse
Blvd. Gustavo Díaz Ordaz
No. 3314-801
Col. Anzures
72530 Puebla, PUE
(22) 469-883

Price Waterhouse
Hidalgo No. 20
Piso 1 Centro
76000 Querétaro, QRO
(463) 216-05

Price Waterhouse
Blvd. Agua Caliente 4558-302
22000 Tijuana, BC
(66) 817-728

Price Waterhouse
Calle 3 No. 803
31000 Chihuahua, CHIH
(14) 157-773

Advertising Agencies

Anuncios ABC de Monterrey
Guerrero 464 Nte.
Monterrey, NL
723-068

Bartres Valdez Wygard y Asociados
Sinaloa 149
Piso 10
06700 Mexico, DF
(5) 525-1443

Brique
16 de Septiembre 730
Guadalajara, JAL
(36) 146-402

Editora Tribuna
I. García 200 Ote.
64000 Monterrey, NL
(83) 742-149

GLM Publicidad
Baja California 177-053
06760 Mexico, DF
(5) 264-6920

Grupo Diseno
Ortiz de Campos 2919
Chihuahua, CHIH
(14) 134-358

Korn Ferry Internacional del Norte
D. Zambrano 525
64030 Monterrey, NL
(83) 337-302

Montenegro Saatchi and Saatchi
Berna 13
06600 Mexico, DF
(5) 525-6265

Ogilvy & Mather
Bahía de Santa Barbara 143
11300 Mexico, DF
(5) 250-1133

Organización Mexicana de Publicidad
P. Moreno 736-9
44100 Guadalajara, JAL
(36) 137-307

Air Cargo and Courier Services

Aero California
López Cotilla 1423
44100 Guadalajara, JAL
(36) 261-889

Aero Despachos Iturbide
U. Aragon Av. 602 Loc. 15
15500 Mexico, DF
(5) 571-0622

Aerolinas Mexicanas
Fuentes 177
01000 Mexico, DF
(5) 683-0687

AeroMéxico
Av. Tahel Esq. Av. Texcoco
Penon de los Baños
15520 Mexico, DF
(5) 784-8077

Aeronica
Paseo de la Reforma No. 322
Col. Juárez
Mexico, DF
(5) 511-2561

Aeronica
Prado de la Rosa No. 4520
Guadalajara, JAL
(36) 474-097

Aeronica
Padre Mier Nol 1607 Pte.

Monterrey, NL
(83) 480-066
Agencia General de Carga Aerea
Isabela la Católica 249
15000 Mexico, DF
(5) 578-2244

Air Express International
J. M. Garza Ote. 1724
64580 Monterrey, NL
(83) 721-840

American Airlines
Aeropuerto Terminal de Carga
Mexico, DF
(5) 571-3471

Martínez Anote y Cía. SC
Aeropuerto Internacional Benito Juarez
Lote 5 Zona Agentes Aduanales
Mexico, DF
(5) 605-1432

Apex Carga Aerea, SA de CV
Tripoli 104-1
03300 Mexico, DF
(5) 605-1432

Avianca
Paseo de la Reforma 195-301
Mexico, DF
(5) 566-8570

Cía. Mexicana de Aviacion
Aeropuerto Internacional de Monterrey
64000 Monterrey, NL
(83) 450-811

DHL Mensajería Mundial
Lope de Vega No. 316
Col. Polanco
11560 Mexico, DF
(5) 254-4900

DHL
Insurgentes Sur 859
Mexico, DF
(5) 705-6164

DHL
Av. Americas 1301
44630 Guadalajara, JAL
(36) 395-156

Federal Express
Melchor Ocampo No. 407

Col. Anzures
11590 Mexico, DF
(5) 255-4708

KLM
Paseo de las Palmas 735
Piso 7
Mexico, DF
(5) 571-8511

Mexicana Airlines
Av. Xola 535
Mexico, DF
(5) 325-0922

Overseas Courier Service
Río de la Plata No. 56-203
Col. Cuauhtémoc
06500 Mexico, DF
(5) 211-1400

Panalpina Transportes Mundiales
Guanajuato 240
06700 Mexico, DF
(5) 574-1555

Reexpedidora Internacional de Carga
Circ. Agustín Yanez 2463-103
Guadalajara, JAL
(36) 301-090

United Parcel Service (UPS)
Tuxpan 10
06760 Mexico, DF
(5) 564-9687

Airlines

Aero California
López Cotilla 1423
44100 Guadalajara, JAL
(36) 261-889

Aero California
Paseo Reforma 332
Mexico, DF
(5) 207-1392

AeroMéxico
Independencia 1205
Chihuahua, CHIH
(14) 160-404

AeroMéxico
Av. Corona 196

Guadalajara, JAL
(36) 156-565

AeroMéxico
Paseo Reforma 445
06500 Mexico, DF
(5) 207-8233
AeroMéxico
Padre Mier y Cuauhtémoc 818
Monterrey, NL
(83) 400-617

America West
Independencia 1205
Chihuahua, CHIH
(14) 160-824

American Airlines
Independencia 1205
Chihuahua, CHIH
(14) 160-404

American Airlines
Paseo Reforma 300
Mexico, DF
(5) 399-9222

American Airlines
Zaragoza 1300 Sur
64000 Monterrey, NL
(83) 403-031

Aviación del Noreste
Jiménez 1204
31000 Chihuahua, CHIH
(14) 165-146

Aviación del Noreste
Hidalgo 480 Pte.
Monterrey, NL
(83) 447-429

Canadian Airlines International
Paseo Reforma 325
06500 Mexico, DF
(5) 208-1654

Canadian Pacific Airlines
Paseo Reforma 87-D
06030 Mexico, DF
(5) 592-1896

Continental Airlines
Independencia 1205
Chihuahua, CHIH
(14) 160-620

Continental Airlines
Astral Plaza Galerias del Hyatt
Local 8
Guadalajara, JAL
(36) 476-672

Continental Airlines
Paseo Reforma 325-11
06500 Mexico, DF
(5) 525-3710

Continental Airlines
Centro Comercial Galerias Monterrey
Monterrey, NL
(83) 332-622

Delta Airlines
Independencia 1205
Chihuahua, CHIH
(14) 160-396

Delta Airlines
López Cotilla 1701
Guadalajara, JAL
(36) 303-530

Delta Airlines
Paseo Reforma 381
Mexico, DF
(5) 202-1608

Japan Airlines
Paseo Reforma 295
Mexico, DF
(5) 533-5515

Lufthansa
Paseo de las Palma 239
11000 Mexico, DF
(5) 202-8866

Mexicana
Av. Mariano Otero 2353
Guadalajara, JAL
(36) 472-222

Mexicana
Xola 535
Mexico, DF
(5) 660-4444

Mexicana
Av. Hidalgo 922
Monterrey, NL
(83) 405-511

Southwest Airlines
Independencia 1205
Chihuahua, CHIH
(14) 160-909

United Airlines
Independencia 1205
Chihuahua, CHIH
(14) 160-909

United Airlines
Poniente 922 G
64750 Monterrey, NL
(83) 448-238

United Airlines
Hamburgo 213
06600 Mexico, DF
(5) 208-8966

Western Airlines
Independencia 1205
Chihuahua, CHIH
(14) 160-404

Attorneys and Legal Assistance

Angulo Enriquez Calvo and González
P.O. Box 9124
El Paso, TX 79982
(16) 660-36

Baker and McKenzie
Av. Ejército Nacional 6515
Piso 29
32530 Cd. Juárez, CHIH
(16) 177-032

Baker and McKenzie
Blvd. M. Avila Camacho
Piso 9
11000 Mexico, DF
(5) 557-8844

Bryan, González-Vargas y González Baz
405 Lexington Ave.
New York, NY 10174
(212) 682-1555

Bryan, González-Vargas y González Baz
Edif. Parque Reforma
Campos Eliseos 400-1802
11560 Mexico, DF
(5) 202-0096

Bryan, González-Vargas y González Baz
Paseo Bolivar 421
Col. Centro
31000 Chihuahua, CHIH
(14) 163-310

Bryan, González-Vargas y González Baz
Ave. 16 de Septiembre 2026, Ote.
32030 Ciudad Juárez, CHIH
(16) 151-515
U.S. Tel: (915) 595-1034

Bryan, González-Vargas y González Baz
Toluca 3835
Col. Mexico
88280 Nuevo Laredo, TAM
(871) 515-15

Bryan, González-Vargas y González Baz
Calle Azucenas 44
Col. Jardin
87330 Matamoros, TAM
(891) 368-06

Bryan, González-Vargas y González Baz
Ave. Justo Sierra 377-1
21200 Mexicali, BC
(65) 681-318

Bryan, González-Vargas y González Baz
Blvd. Agua Caliente 3401
Desp. 205
22420 Tijuana, BC
(66) 864-924

Bufete Internacional
Decartes 55
11590 Mexico, DF
(5) 525-4057

Bufete Sepulveda
Blvd. M. A. Camacho 1
Piso 9
11000 Mexico, DF
(5) 557-8844

Carlsmith, Ball, Wichman, Murray, Case,
  Mukai and Ichiki
555 S. Flower St.
25th Floor
Los Angeles, CA 90071
(213) 955-1234

Castellanos Morfin y Perez de la Torre
Av. Lázaro Cárdenas 1694-308

44900 Guadalajara, JAL
(36) 111-814

Curtis, Mallet-Prevost, Colt & Mosle
Puebla 112
Col. Roma
06700 Mexico, DF
(5) 207-1426

De Buen Bufete
Mariano Escobedo 353-A1402
11560 Mexico, DF
(5) 531-3194

Estrada González y de Ovando
Campos Eliseos 400-701
11560 Mexico, DF
(5) 202-1574

Goodrich Riquelme y Asociados
Paseo Reforma 355
06500 Mexico, DF
(5) 533-0040

Johnson & Gibbs, P.C.
100 Founders Square
900 Jackson St., Ste. 100
Dallas, TX 75202-4499
(214) 977-9008

Laffan, Mues y Kaye
San Jeronimo 500
01900 Mexico, DF
(5) 683-3522

Link Internacional de Mexico
Miguel Laurent 70
Piso 2
03100 Mexico, DF
(5) 575-5120

Maria Eugenia Galvin Antillon
Victoria 1206-4 Altos
31000 Chihuahua, CHIH
(14) 100-363

Ochoa Torres y Asociados
Reforma 2725
Guadalajara, JAL
(36) 157-590

Santos, Elizonado, García, González
Lázaro Cárdenas 2400 Pte.
Edif. Losoles
66220 Garza García, NL
(83) 633-340

Vásquez y Vásquez
Aldama 710-13
31000 Chihuahua, CHIH
(14) 127-927

Trade and Investment Dispute Mediation
Foreign Commercial Service
American Embassy
Paseo de la Reforma 305
Col. Cuauhtemoc
06500 Mexico, DF
(5) 211-0042

Acts as a disinterested mediator in disputes; also provides lists of lawyers from both countries.

Export Legal Assistance Network (ELAIN)
Small Business Administration
409 Third St., SW
Washington, DC 20416
(202) 778-3080

Provides legal assistance to small U.S. businesses on export concerns, with free initial consultations.

Banks (Mexican)

Banca Confia, SNC
Paseo de la Reforma No. 450 PH
06500 Mexico, DF
(5) 207-0197

Banca Cremi, SNC
Paseo de la Reforma No. 93
Piso 15
Col. Lomas
06600 Mexico, DF
(5) 546-0232

Banca Promex
Paseo de la Reforma No. 199
Piso 1
Mexico, DF
(5) 566-0910

Banca Serfin, SNC
Av. 16 de Septiembre No. 38
Col. Centro
06000 Mexico, DF
(5) 512-8201

Banca Serfin, SNC
624 S. Grande, Ste. 1706

Los Angeles, CA 90017
(213) 687-6610

Banca Serfin, SNC
Wall St. Plaza
88 Pine St.
New York, NY 10005
(212) 574-9504

Banco BCH, SNC
Paseo de la Reforma No. 364
Piso 2
Col. Cuauhtémoc
06500 Mexico, DF
(5) 533-0434

Banco de Crédito y Servicio
Paseo de la Reforma 116
Piso 18
Mexico, DF
(5) 535-2571

Banco del Atlantico, SNC
Av. Hidalgo No. 128
Col. Coyoacán
04000 Mexico, DF
(5) 544-5312

Banco de Mexico, SNC (Banxico)
Av. 5 de Mayo 2
Piso 5
Mexico, DF
(5) 512-2266

Fondo de Operación y Financiamiento a la
   Vivienda (FOVI)
Banco de Mexico
Av. Ejército Nacional 180
Col. Anzures
11590 Mexico, DF
(5) 512-2266

*Receives World Bank financing for low-
cost homes*

Banco Internacional, SNC
Paseo de la Reforma No. 156
Col. Juárez
06600 Mexico, DF
(5) 566-2800

Banco Internacional, SNC
45 Broadway Atrium
New York, NY 10006
(212) 480-0111

Banco Internacional, SNC
5210 E. Williams Circle No. 745
Tucson, AZ 85711
(602) 747-4001

Bancomer, SNC
Av. Universidad No. 1200
Del Valle
03339 Mexico, DF
(5) 534-0034

Bancomer, SNC
444 S. Flower St., Ste. 3900
Los Angeles, CA 90071
(213) 489-7245

Bancomer, SNC
115 E. 54th St.
New York, NY 10022
(212) 759-7600

Banco Mexicano Somex, SNC
Gante No. 20
Piso 1
Col. Polanco
06000 Mexico, DF
(5) 512-1289

Banco Mexicano Somex, SNC
235 Fifth Ave.
New York, NY 10016
(212) 679-8000

Banco Nacional de Comercio Exterior,
   SNC (BANCOMEXT)
(Also called Mexican Trade Commission)
Camino a Sta. Teresa No. 1679
Col. Jardines del Pedregal
01900 Mexico, DF
(5) 652-8620

BANCOMEXT
229 Peachtree St., NE
Ste. 917, Cain Tower
Atlanta, GA 30303
(404) 522-5373

BANCOMEXT
8484 Wilshire Blvd., Ste. 808
Beverly Hills, CA 90211
(213) 655-6421

BANCOMEXT
225 N. Michigan Ave., Ste. 708
Chicago, IL 60601
(312) 856-0316

BANCOMEXT
2777 Stemmons Freeway, Ste. 1622
Dallas, TX 75207
(214) 688-4095

BANCOMEXT
New World Tower
100 N. Biscayne Blvd., Ste. 1601
Miami, FL 33132
(305) 372-9929

BANCOMEXT
150 E. 58th St.
17th Floor
New York, NY 10155
(212) 826-2916

BANCOMEXT
Plaza 600 Bldg.
600 Stewart St., Ste. 703
Seattle, WA 98101
(206) 441-2833

Banco Nacional de Credito Rural
Agrarismo 227
Piso 7
Mexico, DF
(5) 515-2813

Banco Nacional de Mexico, SNC
   (BANAMEX)
Andres Bello No. 45
Pisos 10 y 11
Col. Polanco
11560 Mexico, DF
(5) 203-1094

BANAMEX Import Financing Division
Venustiano Carranza No. 64
Piso 1
Col. Centro
06089 Mexico, DF
(5) 709-0920

BANAMEX
800 West Sixth St., Ste. 1616
Los Angeles, CA 90017
(213) 624-6225

BANAMEX
767 Fifth Ave.
8th Floor
New York, NY 10153
(212) 751-5090

BANAMEX
Allied Bank Place
1000 Louisiana St., Ste. 6920
Houston, TX 77002
(713) 651-9091

Banco Nacional de Obras y Servicios
   Publicos, SNC (BANOBRAS)
Av. Insurgentes Norte No. 423
Col. Guerrero
06900 Mexico, DF
(5) 583-0022

Bancresar, SNC
Paseo de la Reforma No. 116
Piso 5
Col. Juárez
06600 Mexico, DF
(5) 566-4213

Banpais, SNC
Av. Insurgentes Sur No. 1443
Piso 9
Col. San Josś Insurgentes
03900 Mexico, DF
(5) 598-6168

Citibank
Paseo Reforma 390
Piso 18
Mexico, DF
(5) 207-3176

Fideicomiso Fondo de Habitaciones
   Populares (FONHAPO)
Homero No. 203
Piso 10
Col. Polanco
11560 Mexico, DF
(5) 254-8765
Trust fund for low-income housing

Fondo de la Vivienda Issste (FOVISSSTE)
Miguel Norena No. 28
Col. San José Insurgentes
03900 Mexico, DF
(5) 680-6142
*Fund for the construction of houses for
Mexican government workers*

Multibanco Comermex, SNC
Avila Camacho No. 1
Col. Polanco
11000 Mexico, DF
(5) 557-8622

Multibanco Comermex, SNC
One Exchange Plaza
16th Floor
New York, NY 10006
(212) 509-4848

Mutibanco Mercantil de México
2000 Post Oak Blvd., Ste. 2150
Houston, TX 77506
(713) 961-5971

Nacional Financiera, SNC (NAFIN)
Av. Insurgentes Sur No. 1971
Col. Guadalupe Inn
01020 Mexico, DF
(5) 550-6911

NAFIN
450 Park Ave., Ste. 401
New York, NY 10022
(212) 753-8030

NAFIN
1615 L St., NW
Washington, DC 20036
(202) 338-9010

Banks (U.S.)

American Express Bank, Ltd.
Campos Eliseos 345
Pisos 9 y 12
Col. Polanco
11560 Mexico, DF
(5) 596-8133

Bank of America
Paseo de la Reforma 116
Piso 12
Col. Juarez
06600 Mexico, DF
(5) 591-0091

Bank of Boston
Campos Eliseos 345, Edif. Omega
Piso 4
Col. Polanco
Mexico, DF
(5) 596-8455

Bankers Trust
Blvd. Manuel Avila Camacho 1
Despacho 806
Piso 8

Col. Chapultepec
01560 Mexico, DF
(5) 540-4855

California Commerce Bank
Andres Bello No. 45
Piso 27
Col. Polanco
11560 Mexico, DF
(5) 584-7125

Chase Manhattan Bank, N.A.
Hamburgo No. 213
Piso 7
Col. Juárez
06600 Mexico, DF
(5) 208-5666

Chemical Bank
Campos Eliseos No. 345
Piso 11
Col. Polanco
11560 Mexico, DF
(5) 202-2306

Citibank, N.A.
Reforma 390
Piso 18
Col. Juárez
06600 Mexico, DF
(5) 211-3030

Continental Illinois
Blvd. M. Avila Camacho 191
Piso 1
Col. Morales Polanco
11560 Mexico, DF
(5) 395-3588

First Interstate Bank of California
Av. Paseo de las Palmas 239
Piso 4
Col. Lomas de Chapultepec
11000 Mexico, DF
(5) 202-8477

First National Bank of Chicago
Campos Eliseos 345
Piso 5
Col. Polanco
11560 Mexico, DF
(5) 540-5801

First National Bank of Commerce
Paseo de la Reforma No. 509

Mexico, DF
(5) 533-7501

First Republic Bank, N.A.
Aristoteles No. 110, PH
Col. Polanco
11560 Mexico, DF
(5) 545-7640

Marine Midland
Campos Eliseos 400
Desp. 601-C
Col. Lomas de Chapultepec
Mexico, DF
(5) 202-0303

Mercantile National/Mellon Bank, N.A.
Reforma 300
Piso 18
Col. Cuauhtémoc
06500 Mexico, DF
(5) 528-7365

Midland Bank, Ltd.
Campos Eliseos 345
11560 Mexico, DF
(5) 596-7839

Morgan Guaranty Trust Co. of New York
Blvd. M. Avila Camacho 1-802
Mexico, DF
(5) 540-6765

NCNB Texas Bank
Paseo de la Reforma No. 590
Piso 3
Col. Cuauhtémoc
06500 Mexico, DF
(5) 533-6155

Northwest Bank Minnesota, N.A.
Sierra Madre 525
Col. Lomas de Chapultepec
11000 Mexico, DF
(5) 520-4566

Pittsburgh National Bank
Presidente Masaryk 120
Col. Polanco
11560 Mexico, DF
(5) 531-0493

Republic Bank Dallas
Paseo de la Reforma 509
Piso 3

Col. Cuauhtémoc
06500 Mexico, DF
(5) 553-6155

Republic National Bank of New York
Av. Juarez No. 4-702 y 705
Col. Centro
06050 Mexico, DF
(5) 521-6426

Security Pacific National Bank
Bosques de Ciruelos 120
Piso 7
Col. Bosques de las Lomas
11700 Mexico, DF
(5) 557-9911

Standard Chartered Bank
Edif. Omega
Campos Eliseos 345-9
Col. Polanco
11560 Mexico, DF
(5) 202-1629

Texas Commerce Bank of Houston
Edif. Omega
Campos Eliseos 345-11
Col. Polanco
11560 Mexico, DF
(5) 202-2306

Wells Fargo, N.A.
Blvd. M. Avila Camacho 1
Piso 4
Desp. 401
Col. Polanco
11560 Mexico, DF
(5) 395-0044

Business Associations

Asociación Mexicana de Comerciante
  Industrial Pequeño
5 de Mayo 57-37
06700 Mexico, DF
(5) 512-7309

Business Coordinating Council (COECE)
1025 Thomas Jefferson St., NW
East Lobby, Ste. 700

Washington, DC 20007
(202) 625-3550

Private-sector NAFTA negotiating team

Consejo Coordinador Empresarial (CCE)
Homero 527
Piso 6
Col. Polanco
11570 Mexico, DF
(5) 250-7755

*Business coordinating council that acts as
a liaison between the private sector and
the government.*

Chambers of Commerce and Business Associations (*Confederacións*)

Cámara Nacional de la Industria de la
  Transformación (CANACINTRA)
Av. San Antonio 256
Piso 3
Col. Ampliación Napoles
03849 Mexico, DF
(5) 563-3400, 611-6238

*National chamber of the manufacturing
industry*

Confederation of industry and agriculture

Confederación de Cámaras Industriales de
  los Estados Unidos Mexicanos
  (CONCAMIN)
Manuel Ma. Contreras 133
Pisos 2 y 8
06590 Mexico, DF
(5) 546-9053

*Confederation of state chambers of
industry*

Confederación de Cámaras Nacionales de
  Comercio (CANACO)
Balderas No. 144
Piso 3
Col. Centro
06070 Mexico, DF
(5) 709-1078, 709-0034

*Confederation of national chambers of
commerce*

Confederación de Comercio Industria y
  Agricultura

Palma 417 Nte.—122
06000 Mexico, DF
(5) 521-6043

Chambers of Commerce (Regional, Manufacturing)

Aguascalientes

Cámara Nacional de Comercio de
  Aguascalientes
Av. Tecnologico 108
20190 Aguascalientes, AGS
(49) 530-63

*Chamber of commerce of the state of
Aguascalientes*

Cámara Nacional Industrial de la
  Transformación
Cristóbal Colón No. 437
Col. Centro
2000 Aguascalientes, AGS
(491) 529-70, 501-33

Manufacturing chamber of commerce

Baja California

Cámara Nacional de Comercio de Baja
  California
Calle de Comercio 254
21100 Mexicali, BC
(65) 534-660

*Chamber of commerce of the state of Baja
California Norte*

Cámara Nacional Industrial de la
  Transformación
Alvarado No. 432
Desp. 10 y 11
Col. Centro
22800 Ensenada, BC
(667) 830-76, 400-16

Manufacturing chamber of commerce

Cámara Nacional Industrial de la
  Transformación
Calzada Justo Sierra S/N
Col. Nueva

21100 Mexicali, BC
(65) 542-46

Manufacturing chamber of commerce

Cámara Nacional Industrial de la
    Transformación
México No. 1970
Col. Fracc. La Perla
23040 La Paz, BC
(682) 216-94

Manufacturing chamber of commerce

Cámara Nacional Industrial de la
    Transformación
Blvd. Gustavo Díaz Ordaz y Bugambi
Col. Fracc. El Prado
22450 Tijuana, BC
(66) 816-101, 816-610

Manufacturing chamber of commerce

Cámara Nacional Industrial de la
    Transformación
Juárez No. 6661
Col. Centro
Tecate, BC
(665) 408-23

Manufacturing chamber of commerce

Campeche

Cámara Nacional de Comercio de
    Campeche
Av. Nva Ley de la Reforma Agraria
24040 Campeche, CAMP
(98) 655-77

*Chamber of commerce of the state of
Campeche*

Cámara Nacional Industrial de la
    Transformación
Calle 25 No. 26
Col. Centro
24100 Cd. del Carmen, CAMP
(938) 210-10

Manufacturing chamber of commerce

Cámara Nacional Industrial de la
    Transformación
Calle 61 No. 20

24000 Campeche, CAMP
(981) 626-81

Manufacturing chamber of commerce

Chiapas

Cámara Nacional de Comercio de Chiapas
Central Norte 225
29000 Tuxtla Gutiérrez, CHIS
(96) 278-83

*Chamber of commerce of the state of
Chiapas*

Cámara Nacional Industrial de la
    Transformación
Sexta Avenida Sur y 24 Calle Pte.
Col. San Sebastián
30790 Tapachula, CHIS
(962) 623-87

Manufacturing chamber of commerce

Cámara Nacional Industrial de la
    Transformación
14 Poniente Sur No. 102
Col. Centro
29000 Tuxtla Gutiérrez, CHIS
(961) 221-04, 204-74

Manufacturing chamber of commerce

Chihuahua

Cámara Nacional de Comercio de
    Chihuahua
Cuauhtémoc 1800
31020 Chihuahua, CHIH
(14) 160-000

*Chamber of commerce of the state of
Chihuahua*

Cámara Nacional de la Industria
    Transformación
Av. Cuauhtémoc No. 1800
Col. Centro
31020 Chihuahua, CHIH
(14) 150-040, 156-044

Manufacturing chamber of commerce

Cámara Nacional Industrial de la
    Transformación
Sexta Oriente 410
Edif. Empresarial

Col. Centro
33000 Cd. Delicias, CHIH
(147) 220-24

Manufacturing chamber of commerce

Cámara Nacional Industrial de la
  Transformación
Centro Comercial Pronaf. Loc. 9 Al. 12
Progresista
23310 Cd. Juárez, CHIH
(16) 163-457, 163-458

Manufacturing chamber of commerce

Coahuila

Cámara Nacional de Comercio de
  Coahuila
Av. Universidad 514
25260 Saltillo, COAH
(84) 556-11

*Chamber of commerce of the state of
Coahuila*

Cámara Nacional Industrial de la
  Transformación
Pasaje González Depto. 28 y 30
Col. Centro
26200 Cd. Acuza, COAH
(877) 203-59

Manufacturing chamber of commerce

Cámara Nacional Industrial de la
  Transformación
Buenos Aires 102
Col. Guadalupe
25700 Monclova, COAH
(863) 366-33, 370-73

Manufacturing chamber of commerce

Cámara Nacional Industrial de la
  Transformación
Periodistas No. 701
Piso 1
Col. Las Fuentes
26020 Piedras Negras, COAH
(878) 214-21

Manufacturing chamber of commerce

Cámara Nacional Industrial de la
  Transformación
Av. Universidad No. 514

25000 Saltillo, COAH
(841) 572-22

Manufacturing chamber of commerce

Cámara Nacional Industrial de la
  Transformación
Blvd. Constitución No. 4 Ote.
Col. Ampl. Los Angeles
27140 Torreón, COAH
(17) 120-760, 126-047

Manufacturing chamber of commerce

Colima

Cámara Nacional de Comercio de Colima
Hidalgo 93
Piso 3
28000 Colima, COL
(33) 200-71

*Chamber of commerce of the state of
Colima*

Cámara Nacional Industrial de la
  Transformación
Morelos No. 179 Altos
28000 Colima, COL
(331) 226-35

Manufacturing chamber of commerce

Distrito Federal

Cámara Nacional de Comercio de la
  Ciudad de Mexico
Paseo de la Reforma 42
Piso 1
Col. Centro
06048 Mexico, DF
(5) 535-2502, 535-0215

Chamber of commerce of Mexico City

Cámara Nacional de Comercio de
  Tlalnepantla
Cuauhtémoc 51
11000 Mexico, DF
(5) 390-3355

*Chamber of commerce of the city of
Tlalnepantla*

Durango

Cámara Nacional de Comercio de
  Durango

Francisco I. Madero 125 Nte.
34000 Durango, DGO
(18) 155-20

Chamber of commerce of the state of Durango

Cámara Nacional Industrial de la
  Transformación
Cobalto Lote 5
Cd. Industrial
34304 Durango, DGO
(181) 809-17, 801-35

Manufacturing chamber of commerce

Cámara Nacional Industrial de la
  Transformación
Av. Hidalgo No. 1370 Sur
Col. Centro
35000 Gómez Palacio, DGO
(17) 140-303, 145-043

Manufacturing chamber of commerce

Guanajuato

Cámara Nacional de Comercio de
  Guanajuato
Juan Valle 15 Bajos
36000 Guanajuato, GTO
(47) 201-61

Chamber of commerce of the state of Guanajuato

Cámara Nacional Industrial de la
  Transformación
Manuel Doblado No. 102
Piso 2
Dep. 202
Col. Centro
38000 Celaya, GTO
(461) 291-51

Manufacturing chamber of commerce

Cámara Nacional Industiral de la
  Transformación
Blvd. Gustavo Díaz Ordaz No. 37
Piso 9
Col. Fracc. Las Reynas
36660 Irapuato, GTO
(462) 543-62, 515-70

Manufacturing chamber of commerce

Cámara Nacional Industrial de la
  Transformación

Blvd. Jaime Nuño No. 6305
Col. San Isidro de Jerez
37000 León, GTO
(471) 321-82, 690-39

Manufacturing chamber of commerce

Guerrero

Cámara Nacional de Comercio de
  Guerrero
Av. Juárez Nte. 35 Altos
39000 Chilpancingo, GRO
(74) 288-44

Chamber of commerce of the state of Guerrero

Cámara Nacional Industrial de la
  Transformación
Calle de la Paz No. 9
Col. Centro
39300 Acapulco, GRO
(748) 219-82, 215-84

Manufacturing chamber of commerce

Hidalgo

Cámara Nacional de Comercio de Hidalgo
Hidalgo 204
42000 Pachuca, HGO
(77) 244-42

Chamber of commerce of the state of Hidalgo

Cámara Nacional Industrial de la
  Transformación
Km. 5.5 de la Carretera a Sahagun
Pachuca, HGO
(771) 426-53, 316-87

Manufacturing chamber of commerce

Cámara Nacional Industrial de la
  Transformación
Yucatan 205 Nte.
Col. Insurgentes
43630 Tulancingo, HGO
(775) 305-12

Manufacturing chamber of commerce

Jalisco

Cámara Nacional de Comercio de Jalisco
Av. Vallarta 4095

44680 Guadalajara, JAL
(36) 471-100

*Chamber of commerce of the state of
Jalisco*

Cámara Nacional de Comercio de
   Guadalajara
Morelos 345
44870 Guadalajara, JAL
(36) 354-03

*Chamber of commerce of the city of
Guadalajara*

Asociación de Usuarios de la Zona
   Industrial de Guadalajara
Calle 12, No. 2991
Guadalajara, JAL
(36) 455-355

Guadalajara industrial zone

Mexico

Cámara Nacional de Comercio de Edo. de
   México
Paseo de Tollocan 308 Ote.
50130 Toluca, MEX
(72) 236-76

*Chamber of commerce of the state of
Mexico*

Cámara Nacional Industrial de la
   Transformación
Av. Morelos Ote. No. 1313
Col. Juan Beltrán
50150 Toluca, MEX
(721) 793-79, 793-55

Manufacturing chamber of commerce

Michoacán

Cámara Nacional de Comercio de
   Michoacán
20 de Noviembre 55
58000 Morelia, MICH
(45) 200-83

*Chamber of commerce of the state of
Michoacán.*

Cámara Nacional Industrial de la
   Transformación
Virrey de Mendoza 2 Pte.

Col. Fracc. la Luneta
Zamora, MICH
(351) 207-65

Manufacturing chamber of commerce

Cámara Nacional Industrial de la
   Transformación
Gral. Enrique Ramírez No. 74
Col. Centro
59300 La Piedad, MICH
(352) 270-70

Manufacturing chamber of commerce

Cámara Nacional Industrial de la
   Transformación
Allende No. 15
Col. Centro
59000 Sahuayo, MICH
(353) 224-70

Manufacturing chamber of commerce

Cámara Nacional Industrial de la
   Transformación
Paseo Lázaro Cárdenas 1666
Piso 1
Col. Los Angeles
60160 Uruapan, MICH
(452) 354-40

Manufacturing chamber of commerce

Cámara Nacional Industrial de la
   Transformación
Pino Juárez No. 232
Col. Centro
58000 Morelia, MICH
(451) 206-35

Manufacturing chamber of commerce

Morelos

Cámara Nacional de Comercio de Morelos
Morelos Sur 609
62050 Cuernavaca, MOR
(73) 120-131

*Chamber of commerce of the state of
Morelos*

Cámara Nacional Industrial de la
   Transformación
Av. Emiliano Zapata No. 200
Col. Tlaltenango

62170 Cuernavaca, MOR
(73) 139-009, 170-191

Manufacturing chamber of commerce

Nayarit

Cámara Nacional de Comercio de Nayarit
Morelos 87 Pte.
Piso 2
63000 Tepic, NAY
(32) 236-46

Chamber of commerce of the state of Nayarit

Cámara Nacional Industrial de la
  Transformación
Puebla Norte No. 89
Col. Centro
63000 Tepic, NAY
(321) 204-09, 259-96

Manufacturing chamber of commerce

Nuevo León

Cámara Nacional de Comercio de Nuevo
  León
Ocampo Pte. 250
Piso 1
64000 Monterrey, NL
(83) 422-166

Chamber of commerce of the state of Nuevo León

Cámara Nacional de Comercio de
  Monterrey
Ocampo 250 Pte.
64000 Monterrey, NL
(83) 403-771

Chamber of commerce of the city of Monterrey

Oaxaca

Cámara Nacional de Comercio de Oaxaca
4a Calle de Guerrero No. 402
68000 Oaxaca, OAX
(95) 657-33

Chamber of commerce of the state of Oaxaca

Cámara Nacional Industrial de la
  Transformación
Av. Hidalgo No. 911 Desp. 200
Col. Centro
68000 Oaxaca, OAX
(951) 614-34, 614-49

Manufacturing chamber of commerce

Puebla

Cámara Nacional de Comercio de Puebla
Av. Reforma 2704
Piso 7
72160 Puebla, PUE
(22) 486-435

Chamber of commerce of the state of Puebla

Cámara Nacional Industrial de la
  Transformación
Av. Reforma No. 2704 Esq. D. Defensores
Col. De la Republica Edif. Empre.
72000 Puebla, PUE
(22) 482-233, 482-630

Manufacturing chamber of commerce

Cámara Nacional Industrial de la
  Transformación
Av. Uno Norte No. 218
Col. Centro
75700 Tehuacán, PUE
(238) 204-17, 246-79

Manufacturing chamber of commerce

Querétaro

Cámara Nacional de Comercio de
  Querétaro
Paseo de las Balaustradas No. 405
76000 Querétaro, QUE
(46) 203-32

Chamber of commerce of the state of Querétaro

Quintana Roo

Cámara Nacional de Comercio de
  Quintana Roo
22 de Enero con Reforma

77000 Chetumal, QROO
(98) 200-88

Chamber of commerce of the state of Quintana Roo

Cámara Nacional Industrial de la
    Transformación
Av. Xel-Ha No. 5, Altos 10
Cancun, QROO
(988) 441-63

Manufacturing chamber of commerce

Cámara Nacional Industrial de la
    Transformación
Alvaro Obregón No. 326
Col. Centro
77000 Chetumal, QROO
(983) 223-45

Manufacturing chamber of commerce

Cámara Nacional Industrial de la
    Transformación
Av. 5 de Febrero No. 308 Nte.
Col. Zona Indl. B. Juárez
76120 Querétaro, QROO
(463) 800-30

Manufacturing chamber of commerce

Cámara Nacional Industrial de la
    Transformación
Av. Juárez Pte. No. 10 Altos
Col. Centro
76800 San Juan del Río, QROO
(467) 232-10

Manufacturing chamber of commerce

San Luis Potosí

Cámara Nacional de Comercio de San Luis
    Potosí
Av. Venustiano Carranza 1325
78250 San Luis Potosí, SLP
(48) 349-66

Chamber of commerce of the state of San Luis Potosí

Cámara Nacional Industrial de la
    Transformación
Venustiano Carranza No. 64-A Sur
Col. Centro

79000 Cd. Valles, SLP
(138) 225-35

Manufacturing chamber of commerce

Cámara Nacional Industrial de la
    Transformación
Av. Venustiano Carranza No. 1325
Col. Barrio Tequisquiapan
78250 San Luis Potosí, SLP
(481) 356-87, 354-07

Manufacturing chamber of commerce

Sinaloa

Cámara Nacional de Comercio de Sinaloa
Av. Obregón Nte. 732
80000 Culiacán, SIN
(67) 323-08

Chamber of commerce of the state of Sinaloa

Cámara Nacional Industrial de la
    Transformación
Blvd. Leyva Solano S/N y Rodolfo G.
Col. Centro
80000 Culiacán, SIN
(671) 208-59, 255-61

Manufacturing chamber of commerce

Cámara Nacional Industrial de la
    Transformación
Francisco I. Madero No. 573 Sur
Col. Centro
81000 Guasave, SIN
(687) 233-76

Manufacturing chamber of commerce

Cámara Nacional Industrial de la
    Transformación
Guillermo Prieto 728 Sur Altos
Col. Centro
81200 Los Mochis, SIN
(681) 245-53, 245-67

Manufacturing chamber of commerce

Cámara Nacional Industrial de la
    Transformación
Emilio Barragan 147
Col. Centro

82000 Mazatlán, SIN
(678) 277-18, 283-06

Manufacturing chamber of commerce

Cámara Nacional Industrial de la
Transformación
Blvd. Leyva Solano S/N y Rodolfo G.
Col. Centro
80000 Culiacán, SIN
(671) 208-59, 255-61

Manufacturing chamber of commerce

Cámara Nacional Industrial de la
Transformación
Francisco I. Madero No. 573 Sur
Col. Centro
81000 Guasave, SIN
(687) 233-76

Manufacturing chamber of commerce

Cámara Nacional Industrial de la
Transformación
Guillermo Prieto 728 Sur Altos
Col. Centro
81200 Los Mochis, SIN
(681) 245-53, 245-67

Manufacturing chamber of commerce

Cámara Nacional Industrial de la
Transformación
Emilio Barragan 147
Col. Centro
82000 Mazatlán, SIN
(678) 277-18, 283-06

Manufacturing chamber of commerce

Sonora

Cámara Nacional de Comercio de Sonora
Gaston Madrid 31
83000 Hermosillo, SON
(62) 240-68

*Chamber of commerce of the state of
Sonora*

Cámara Nacional Industrial de la
Transformación
Blvd. Benito Juárez 100 Ote.
83600 Caborca, SON
(637) 213-37, 224-03

Manufacturing chamber of commerce

Cámara Nacional Industrial de la
Transformación

Av. Aquiles Serdan No. 776 Pte.
Col. Contiguo Obelisco
85400 Guaymas, SON
(622) 258-70, 250-52

Manufacturing chamber of commerce

Cámara Nacional Industrial de la
Transformación
Av. Circunvalación SN y Calle Torno
Parque Industrial
Cd. Obregón, SON
(641) 377-00, 528-29

Manufacturing chamber of commerce

Cámara Nacional Industrial de la
Transformación
Periferico Pte. No. 2
Col. Esq. Blvd. Navarrete
83270 Hermosillo, SON
(621) 660-23, 647-71

Manufacturing chamber of commerce

Cámara Nacional Industrial de la
Transformación
Pesqueira 218 Nte. Desp. 6
Col. Centro
85800 Navojoa, SON
(642) 244-14

Manufacturing chamber of commerce

Cámara Nacional Industrial de la
Transformación
Av. Obregón No. 1696 Local 6
Col. Centro
84000 Nogales, SON
(631) 315-86, 315-89

Manufacturing chamber of commerce

Cámara Nacional Industrial de la
Transformación
Av. Obregón Entre 14 y 15 Edif. Canac
Col. Centro
83400 San Luis Río Colorado, SON
(653) 421-47

Manufacturing chamber of commerce

Tabasco

Cámara Nacional de Comercio de Tabasco
Malecón CAM 677

86000 Villahermosa, TAB
(93) 213-60

Chamber of commerce of the state of
Tabasco

Cámara Nacional Industrial de la
  Transformación
Aldam No. 530 Altos
Col. Centro
86000 Villahermosa, TAB
(931) 214-34

Manufacturing chamber of commerce

Tamaulipas

Cámara Nacional de Comercio de
  Tamaulipas
Av. Francisco I. Madero 510 Ote.
89000 Tampico, TAM
(12) 121-540

Chamber of commerce of the state of
Tamaulipas

Cámara Nacional Industrial de la
  Transformación
Matias Canales No. 603
Col. Riberena
88620 Cd. Reynosa, TAM
(892) 362-59, 360-95

Manufacturing chamber of commerce

Cámara Nacional Industrial de la
  Transformación
Hidalgo Ote. 830 Altos Desp. 1
87000 Cd. Victoria, TAM
(131) 213-63

Manufacturing chamber of commerce

Cámara Nacional Industrial de la
  Transformación
Herrerea No. 6
Piso 2
Col. Centro
87300 Matamoros, TAM
(891) 213-27, 232-28

Manufacturing chamber of commerce

Cámara Nacional Industrial de la
  Transformación
Blvd. Constitución No. 1020 Nte.
Col. del Pueblo

89190 Tampico, TAM
(12) 128-350, 120-353

Manufacturing chamber of commerce

Cámara Nacional Industrial de la
  Transformación
Av. Guerrero No. 810
Col. Centro
88000 Nuevo Laredo, TAM
(871) 258-88

Manufacturing chamber of commerce

Cámara Nacional Industrial de la
  Transformación
Niños Heroes y Saltillo No. 410
Col. Centro
88900 Río Bravo, TAM
(893) 430-27, 437-11

Manufacturing chamber of commerce

Tlaxcala

Cámara Nacional Industrial de Comercio
  de Tlaxcala
Calle Uno Lado Sur C Camionera
90000 Tlaxcala, TLAX
(24) 248-60

Chamber of commerce of the state of
Tlaxcala

Cámara Nacional Industrial de la
  Transformación
Calle 12 No. 12
Col. La Loma Xicohténcatl
90070 Tlaxcala, TLAX
(246) 219-71, 212-39

Manufacturing chamber of commerce

Veracruz

Cámara Nacional de Comercio de
  Veracruz
Lucio Esq. Enriquez Edif. Tanos
91000 Jalapa, VER
(28) 721-45

Chamber of commerce of the state of
Veracruz

Cámara Nacional Industrial de la
  Transformación
Nicolas Bravo No. 3

Col. Buenavista Sur
96739 Minatitlán, VER
(922) 419-23, 434-55

Manufacturing chamber of commerce

Cámara Nacional Industrial de la
   Transformación
Sur 15 No. 222
Col. Centro
94300 Orizaba, VER
(272) 430-99

Manufacturing chamber of commerce

Cámara Nacional Industrial de la
   Transformación
5 de Mayo No. 305A
Col. Tajin
93330 Poza Rica, VER
(782) 339-48

Manufacturing chamber of commerce

Cámara Nacional Industrial de la
   Transformación
Gral. Arteaga No. 86
Col. Centro
92800 Tuxpan, VER
(783) 413-99

Manufacturing chamber of commerce

Cámara Nacional Industrial de la
   Transformación
Emparan No. 250
Piso 1
Col. Centro
91700 Veracruz, VER
(29) 325-990

Manufacturing chamber of commerce

Cámara Nacional Industrial de la
   Transformación
Calle 5 No. 304 P.B. Edif. Canaco
Col. Centro
94500 Cordoba, VER
(271) 272-43, 442-88

Manufacturing chamber of commerce

Cámara Nacional Industrial de la
   Transformación
Zaragoza S/N Esq. Primo Verdad

Col. Edif. Estela Desp. 304
91000 Jalapa, VER
(281) 739-82, 701-02

Manufacturing chamber of commerce

Yucatán

Cámara Nacional de Comercio de Yucatán
Calle 32-273
97119 Mérida, YUC
(99) 253-122

*Chamber of commerce of the state of
Yucatán*

Cámara Nacional Industrial de la
   Transformación
Calle 30 No. 151
Col. García Gineres
97070 Mérida, YUC
(992) 534-00, 558-33

Manufacturing chamber of commerce

Zacatecas

Cámara Nacional de Comercio de
   Zacatecas
Blvd. Adolfo López Mateos 613
98000 Zacatecas, ZAC
(49) 200-29

*Chamber of commerce of the state of
Zacatecas*

Cámara Nacional Industrial de la
   Transformación
Antihua Matamoros No. 219-1
98000 Zacatecas, ZAC
(492) 201-07, 200-39

Manufacturing chamber of commerce

Chambers and Associations (by Industry)

Advertising

Asociación Mexicana de Agencia de
   Publicidad
Plaza Carlos J. Finlay 6
Piso 4
Col. Cuauhtémoc
06500 Mexico, DF
(5) 535-0139

Advertising agencies

Agriculture *(See also* Food)

Asociación Algodonera de Mexico, DF
López 15-301
06700 Mexico, DF
(5) 518-6189

Cotton growers

Asociación Hereford Mexicana
N. Bravo 3700
31350 Chihuahua, CHIH
(14) 164-340

Herefords

Asociación Mexicana de Criadores de
   Ganado Suizo
Andalucia 162
03400 Mexico, DF
(5) 538-1906

Swiss cattle breeders

Asociación Mexicana de Exportadores de
   Cafe
Insurgentes Sur 682-803
Mexico, DF
(5) 536-7767

Coffee exporters

Asociación Mexicana de Industria
   Plagicidas y Fertilizantes
San Antonio 256
Piso 8
03910 Mexico, DF
(5) 598-9095

Fertilizer and pesticides

Asociación Nacional de Especialidad en
   Ciencias Avicolas
Hacienda Canutillo 8-4
04960 Mexico, DF
(5) 673-6447

Poultry science

Cámara Nacional de Industriales de la
   Leche
Benjamin Franklin 134
11800 Mexico, DF
(5) 271-3798

Dairy products

Comisión Nacional del Cacao
Talleres Gráficos 64

08100 Mexico, DF
(5) 763-9747

Cocoa commission

Confederación Nacional Ganadera
Mariano Escobedo 714
11590 Mexico, DF
(5) 203-3506

Cattlemen's confederation

Federación Mexicana de Organizaciones
   Agricolas
Tacuba 37
06000 Mexico, DF
(5) 521-7899

Agricultural organizations

Unión Agricoloa Regional de Fruticultores
Av. Division del Norte 2908
Chihuahua, CHIH
(14) 136-344

Fruit growers

Unión Ganadera Regional de Chihuahua
Carr a Cuauhtémoc Km. 8.5
31000 Chihuahua, CHIH
(14) 180-286

Cattlemen in the Chihuahua region

Unión Ganadera Regional de Nuevo León
V. Juárez
67150 Monterrey, NL
(83) 370-876

Cattlemen in Nuevo León

Applied Mechanics

Sociedad Industrial de Mecánica Aplicada
Madero 2333 Pte.
64630 Monterrey, NL
(83) 469-377

Automotive Industry

Asociación Mexciana de la Industria
   Automotriz, A.C.
Ensenada 90
Col. Condesa
04200 Mexico, DF
(5) 272-1144

Industria Nacional de Autopartes
Shakespeare No. 15
Piso 3
Col. Nueva Anzures
11590 Mexico, DF
(5) 254-7766

Automotive parts manufacturers

Banking

Asociación Mexicana de Bancos
Lázaro Cárdenas 2
Piso 9
Torre Latinoamericana
Col. Centro
06007 Mexico, DF
(5) 512-3103

Beverages

Asociación Nacional de la Industria del
   Cafe
Sierra Picacho 14-PB
Col. Lomas de Chapultepec
11000 Mexico, DF
(5) 259-1528

Coffee

Asociación Nacional de Productores de
   Aguas Envasadas
Paseo de la Reforma 195-1301
Piso 13
Col. Cuauhtémoc
06500 Mexico, DF
(5) 566-2294

Soft-drink bottling, bottled water

Asociación Nacional de Vitivinicultores,
   A.C.
Calz. de Tlalpán 3515
Col. Santa Ursula Coapa
04650 Mexico, DF
(5) 606-9724

Grape growers and wine producers

Cámara Nacional de la Industria
   Azucarera y Alcoholera
Río Niagara No. 11
Col. Cuauhtémoc

06500 Mexico, DF
(5) 533-3040

Sugar and alcohol

Cámara Nacional de la Industria de la
   Malta y la Cerveza
Horacio 1556
Col. Polanco
11570 Mexico, DF
(5) 520-6283

Malt and beer

Chemicals

Asociación Nacional de la Industria
   Química
Av. Providencia 1118
03100 Mexico, DF
(5) 559-7833, 559-1979

Chemical industry

Consejo Coord de la Industria Química y
   Petroquímica
Av. San Antonio 256
Piso 4
53000 Mexico, DF
(5) 563-3164

Chemical and petrochemical

Cinematography/Photography

Cámara Nacional de la Industria
   Cinematográfica
Calle 7 No. 743-1
44100 Guadalajara, JAL
(36) 254-194

Cinematography

Asociación Mexicana de Laboratorios de
   Fotoacabado
Madero 23-C
Mexico, DF
(5) 521-1327

Photo labs

Clothing

Cámara Nacional de la Industria del
   Vestido
Tolsa 54

Col. Centro
06040 Mexico, DF
(5) 588-7822, 588-7664

Garment industry

Cámara Nacional de la Industria del
Vestido
Calle 37 No. 1545-151
44170 Guadalajara, JAL
(36) 256-078

Garment industry

Cámara Nacional de la Industria del
Vestido
M. Arreola 905 Ote.
64000 Monterrey, NL
(83) 422-633

Garment industry

Construction

Centro de la Vivendo y Estudios Urbanos
Violeta 27
04340 Mexico, DF
(5) 550-4099

Center of Housing and Urban Studies

Cámara Nacional del Cemento
Leibnitz 77
Col. Anzures
11590 Mexico, DF
(5) 533-0133

Cement

Asociación Mexicana de la Industria del
Concreto Premezclado
Blvd. A López Mateos 1135
03800 Mexico, DF
(5) 516-0902

Premixed concrete industry

Cámara Nacional de la Industria de la
Construcción
Periferico Sur 4839
Col. Parques del Pedregal
14010 Mexico, DF
(5) 606-8568, 652-3016

Construction industry

Cámara Nacional de la Industria de la
Construcción
Lerdo de Tejada 2151

Guadalajara, JAL
(36) 154-761

Construction industry

Sociedad Mexicana de Ingenieria
Sanitaria y Ambiental
Mexico 5682
16030 Mexico, DF
(5) 653-5082

Sanitary and environmental engineers

Sociedad de Arquitectos del IPN
Homero 1425-301
Col. Lomas Altas
11560 Mexico, DF
(5) 395-6959

Architects

Asociación de Ingenieros y Arquitectos de
Guadalajara
Calle 35 No. 1943
Guadalajara, JAL
(36) 263-289

Engineers and architects of Guadalajara

Asociación de Ingenieros y Arquitectos de
Mexico
Puente de Alvarado 58
06030 Mexico, DF
(5) 535-1213

Engineers and architects

Sociedad de Ingenieros y Tecnicos de
Monterrey
Cond Acero Monterrey 604
64000 Monterrey, NL
(83) 432-574

Engineers and technicians

Containers

Asociación Nacional de Fabricantes de
Cajas y Empaques de Carton
Palmas 765-401
06000 Mexico, DF
(5) 520-0835

*Packaging and cardboard box
manufacturers*

Asociación de Fabricantes de Envases
Metalicos
Bosque de Ciruelos 190-301

11700 Mexico, DF
(5) 251-9223

Metal container manufacturers

Cosmetics

Cámara Nacional de la Industria de
   Perfumería y Cosméticos
Gabriel Mancera 1134
03100 Mexico, DF
(5) 575-2121

Perfume and cosmetics

Credit

Asociación Nacional de Ejecutivos de
   Crédito
Puebla 402-A
México, DF
(5) 566-3873

Credit Executives

Asociación Nacional de Control del
   Crédito
Calle 5 No. 1458-201
Guadalajara, JAL
(36) 303-137

Credit control

Customs Brokers

Asociación de Agentes Aduanales
Xola 1707-A
03300 Mexico, DF
(5) 530-6804

Domestic Wares

Asociación Nacional de Fabricantes de
   Aparatos Domesticos
Bahía de Ballenas No. 88
Piso 2
Col. Nueva Anzures
11590 Mexico, DF
(5) 531-2375

Household appliance manufacturers

Cámara de la Industria de Baños del D.F.
Morelia 38-104

06700 Mexico, DF
(5) 533-1213

Bath industry

Electric/Electronic

Cámara Nacional de las Manufacturas
   Electricas (CANAME)
Ibsen 13
Col. Chapultepec Polanco
11560 Mexico, DF
(5) 202-1440

Electrical Manufacturers

Asociación Mexicana de Fabricantes de
   Transformadores Eléctricos
Thiers 251
Piso 7
11000 Mexico, DF
(5) 250-4171

Electrical transformer manufacturers

Asociación Mexicana de Fabricantes de
   Conductores Eléctricos
Sonora 166
Piso 1
06100 Mexico, DF
(5) 207-2254

Electrical conductor manufacturers

Asociación de Ingenieros Mecanicos y
   Eléctricos
Tacuba 5
06700 Mexico, DF
(5) 512-2046

Electrical and mechanical engineers

Cámara Nacional de la Industria
   Electronica y de Comunicaciones
   Eléctricas (CANIECE)
Guanajuato 65
Col. Roma
06700 Mexico, DF
(5) 574-7411

Electronic and electric communications

Food (for sugar and alcohol products, see Beverages)

Cámara Nacional de Conservas
   Alimenticias

Calderón de la Barca 359-200
11560 Mexico, DF
(5) 250-9679

Grocery industry

Cámara Nacional de la Industria
    Panificadora
Dr. Liceaga 96
06720 Mexico, DF
(5) 578-9051, 578-8924

Bakery industry

Cámara Nacional de la Industria Pesquera
Manuel Ma. Contreras No. 133
Piso 4
Col. Cuauhtémoc
06500 Mexico, DF
(5) 566-9411

Seafood, fishing industry

Confederación Nacional de Productores
    del Coco
Paseo Reforma 122
Piso 4
Mexico, DF
(5) 546-4830

Cocoa products

Cámara de Productos Alimenticios
    Elaborados con Leche
Benjamin Franklin 134
Col. Escandon
11800 Mexico, DF
(5) 271-2100

Dairy food products

Asociación Mexicana de la Industria
    Salinera, A.C.
Tacuba No. 37-332
Col. Centro
06000 Mexico, DF
(5) 518-3653

Salt

Cámara de la Industria Alimenticia de
    Jalisco
Washington 1920
Piso 2

44100 Guadalajara, JAL
(36) 104-177

Food industry of Jalisco

Footware

Asociación Nacional de Proveedores para
    la Industria del Calzado, A.C.
Av. del Obrero No. 403
Fracc. Industrial Julian de Obregón
37290 León, GTO
(471) 633-55

Footwear suppliers

Asociación Nacional de Proveedores de la
    Industria Calzado
Progreso 271
Piso 2
44140 Guadalajara, JAL
(36) 262-572

Footwear suppliers

Cámara Nacional de la Industria del
    Calzado
Durango 245-1104
Col. Roma
06700 Mexico, DF
(5) 533-6255, 525-4960

Footware industry

Cámara Nacional de la Industria del
    Calzado
Edif. Sociedad de Viajante 3
64000 Monterrey, NL
(83) 401-464

Footware industry

Forestry

Asociación Nacional de Fabricantes de
    Tableros de Madera, A.C. (ANAFATA)
Viaducto Miguel Alemán No. 277
Col. Escandon
11800 Mexico, DF
(5) 516-2545

Lumber manufacturers

Cámara Nacional de la Industria Forestal
Viaducto Miguel Alemán 277

11800 Mexico, DF
(5) 516-2545

Forest industry

Cámara Nacional de Silvicultura y
   Industria Derivadas
Baja California 255
Piso 12
Edif. A
06170 Mexico, DF
(5) 584-4044

Forest products

Cámara Nacional de la Industria Maderera
   y Similares
Santander No. 15-301
03920 Mexico, DF
(5) 598-6725

Lumber and related products

Cámara Nacional de la Industria Maderera
   y Similares
Colón 507 Ote.
64000 Monterrey, NL
(83) 721-171

Lumber and related products

Cámara Nacional de la Industria Maderera
   y Similares
Calle 18
Guadalajara, JAL
(36) 142-848

Lumber and related products

Cámara Nacional de las Industrias de la
   Celulosa y el Papel
Privada San Isidro 30
Col. Reforma Social
11650 Mexico, DF
(5) 202-8603

Paper and cellulose

Furniture

Asociación Metropolitana de Fabricantes
   de Muebles
Santander No. 15-102

03920 Mexico, DF
(5) 611-1787

Furniture manufacturers

Graphic Art

Cámara Nacional de la Industria de Artes
   Gráficas
Av. Río Churubusco 428
Piso 2
Col. del Carmen
04100 Mexico, DF
(5) 554-3500

Graphic art

Cámara Nacional de la Industria de Artes
   Gráficas
Alameda 640
44280 Guadalajara, JAL
(36) 149-474

Graphic art

Handicrafts

Asociación Nacional de Fabricantes de
   Regalos y Decoración y Artesanias
Monterrey 149
06700 Mexico, DF
(5) 564-8961

Hotels

Asociación Mexicana de Hoteles y Moteles
   de la Republica, A.C.
Balderas 33-414
Col. Centro
06040 Mexico, DF
(5) 510-8874

Hotels and motels

Asociación Nacional Hotelera, S.A.
Edison 84
Piso 2
Col. Tabacalera
06030 Mexico, DF
(5) 535-9341

Hotels

Insurance

Asociación de Compañías Afianzadoras
Adolfo Prieto 1012

Piso 4
03100 Mexico, DF
(5) 523-6854

Insurance companies

Asociación Mexicana de Agentes de
  Seguros y Fianzas
Florencia 18
Piso 1
06600 Mexico, DF
(5) 511-3118

Insurance and warranty agents

Laundry

Cámara Nacional de la Industria de
  Lavanderías
Río Danubio 38
06500 Mexico, DF
(5) 511-3823

Leather

Cámara Nacional de la Industria de la
  Curtiduría
Tehuantepec 255
Piso 1
Col. Roma Sur
06760 Mexico, DF
(5) 564-6600

Tannery industry

Cámara Nacional de la Industria de la
  Curtiduría
Eje Norte 2178
44700 Guadalajara, JAL
(36) 382-503

Tannery industry

Lubricants/Soap

Cámara Nacional de la Industria de
  Aceites, Grasa y Jabones
Melchor Ocampo No. 193-A-801
Col. Veronica Anzures
11320 Mexico, DF
(5) 203-1640, 254-0325

Oil, grease, and soap

Cámara Nacional de la Industria de
  Aceites, Grasa y Jabones

Rosario 836
Guadalajara, JAL
(36) 228-096

Oil, grease, and soap

Medical and Health

Asociación Dental Mexicana
E Montes 92
06400 Mexico, DF
(5) 546-0594

Dental

Asociación de Medicos Mexicanos
Dr. Vertiz 692
06700 Mexico, DF
(5) 519-9600

Doctors

Asociación Medico Diagnostico Nacional
Cipres 187
06400 Mexico, DF
(5) 541-5190

Diagnostic medicine

Asociación Mexicana de Bioquímica
  Clinica
Torres Adalid 508
Mexico, DF
(5) 523-2256

Clinical biochemistry

Asociación Mexicana de Ginecología y
  Obstetricia
Baja California 311
06100 Mexico, DF
(5) 515-3668

Gynecologists and obstetricians

Asociación Mexicana de Higiene y
  Seguridad
Lirio 7
6400 Mexico, DF
(5) 541-1566

Health and safety

Asociación Mexicana de Hospitales
Querétaro No. 210
Col. Roma

06700 Mexico, DF
(5) 574-0128

Hospitals

Cámara Nacional de Hospitales
Circuito Fundadores No. 19
Cd. Satelite
Naucalpan de Juárez
53100 Estado de México
(5) 562-8932

Hospitals

Cámara Nacional de la Industria de Lab
   Químicos y Farmacéuticos
Cuauhtémoc 1481
Mexico, DF
(5) 688-9477

*Lab chemicals and pharmaceutical
industry*

Cámara Nacional de la Industria del
   Embellecimiento Físico
Salamanca No. 5
Col. Roma
06700 Mexico, DF
(5) 533-2707

Physical fitness

Cámara Nacional de la Industria
   Farmacéutica (CANIFARMA)
Av. Cuauhtémoc 1481
Col. Santa Cruz Atoyac
03310 Mexico, DF
(5) 688-9477, 604-9808

Pharmaceutical industry

Sociedad Farmacéutica de Monterrey
M Arreola 717 Ote.
64000 Monterrey, NL
(83) 424-923

Pharmaceutical industry

Consejo Mexicano de Cirugía General
Av. Veracruz 93-201
06140 Mexico, DF
(5) 515-3668

General surgeons

Ortopedia Traumatologia y Cirujía de
   Urgencia
Candelaria 54

06400 Mexico, DF
(5) 544-0093

*Orthopedics, trauma, and emergency
surgery*

Sociedad Mexicana de Optometría
Madero 26-206
06000 Mexico, DF
(5) 510-4002

Optometry

Sociedad Mexicana de
   Otorrinolaringología
Eugenia 13-403
03810 Mexico, DF
(5) 669-0263

Ear, nose, and throat doctors

Sociedad Mexicana de Pediatría
Tehuantepec 86-503
53000 Mexico, DF
(5) 564-7739

Pediatrics

Mining/Minerals

Instituto del Aluminio
Francisco Petrarca 133
Piso 9
Col. Polanco
11560 Mexico, DF
(5) 531-7892, 531-2614

Aluminum

Cámara Nacional de la Industria del Hierro
   y del Acero
Amores 338
Col. del Valle
03100 Mexico, DF
(5) 543-4443, 523-3150

Iron and steel

Asociación de Distribuidores de Acero de
   Monterrey
Cond. Acero Monterrey 506
64000 Monterrey, NL
(83) 449-378

Steel distributors

Instituto Mexicano del Zinc, Plomo y
   Coproductos, A.C.
Sonora 166

Piso 1
Col. Condesa
06140 Mexico, DF
(5) 533-4191

Zinc and lead

Cámara Minera de México
Sierra Vertientes 369
Col. Lomas de Chapultepec
11000 Mexico, DF
(5) 540-6788, 540-6061

Mining

Asociación Minera de Chihuahua
Independencia 1003-509-B
31000 Chihuahua, CHI
(14) 150-093

Mining

Cámara Nacional de la Industria de la
   Platería y la Joyería
Reynosa 13-2
Col. Condesa
06100 Mexico, DF
(5) 516-8481, 516-1067

Silver and jewelry

Asociación Mexicana del Cobre, A.C.
Av. Sonora No. 166
Piso 1
Col. Hipodromo Condesa
06100 Mexico, DF
(5) 207-2254, 533-4441

Copper

Asociación de Ingenieros de Minas,
   Metalurgistas y Geólogos de Mexico,
   A.C.
Jaime Torres Bodet No. 176
Col. Santa Ma. La Ribera
06400 Mexico, DF
(5) 547-0751, 541-3694

*Mining engineers, metallurgists, and
geologists*

Personnel

Secretarías Ejecutivas de Guadalajara
Calle 12 No. 380-A-302

44100 Guadalajara, JAL
(36) 132-889

Executive secretaries

Secretarías Profesionales de Chihuahua
Av. Leyes de Reforma y Calle 4
31000 Chihuahua, CHIH
(14) 166-335

Secretaries

Ejecutivos de Ventas y Mercadotecnia
Río Niagara 26
06000 Mexico, DF
(5) 525-0942

Sales and marketing executives

Ejecutivos de Ventas y Mercadotecnia de
   Monterrey
San Francisco 2301-25
64710 Monterrey, NL
(83) 473-397

Sales and marketing executives

Ejecutivos de Ventas y Mercadotecnia de
   Guadalajara
Calle 5 No. 4000
Guadalajara, JAL
(36) 225-040

Sales and marketing executives

Ejecutivos de Ventas y Mercadotecnia de
   Chihuahua
Blvd. Ortiz Mena
Chihuahua, CHIH
(14) 182-241

Sales and marketing executives

Asociación Mexicana de Capacitación de
   Personal
Cordoba 76
Piso 2
06700 Mexico, DF
(5) 533-1375

Personnel training

Asociación de Ejecutivos de Personal del
   Edo. de NL
Ocampo 250-603 Pte.
Monterrey, NL
(83) 432-162

*Personnel executives of Nuevo
León*

Petroleum

Asociación Mexicana de Distribuidoras de
  Gas Licuado
Juan Jacobo Rasseau No. 44
Cd. Nueva Anzures
11560 Mexico, DF
(5) 545-5864

Gas distributors

Plastics

Asociación Nacional de Industrias del
  Plastico, A.C. (ANIPAC)
Sullivan 165
53000 Mexico, DF
(5) 566-7466

Publishing

Cámara Nacional de la Industria Editorial
  Mexicana
Holanda 13
Col. San Diego Churubusco
04120 Mexico, DF
(5) 688-2221, 688-2011

Publishing

Corresponsales de la Prensa de la Rep.
  Mexicana
F Mata 8-301
06700 Mexico, DF
(5) 518-5886

Press correspondents

Asociación de Relaciones Publicas y
  Comunicación
Ocampo 250-601 Pte.
64000 Monterrey, NL
(83) 401-363

Public relations

Asociación Mexicana de Agencias de
  Publicidad
Plaza Carlos J. Finlay 6
Piso 4

06500 Mexico, DF
(5) 535-0439

Public relations

Radio

Cámara Nacional de la Industria de Radio
  y Televisión
Guanajuato 65
15000 Mexico, DF
(5) 547-7485, 254-1809

Radio and television industry

Real Estate

Cámara de Propietarios de Bienes Raíces
  de Nuevo León
Ocampo 250-501 Pte.
64000 Monterrey, NL
(83) 403-764

*Real estate owners of Nuevo
León*

Asociación Hipotecaria Mexicana
Unidad Plateros Edif. A-9
11000 Mexico, DF
(5) 593-2007

Mortgage brokers

Colegio de Ingenieros Topográficos
Tacuba 5-7
06700 Mexico, DF
(5) 512-1774

Surveyors

Restaurants

Asociación Mexicana de Restaurantes
Torcuato Tasso 325-103
Col. Polanco
11560 Mexico, DF
(5) 250-1146

Restaurants

Rubber

Cámara Nacional de la Industria Hulera
Manuel Ma. Contreras 133-115
Piso 1

Col. Cuauhtémoc
06500 Mexico, DF
(5) 535-8917, 535-2266

Rubber

Cámara Nacional de la Industria Hulera
Calle 5 No. 1835-7
44650 Guadalajara, JAL
(36) 168-269

Rubber

Television (see also Radio)

Agrupación Mexicana de la TV Mexicana
Quintana Roo 142
Mexico, DF
(5) 564-2065

Television

Textiles

Cámara Nacional de la Industria Textil
Plinio 220 Esq. Horacio
Col. Polanco
11510 Mexico, DF
(5) 202-2801, 202-2567

Textiles

Cámara Textil de Occidente
Calle 37 No. 2208
44600 Guadalajara, JAL
(36) 156-646

Textiles—western region

Cámara Regional Textil del Norte
Calle Padre Mier 893 Ote.
64000 Monterrey, NL
(83) 407-410

Textiles—northern region

Transportation/Infrastructure

Cámara Nacional del Aerotransporte
Paseo de la Reforma 76
Piso 17
Col. Juárez

06600 Mexico, DF
(5) 592-4472

Air transportation

Cámara Nacional de Autotransportes de
    Carga (CANACA)
Pachuca 158
Piso 5
Col. Condesa
06140 Mexico, DF
(5) 553-2593, 553-2682

Trucking

Asociación Mexicana de Caminos
Rio Tiber 103
Piso 2
Col. Cuautémoc
06500 Mexico, DF
(5) 207-8090

Roads

Cámara Regional de la Industria de
    Transportes
Calle 53A-No. 1920
Guadalajara, JAL
(36) 142-848

Transportation industry of Guadalajara

Asociación Mexicana de Agentes de
    Navieros
Insurgentes Sur 421-A1301
15000 Mexico, DF
(5) 574-7833

Maritime agents

Travel Agencies

Asociación Mexicana de Agencias de
    Viajes
Ameyalco 10-646
03100 Mexico, DF
(5) 660-4403

Valves

Asociación Mexicana de Fabricantes de
    Válvulas y Conexos, S.A.
Copérnico No. 47
Col. Anzures

11590 Mexico, DF
(5) 203-8223

Valve manufacturers

Consulates *(Consulados)*, Mexican, in the United States

Arizona

60 N. Terrace Ave.
Nogales, AZ 85621
(602) 287-2521

553 S. Stone Ave.
Tucson, AZ 85701
(602) 882-5595

California

331 W. Second St.
Calexico, CA 92231
(619) 357-3863

905 N. Fulton St.
Fresno, CA 93728
(209) 233-3065

2401 W. Sixth St.
Los Angeles, CA 90057
(213) 351-6800

Oxnard Transportation Center
201 E. Fourth St., Ste. 2
Oxnard, CA 93030
(805) 483-4684

9812 Old Winery Pl.
Sacramento, CA
(916) 363-3885

558 W. Sixth St.
San Bernardino, CA 92401
(714) 888-2500

601 A St., Ste. 100
San Diego, CA 92101
(619) 231-0337

870 Market St., Ste. 528
San Francisco, CA 94102
(415) 392-5554

380 N. First St., Ste. 102
San Jose, CA 95112
(408) 294-3414

406 W. Fourth St.
Santa Ana, CA 92701
(714) 835-3069

Colorado

707 Washington St., Ste. A
Denver, CO 80203
(303) 830-0523

District of Columbia

2827 16th St., NW
Washington, DC 20009
(202) 736-1000

Florida

780 NW Le Jeune Rd., Ste. 525
Miami, FL 33126
(305) 441-8781

Georgia

410 South Tower
One CNN Center
Atlanta, GA 30303
(404) 688-3258

Illinois

300 N. Michigan Ave.
2nd Floor
Chicago, IL 60601
(312) 855-1380

Louisiana

World Trade Center Bldg.
2 Canal St., Ste. 114
New Orleans, LA 70130
(504) 522-3596

Massachusetts

20 Park Plaza, Ste. 1212
Boston, MA 02116
(617) 426-4942

Michigan

600 Renaissance Center, Ste. 1510
Detroit, MI 48243
(313) 567-7709

Missouri

1015 Locust St., Ste. 922
St. Louis, MO 63101
(314) 436-3233

New Mexico

401 Fifth St., NW
Western Bank Bldg.
Albuquerque, NM 87102
(505) 247-2139

New York

8 E. 41st St.
New York, NY 10017
(212) 689-0456

Pennsylvania

575 Bourse Bldg.
21 S. Fifth St.
Philadelphia, PA 19106
(215) 922-4262

Puerto Rico

Edif. Bankers Finance Tower
Ave. Muñoz Rivera
San Juan, PR 00918
(809) 764-0258

Texas

200 E. Sixth St., Ste. 200
Austin, TX 78701
(512) 478-9031

Elizabeth and East 7th
Brownsville, TX 78520
(512) 542-2051

800 North Shoreline Blvd.
One Shoreline Plaza

Corpus Christi, TX 78401
(512) 882-3375

1349 Empire Central, Ste. 100
Dallas, TX 75244
(214) 630-7341

140 Adams St.
Eagle Pass, TX 78853
(512) 773-9255

910 E. San Antonio St.
El Paso, TX 79901
(915) 533-3644

3015 Richmond, Ste. 100
Houston, TX 77098
(713) 524-4861

1612 Farragut St.
Laredo, TX 78040
(512) 723-6360

1418 Beech St.
McAllen, TX 78501
(512) 686-0243

511 W. Ohio, Ste. 121
Midland, TX 79701
(915) 687-2334

127 Navarro St.
San Antonio, TX 78205
(512) 227-9145

Utah

182 South 600 East, Ste. 202
Salt Lake City, UT 84102
(801) 521-8502

Washington

2132 Third Ave.
Seattle, WA 98121
(206) 448-6819

Consulates, U.S., in Mexico

Ciudad Juárez, CHIH

Av. López Mateos 924
Ciudad Juárez, CHI
(16) 340-48

Guadalajara, JAL

Progreso 175
Guadalajara, JAL
(36) 252-700

Hermosillo, SON

Monterrey 141
Hermosillo, SON
(62) 389-23

Matamoros, TAM

Av. Primera 2002
Matamoros, TAM
(891) 672-702

Mérida, YUC

Paseo Montejo 453
Mérida, YUC
(99) 255-011

Mexico, DF

American Consulate General
Paseo de la Reforma 305
Mexico City, DF
(5) 211-0042

Nuevo Laredo, TAM

Avenida Allende 3330
Col. Jardin
Nuevo Laredo, TAM
(871) 405-12

Tijuana, BC

Tapachula 96
Tijuana, BC
(66) 817-400

Consulting Companies (*Empresas Consultorias*)

Employee Benefits

Benefit
Av. Contreras 407
10200 Mexico, DF
(5) 681-1738

Consultores en Compensación
Lago Mero 32
Piso 6
11520 Mexico, DF
(5) 255-0184

Consultores y Servicios Actuariales
Zaragoza Sur 1300-325
64000 Monterrey, NL
(83) 402-205

TPFYC de México
Independencia 911-204
31000 Chihuahua, CHIH
(14) 161-959

Franchising

Asociación Mexicana de Franquicias
Insurgentes Sur No. 1783-303
Col. Guadelupe Inn
01020 Mexico, DF
(5) 524-8043

Centro Internacional de Franquicias
José Ma Rico 55
03100 Mexico, DF
(5) 534-9021

International Franchise Association
World Headquarters
1350 New York Ave., NW
Ste. 900
Washington, DC 20005
(202) 628-8000

Promotora de Franquicias Praxis
Lázaro Cárdenas 2465-E4
Garza García, NL
(83) 632-934

Rudnick & Wolfe
203 North LaSalle St.

Chicago, IL 60601-1293
(312) 368-4000

Sonabend y Asociados
Montes Urales 739
11000 Mexico, DF
(5) 520-3909

Government Affairs

Consultores Internacionales
José María Rico 55
Piso 2
03100 Mexico, DF
(5) 524-3179

Dynamics Enterprises de México
Sonora 141
Piso 2
06140 Mexico, DF
(5) 211-9375

González Zucieta y Asociados
Av. Gómez Morin 400 Nte. 6
66220 Monterrey, NL
(83) 785-042

Intercapta
Calle 6, 2234
31000 Chihuahua, CHI
(14) 162-602

Tennessee Associated Int. de México
Zaragoza Sur 1300-315
64000 Monterrey, NL
(83) 400-093

Urbanismo y Sistemas de Transporte
Revolución 2042-2C
01090 Mexico, DF
(5) 550-2523

Market Research and Feasibility Studies

Alfa Consultores Alimentarios, S.C.
Libertad No. 107-402
San Simón
03660 Mexico, DF
(5) 539-5737

Market research

A. Corella y Asociados, S.A. de C.V.
Gonzalitos Sur 298

Piso 3
64640 Monterrey, NL
(83) 469-866

Feasibility studies

Buro de Investigaciones de Mercado, S.A.
Irrigación No. 108
11500 Mexico, DF
(5) 557-4433

Market research, feasibility studies

Consultoría Mexicana, S.A. de C.V.
Monte Elbruz No. 134
Piso 1
Lomas de Chapultepec
11000 Mexico, DF
(5) 540-1861

Feasibility studies

Consultoría y Promoción
Av. Insurgentes Sur No. 421-1101
Col. Condesa
06140 Mexico, DF
(5) 564-5800

Market research, feasibility studies

Consultoría y Proyectos Empresariales, S.C.
2 Poniente Sur No. 355
Col. Centro
29000 Tuxtla Gutiérrez, CHIS
(961) 281-41

Market research, feasibility studies

Duran Juárez y Asocdiados, S.C.
Av. Lerdo de Tejada No. 2641
Arcos Vallarta
44100 Guadalajara, JAL
(36) 301-354

Market research, feasibility studies

Flores Zaher y Asociados, S.C.
Puerto Vallarta No. 4228-B
Valle de las Brisas
64790 Monterrey, NL
(83) 571-753

Market research, feasibility studies

Grupo de Consultoría Técnica Industrial
Virrey No. 24
Col. Satelite

53120 Naucalpan, Edo. de Mex.
(5) 393-5524

Market research

Guzmán Clemente Ibarra
Av. Las Americas No. 105-204
Fracc. Las Americas
20230 Aguascalientes, AGS
(491) 564-05

Feasibility studies

Indermec (Compañía de Investigación de
  Mercado)
Zamora No. 98
Col. Condesa
06140 Mexico, DF
(5) 553-5888

Market research, feasibility studies

Infotec
Av. San Fernando No. 37
Toriello Guerra
14050 Mexico, DF
(5) 606-0011

Market research, feasibility studies

McKinsey and Co., Inc.
Blvd. Avila Camacho No. 1-13
Chapultepec Polanco
11560 Mexico, DF
(5) 557-7833

Feasibility studies

Price Waterhouse
Río de la Plata No. 48
Col. Cuauhtémoc
06500 Mexico, DF
(5) 211-7883

Market research, feasibility studies

(For other locations, see *Accountants*)

Patentability, Development, and Technology Transfer

Becerril y Becerril, S.C.
Thiers No. 251-12
Col. Anzures
11590 Mexico, DF
(5) 254-0400

Technology transfer

Gutiérrez Tello y Compañía, S.A. de C.V.
Dakota No. 423

Piso 1
Col. Napoles
03810 Mexico, DF
(5) 363-7709

Technological patentability and development

Infotec
Av. San Fernando No. 37
Toriello Guerra
14050 Mexico, DF
(5) 606-0011

Technological patentability, development, and transfers

Proyectos de Ingenieria Computacional,
  S.C.
Calle del Ejido No. 4621
Col. Nogales
32350 Cd. Juárez, CHIH
(16) 132-002

Technological development

Tecnologías en Obras y Proyectos, S.A.
Providencia No. 334-401
Del Valle
03100 Mexico, DF
(5) 543-8447

Technological development

Tourism

Consultores Desarollo Turistico
Newton 186-503
06400 Mexico, DF
(5) 545-8361

Hoteles y Restaurantes Soberanis
Londres 175
Piso 2
06360 Mexico, DF
(5) 525-5901

Credit Reporting Agencies

Análisis y Evaluación Crediticia
Tabasco 275 Desp. 101
06700 Mexico, DF
(5) 525-6730

Buro Central de Informatica de Crédito
Insurgentes Sur 421, Edif. A-113-A

15000 Mexico, DF
(5) 574-9264

Dun & Bradstreet
Durango 263
Pisos 4 y 5
06700 Mexico, DF
(5) 511-5643

Dun & Bradstreet
Dr. Coss 843 Sur
64000 Monterrey, NL
(83) 453-495

Dun & Bradstreet
López Cotilla 1713-203
44160 Guadalajara, JAL
(36) 259-797

The Foreign Credit Interchange Bureau
  (FCIB)
520 Eighth Ave.
22nd Floor
New York, NY 10018
(212) 947-5368

Customs Brokers (*Agentes Aduanales*)

Aerofletes Internacionales, S.A.
Av. 602 Loc. 4, Aduana del Aeropuerto
  Internacional
Moctezuma
15620 Mexico, DF
(5) 762-1522

Knowledgeable about all Mexican states

Agencia Aduanal Antonio Escalante
  Castera
Edif. de Agentes Aduanales
Loc. 13
Penon de los Baños
15520 Mexico, DF
(5) 571-8844

Knowledgeable about all Mexican states

Agencia Aduanal Martínez Vara
Bajio No. 282 y 603
Piso 6
Roma Sur
06760 Mexico, DF
(5) 584-5231

Agencia Aduanal Nogueira de
  Guadalajara, S.A. de C.V.

Independencia Sur No. 1281-A
44460 Guadalajara, JAL
(36) 190-802

Agencia Aduanal Super Cargo de
  Occidente, S.A.
Heroes Ferrocarrileros No. 1290
44220 Guadalajara, JAL
(36) 197-015

Agencia Aduanal Woodward, S.C.
Tula No. 3
06140 Mexico, DF
(5) 553-0826

Central de Aduanas de Monterrey, S.A.
Ruperto Martínez Pte. No. 1613
64000 Monterrey, NL
(83) 438-530

Emery Air Freight Corp.
Irapuato 188
15520 Mexico DF
(5) 785-4756

Emery Air Freight Corp.
Av. de la Paz 2183-A
44770 Guadalajara, JAL
(36) 165-930

Emery Air Freight Corp.
Carr. Miguel Alemán Km. 1107
67110 Guadelupe, NL
(83) 795-150

Tecnicos Aduanales Asociados, S.C.
Libertad No. 1925
44100 Guadalajara, JAL
(36) 261-402

Transcarga Internacional, S.C.
Norte 196 No. 694
Pensador Mexicano
15510 Mexico, DF
(5) 760-1422

Customs Service Representatives (U.S.)

U.S. Customs Attaché
American Embassy
Paseo Reforma 305
Mexico, DF
(5) 211-0042

U.S. Customs Representative
Av. Construcción 411 Pte.
Monterrey, NL
(83) 452-120

U.S. Customs Representative
Paseo Montejo 453
Mérida, YUC
(99) 258-235

U.S. Customs Representative
Morelia 139
Hermosillo, SON
(621) 752-58

Department Stores

Director de Compras
Aurrera S.A. de C.V.
Masaryk 111
Piso 7
Col. Polanco
11560 Mexico, DF
(5) 254-5581

Director de Compras y Operación
Blanco Sucesores, S.A. de C.V.
Av. Jardin No. 245
Col. Tlatilco
Delegación Atzcapozalco
02860 Mexico, DF
(5) 355-7555, ext. 19

Director General
Centro Comercial de Todo
San Francisco No. 1621
Col. del Valle
03100 Mexico, DF
(5) 534-8100

Director General
Class, S.A.
Insurgentes Sur 1235
Col. Insurgentes Mixcoac
Mexico, DF
(5) 563-8133

Clothes only

Jefe de Compras de Importación
Comercial Mexican, S.A.
Calz. Chabacano 43
Col. Asturias
Mexico, DF
(5) 538-1145

Director General
Compañía Hermanos Vázquez
Av. Universidad 2014
Esq. Copilco
Copilco Universidad
04360 Mexico, DF
(5) 591-1200

Household furniture

Director General
Compañía Mercantil El Refugio, S.A.
Av. Felix Cuevas 231
Esq. Recreo 151
Col. del Valle
03100 Mexico, DF
(5) 652-0573

Jefe de Importaciones Gigante, S.A.
Ejercito Nacional 769-A
Col. Nueva Granada
11560 Mexico, DF
(5) 250-3011

Grupo Pali-Pali Lomas
Blvd. Avila Camacho 138
Col. Lomas de Chapultepec
01000 Mexico, DF
(5) 202-2295

Director General
High Life, S.A.
Gante 4
Piso 6
Zona Centro
06000 Mexico, DF
(5) 510-1032

Director de Compras
Liverpool Mexico, S.A. de C.V.
Mariano Escobedo 425
11510 Mexico, DF
(5) 531-3440, ext. 318

El Palacio de Hierro, S.A.
Durango 230
Col. Condesa
06700 Mexico, DF
(5) 525-9000

Robert's
Tejocotes No. 164
Col. del Valle

03100 Mexico, DF
(5) 559-2996, 575-3212

Men's clothes only

Director de Compras
Salinas y Rocha, S.A.
Presidente Masaryk 169
Col. Chapultepec Morales
11570 Mexico, DF
(5) 203-8303

Director General
Sanborn's Hermanos, S.A.
Calvario No. 100
Col. Tlalpán
14000 Mexico, DF
(5) 655-0200

Director de Compras
Soriana Corporativo, S.A.
Av. de los Angeles 1732
Col. Juana de Arco
64000 Monterrey, NL
(83) 310-410, 310-019

Director General
Viana y Cía., S.A.
Insurgentes Norte No. 3
Col. Guerrero
06300 Mexico, DF
(5) 566-3666

Household furniture

Woolworth Mexicana, S.A. de C.V.
Suderman 250
Piso 2
Col. Chapultepec Morales
11550 Mexico, DF
(5) 250-5099

Embassies (*Embajadas*)

Embassy of Mexico
1911 Pennsylvania Ave.
Washington, DC 20006
(202) 728-1600

American Embassy
Col. Cuauhtémoc
Paseo de la Reforma 305
Mexico City, DF
(5) 211-0042

Engineers

Consultores en Planeación y Diseno
    Urbano, S.C.
Fernando Villapando No. 43-2
Guadalupe Inn
01020 Mexico, DF
(5) 548-3347

Dirección Técnica de Ingenieria, S.C.
Río Volga No. 3-6 Bis
Col. Cuauhtémoc
06500 Mexico, DF
(5) 525-3977

Grupo Bufete Industrial
Moras No. 850
Del Valle
03100 Mexico, DF
(5) 658-5299

Industria del Hierro, S.A. de C.V.
Viaducto Río Becerra No. 27
Pisos 1 y 2
Col. Napoles
03810 Mexico, DF
(5) 660-3596

Ingenieros y Desarrollo Las Truchas, S.A.
    de C.V.
Av. Insurgentes Sur No. 1799-301
Guadalupe Inn
01020 Mexico, DF
(5) 534-5175

Instituto Mexicano del Petróleo
Lázaro Cárdenas Nte. No. 152
San Bartolo Atephuaca
07730 Mexico, DF
(5) 567-6600

Export Finance Organizations (Noncommercial banks, private sector)

ADF Trade Finance
11611 San Vincente Blvd., Ste. 840
Los Angeles, CA 90049
(310) 820-8185

American Credit Institute, Inc.
7 Penn Plaza
New York, NY 10001
(212) 563-1036

Amerimex Maquiladora Fund
Warwick Group
300 W. Clarendon, Ste. 230
Phoenix, AZ 85013
(602) 277-8006

ExIm Corporation
6620 W. Broad St., Ste. 270
Richmond, VA 23230
(804) 289-6006

InterAmerican Holdings
1551 Fourth Ave., Ste. 301
San Diego, CA 92101
(619) 237-0433

Trading Alliance Corp.
47 E. 44th St.
New York, NY 10015
(212) 953-0400

World Trade Finance, Inc.
875 N. Virgil
Los Angeles, CA 90029
(213) 660-1277

U.S. World Trade Corp.
P.O. Box 6095
Portland, OR 97228
(503) 275-4100

Foreign Trade Associations

Cámara Americana de Comercio, S.A.
Lucerna 78
Piso 3 y 4
Col. Juárez
06600 Mexico, DF
(5) 705-0995

American Chamber of Commerce

Cámara Americana de Comercio, S.A.
Marsella 570-206
44370 Guadalajara, JAL
(36) 150-074

American Chamber of Commerce

Cámara Americana de Comercio, S.A.
Picachos 760-6
64060 Monterrey, NL
(83) 481-519

American Chamber of Commerce

Cámara de Comercio Mexicana Argentina
Temístocles 103

11550 Mexico, DF
(5) 280-4213

Chamber of Commerce of Argentina

Cámara de Comercio Britanica, A.C.
Río de la Plata 30
Col. Cuauhtémoc
06500 Mexico, DF
(5) 286-9918, 286-2705

Chamber of Commerce of Great Britain

Cámara Franco-Mexicana de Comercio y
   Industria, A.C.
Río Nilo 80
Piso 6
06500 Mexico, DF
(5) 511-9963

Chamber of Commerce of France

Cámara Mexicano-Alemána de Comercio e
   Industria, A.C.
Bosques de Ciruelos 130
Piso 12
Col. Bosques de las Lomas
11700 Mexico, DF
(5) 251-4022

Chamber of Commerce of Germany

Cámara de Comercio Italiana en México
Marsella 39
Piso 1
Col. Juárez
06600 Mexico, DF
(5) 511-5257

Chamber of Commerce of Italy

Cámara Mexico-Israel de Comercio e
   Industria, A.C.
Av. de las Fuentes No. 35 Desp. 201
Col. Lomas de Tacamachalco
Naucalpan de Juárez
53950, Edo. de Mex.
(5) 294-2278

Chamber of Commerce of Israel

Cámara Japonésa de Comercio e Industria
Sevilla 9
Piso 2
Col. Juárez

06600 Mexico, DF
(5) 207-5110

Chamber of Commerce of Japan

North American Free Trade Association
1130 Connecticut Ave., NW, Ste. 500
Washington, DC 20036
(202) 296-3019

Asociación Escandinava de México
Presa Salinillas 178
15900 Mexico, DF
(5) 557-1625

Scandinavian Association of Mexico

U.S.-Mexico Chamber of Commerce
Homero No. 572
Piso 7
Col. Chapultepec Morales
11570 Mexico, DF
(5) 250-7033

U.S.-Mexico Chamber of Commerce
1211 Connecticut Ave., NW, Ste. 510
Washington, DC 20036
(202) 296-5198

U.S.-Mexico Chamber of Commerce
400 E. 59th St., Ste. 8-B
New York, NY 10022
(212) 750-2638

U.S.-Mexico Chamber of Commerce
3000 Carlisle, Ste. 210
Dallas, TX 75204
(214) 754-8060

U.S.-Mexico Chamber of Commerce
555 S. Flower St.
25th Floor
Los Angeles, CA 90071-2326
(213) 623-7725

Asociación Nacional de Importadores y
Exportadores de la República Mexicana
(ANIERM)
Monterrey 130
Col. Roma
06700 Mexico, DF
(5) 564-9379

*National association of importers and
exporters*

Asociación de Ind de Transporte y
Comercio Internacional

Pres. Masaryk 134-204
11560 Mexico, DF
(5) 254-1863

*Foreign trade and transportation
association*

Asociación Nacional de Consorcios y Cías
Comercio Exterior
Tlaxcala 177-803
06170 Mexico, DF
(5) 286-8744

*National association of foreign trade
consortiums and companies*

Asociación de Representantes de Casas
Extranjeras
López 15-502
06050 Mexico, DF
(5) 518-5962

*Foreign company representatives
association*

Centro Internacional de Negocios
Adolfo Prieto y Av. Nueva Fundidor
64000 Monterrey, NL
(83) 457-260

International Trade Center

Consejo Empressarial Mexicano para
Asuntos Internacionales (CEMAI)
Homero 527
Piso 7
Col. Polanco
11570 Mexico, DF
(5) 250-7033

*Mexican Coordinating Council for
International Business*

Consejo Mexicano de Inversión
Paseo de la Reforma 915
Lomas de Chapultepec
11000 Mexico, DF
(5) 202-7804

Mexican Investment Council

Consejo Nacional de Comercio Exterior
(CONACEX)
Tlaxcala 177, Ste. 803
Col. Condesa
06140 Mexico, DF
(5) 286-8744

*The National Council on Foreign Trade;
provides trade information on
nonpetroleum commerce*

Consejo Nacional de Comercio Exterior
Calz Lázaro Cárdenas 3294
Piso 2
45040 Guadalajara, JAL
(36) 221-090

National Foreign Trade Council

Consejo Nacional de Comercio Exterior
Altamirano 2306
31320 Chihuahua, CHIH
(14) 139-098

National Foreign Trade Council

Coordinadora de Organizaciones
  Empresariales de Comercio Exterior
  (COECE)
1025 Thomas Jefferson St., NW
East Lobby, Ste. 700
Washington, DC 20007
(202) 625-3550

*Mexican Coordinating Committee for
Foreign Trade*

Fom y Des del Comercio Exterior de
  Occidente
Lázaro Cárdenas 3294
Guadalajara, JAL
(36) 221-091

*Foreign Trade Association of Western
Mexico*

Sociedad Mexicana de Comercio Exterior
Popocatépetl 32
Mexico, DF
(5) 584-5528

Mexican Foreign Trade Society

Freight Forwarding *(Consilidores de Carga)*

Aerodocumentación Aduanal, S.C.
Asturias No 94-B
Álamos
03400 Mexico, DF
(5) 530-4366

Agencia Aduanal Mexicana, S.C.
Av. Insurgentes Sur No. 1180-602
Del Valle
03100 Mexico, DF
(5) 575-1686

Carga de Mexico, S.A. de C.V.
Londres No. 38
Piso 2
Col. Juárez
06600 Mexico, DF
(5) 533-0495

Central de Fletes Monterrey
Matamoros 547
Guadalajara, JAL
(36) 390-120

Central de Fletes Monterrey
Lago Chapula 4620
Nuevo Laredo, TAM
(87) 558-57

Circle Air Freight de Mexico, S.A. de C.V.
Av. Texcoco No. 18
Peñon de los Baños
15520 Mexico, DF
(5) 571-1495

Coordinadores Maritimos Internacionales,
  S.A. de C.V.
Manzanillo No. 83-401
Roma Sur
06760 Mexico, DF
(5) 574-8156

Flores Tello y Cía.
Gral San Martín 204 Sur
09000 Tampico, TAM
(12) 127-144

Importaciones y Exportaciones Mexicanas,
  S.A. de C.V.
Genova No. 33-401
Col. Juárez
06600 Mexico, DF
(5) 514-7212

Ramon Barrios y Cía.
Maclovio Herrera 4028
88000 Nuevo Laredo, TAM
(87) 224-89

Trafico Aereo Internacional
Av. Nogalar 123 Sur
64000 Monterrey, NL
(83) 504-665

Villasana
Calz del Valle 400-817
66200 Monterrey, NL
(83) 354-972

Government Agencies *(Agencias Del Gobierno)*

Secretariat of Agriculture and Water Resources (SARH)

Secretaría de Agricultura y Recursos
   Hidraulicos (SARH)
Insurgentes Sur No. 476
Piso 13
Col. Roma Sur
06768 Mexico, DF
(5) 584-0096

Secretary's office

Embassy of Mexico
SARH
1911 Pennsylvania Ave., NW
7th Floor
Washington, DC 20006
(202) 728-1720

U.S. office

Dirección de Importaciones y
   Exportaciones
SARH
Lope de Vega No. 125
Piso 10
Col. Chapultepec Morales
11570 Mexico, DF
(5) 254-2269

Office of Importing and Exporting

Dirección General de Asuntos
   Internacionales
SARH
Benjamin Franklin No. 146, PB
Col. Escandon
11800 Mexico, DF
(5) 515-3640

Office of International Agricultural Affairs

Dirección General de Sanidad Forestal
SARH
Av. Progreso No. 5
Piso 2
Edif. Principal, PB
Col. Viveros de Coyoacan

04000 Mexico, DF
(5) 658-8974

Office of Forest Policy

Dirección General de Salud Animal
SARH
Recreo 51
Piso 11
03230 Mexico, DF
(5) 534-3985

Office of Animal Health

Dirección General de Sanidad Vegetal
SARH
Guillermo Pérez Valenzuela 127
Piso 2
04110 Mexico, DF
(5) 554-0512

Office of Phytosanitary Affairs

Secretary of Agrarian Reform

Secretario de la Reforma Agraria (SRA)
Calz. de la Viga 1174
Torre B
Piso 15
09430 Mexico, DF
(5) 650-6077

Main office

Secretary of Trade and Industrial Development (SECOFI)

Embassy of Mexico
SECOFI Office
1911 Pennsylvania Ave., NW
7th Floor
Washington, DC 20006
(202) 728-1700

U.S. office

Dirección General de Asuntos Fronterizos
SECOFI
Periferico Sur 3025
Piso 7
Col. Heroes de Padierna
Del. Ma. Contreras
Mexico, DF
(5) 683-4394, 683-7055, ext. 2706

Office of Quotas

Dirección General de Inversiones
   Extranjeras

SECOFI
Blvd. Manuel Ávila Camacho 1
Torre Comermex
11560 Mexico, DF
(5) 540-1426

Office of Foreign Investment

Dirección General de Servicios al
   Comercio Exterior
SECOFI
Blvd. Adolfo López Mateos 3025
Piso 5
10700 Mexico, DF
(5) 683-4344, 683-5066

*Office of Foreign Trade & Import
Procedures*

Dirreción General de Negociaciones
   Comerciales e Internacionales
SECOFI
Blvd. Adolfo López Mateos 3025
Piso 11
10700 Mexico, DF
(5) 683-4035

Office of International Investment

Dirección General de Asuntos Jurídicos
SECOFI
Av. Yucatán 23
Piso 7
06170 Mexico, DF
(5) 533-4909

Office of Legal Affairs

Dirección General de Planeación e
   Informatica
SECOFI
Alfonso Reyes 30
Piso 5
06179 Mexico, DF
(5) 286-0080

Office of Planning and Information

Dirección General de Abasto y Productos
SECOFI
Dr. Navarro 180
Piso 1
06720 Mexico, DF
(5) 578-8275

Office of Supply and Products

Dirección General de Desarrollo
   Tecnológico

SECOFI
Azafran No. 18
Piso 6
Col. Granzas
08400 Mexico, DF
(5) 657-3751

*Office for trademark, patent, and
technological registration*

Dirección General de Normas
SECOFI
Puente de Tecamachalco No. 6
Piso 1
Col. Fuentes
de Tecamachalco
53950 Naucalpan
Edo. de Mex.
(5) 540-2620, 589-9877, ext. 130

Office of Standardization

Subsecretario de Industria e Inversiones
   Extranjeras
SECOFI
Alfonso Reyes 30
Piso 13
06179 Mexico, DF
(5) 286-1471

*Undersecretary of Industry and Foreign
Investment*

Subsecretario de Comercio Exterior
SECOFI
Alfonso Reyes 30
Piso 12
06179 Mexico, DF
(5) 286-1461

Undersecretary of Foreign Trade

SECOFI Industry and Sector Specialists

Agrochemical:	(5) 683-4417
Audiovisual:	(5) 593-6563
Automotive Parts:	(5) 683-5168
Automotive Technical Control:	(5) 683-5168
Automotive Transportation and Control:	(5) 683-4449
Basic Chemicals:	(5) 683-4046
Maquiladora and Border Industry:	(5) 595-5136
Capital and Consumption Goods:	(5) 683-3251

Cellulose and Paper: (5) 683-4046
Chemicals: (5) 683-3001
Commercial and Office
  Equipment: (5) 595-6563
Computers: (5) 683-4521
Diversified Transportation: (5) 683-8402
Dress and Apparel Industry: (5) 683-4985
Electronics and Components: (5) 683-4521
Electronics: (5) 683-4644
Electronic Machinery and
  Equipment: (5) 595-9667
Food Additives: (5) 683-4417
Food and Beverages: (5) 683-4417
Forest-Related Industries: (5) 683-4985
Health Auxiliary Products: (5) 595-1628
Heavy Machinery: (5) 683-7055
Industrial Coordination: (5) 683-4521
Iron and Steel Products: (5) 683-7055
Machinery and Equipment: (5) 595-9667
Maquiladora Industry: (5) 683-2982
Mechanical Equipment and
  Machinery: (5) 595-9667
Medicine and Health
  Products: (5) 595-1628
Metal Products: (5) 683-7055
Microindustries: (5) 595-3091
Nonmetallic Minerals: (5) 683-4046
Petrochemicals: (5) 683-3375
Pharmaceuticals and
  Foodstuffs: (5) 595-1628
Plastic Resin and Fiber: (5) 683-3375
Regional Development: (5) 683-2982
Rubber and Petroleum
  Derivatives: (5) 683-3375
Small and Medium
  Industries: (5) 595-1941
Tanning and Leather: (5) 683-4985
Telecommunications: (5) 595-6563
Textiles: (5) 683-4985

SECOFI State Offices

Aquascalientes

SECOFI
Morelos 224
20000 Aguascalientes, AGS
(49) 520-24

Baja California Sur

SECOFI
5 de Mayo y Madero 190

23000 La Paz, BCS
(682) 206-44

Baja California Norte

SECOFI
Calle 3-A-1030
22800 Ensenada, BC
(65) 401-18

SECOFI
Palacio Federal
Piso 1, Cuerpo A
21000 Mexicali, BC
(65) 574-891

SECOFI
Calle 6 y Av. Ocampo 2214
22000 Tijuana, BC
(66) 851-621

Campeche

SECOFI
Av. 16 de Septiembre
24000 Campeche, CAM
(981) 621-30

Chiapas

SECOFI
Palacio Federal
Piso 3
29000 Tuxtla Gutiérrez, CHIS
(961) 203-98

Chihuahua

SECOFI
Av. Universidad 3705
31170 Chihuahua, CHI
(14) 138-047

SECOFI
Tomas Alba Edison Esq. Malecón
32000 Juárez, CHI
(161) 675-62

Coahuila

SECOFI
Matamoros y Galeana Loc. 4 y 5
26000 Cd. Acuña, COA
(877) 224-41

SECOFI
Aldama 709 Pte.
25000 Saltillo, COA
(841) 203-04

SECOFI
Blvd. Independencia 2029 Ote.
27100 Torreón, COA
(17) 737-83

Colima

SECOFI
Av. Rialfer y Blvd. D. Ordaz
30730 Tapachula, COL
(962) 531-89

Durango

SECOFI
Av. Circunvalación y Av. Normal 99
34000 Durango, DUR
(181) 231-98

SECOFI
Morelos 326 Ote.
Piso 5
35000 Gómez Palazio, DUR
(171) 425-65

Guanajuato

SECOFI
Carr. Guanajuato Marfil Km. 1, 5
36000 Guanajuato, GTO
(473) 239-45

SECOFI
Constitución 103 y Pino Suárez
37000 León, GTO
(471) 471-97

Guerrero

SECOFI
José Valdes Arévalo 7
39300 Acapulco, GRO
(748) 361-12

SECOFI
5 de Mayo e Hidalgo 9
39000 Chilpancingo, GRO
(747) 220-77

SECOFI
Av. John Kennedy 124
42000 Taxco de Alarcón, GRO
(732) 231-58

Hidalgo

SECOFI
Plaza Independencia Sur 1035

42000 Pachuca, HID
(36) 190-098

Jalisco

SECOFI
Calz. Independencia Sur 1035
44460 Guadalajara, JAL
(36) 192-204

Mexico

SECOFI
Plaza Fray Andres de Castro
5000 Toluca, MEX
(721) 587-74

SECOFI
Bravo Esq. 2a Cda de Bravo
Piso 2
56100 Texcoco, MEX
(595) 416-73

Michoacán

SECOFI
Blvd. Garciá de León 1521
58000 Morelia, MIC
(451) 514-58

SECOFI
Andador Río Cutzamala 1
60950 Cd. Lázaro Cárdenas, MIC
(743) 214-20

Morelos

SECOFI
Av. Heroico Colegio Militar
62250 Cuernavaca, MOR
(73) 170-741

Nayarit

SECOFI
Allende 100 Ote.
Piso 1
63000 Tepic, NAY
(321) 250-32

Nuevo León

SECOFI
Margarita Maza de Juárez y Corregidora
67100 Cd. Guadelupe, NL
(83) 544-096

Oaxaca

SECOFI
Gardenias 15
7000 Juchitán, OAX
(971) 201-79

SECOFI
Xicoténcatl 419
68000 Oaxaca, OAX
(951) 626-86

Puebla

SECOFI
Calle 13 Sur 301
72000 Puebla, PUE
(22) 420-391

Querétaro

SECOFI
Wenceslao de la Barquera 13
76000 Querétaro, QUE
(463) 438-68

Quintana Roo

SECOFI
Av. Xel-ha Super Manzana 28
77500 Benito Juárez, QROO
(988) 417-47

SECOFI
Av. Heroes y Lázaro Cárdenas
77000 Othon P. Blanco, QROO
(983) 230-56

San Luis Potosí

SECOFI
Zamarripa 1381
78000 Cd. Valle, SLP
(481) 508-98

Sinaloa

SECOFI
Nicolas Bravo 402 Esq. Juan
  José Rios
80200 Culiacan, SIN
(671) 665-85

SECOFI
Angel Flores 117 Nte.
81200 Los Mochis, SIN
(681) 234-19

SECOFI
21 de Marzo 808 Pte.
82000 Mazatlán, SIN
(678) 139-72

Sonora

SECOFI
5 de Febrero 634 y 636 Sur
85000 Cd. Obregón, SON
(641) 440-44

SECOFI
Blvd. Navarrete 138-B
83200 Hermosillo, SON
(621) 639-96

SECOFI
Av. Obregón 360
84000 Nogales, SON
(631) 314-55

Tabasco

SECOFI
Vía B. Méndez 722-A
86000 Villa Hermosa, TAB
(931) 213-58

Tamaulipas

SECOFI
Pedro Méndez Ote. 308
89800 Cd. Mante, TAM
(123) 213-88

SECOFI
Palacio Federal
Piso 1
87000 Cd. Victoria, TAM
(131) 270-62

SECOFI
Lauro Villar 198
87390 Matamoros, TAM
(891) 323-19

SECOFI
Av. Guerrero 2902
88250 Nuevo León, TAM
(871) 401-96

SECOFI
Blvd. Morelos 1020
88630 Peynosa, TAM
(892) 432-37

SECOFI
Av. Hidalgo 2808
Piso 1
89230 Tampico, TAM
(121) 368-33

Tlaxcala

SECOFI
Av. Juarez 24
90000 Tlaxcala, TLA
(246) 257-25

Veracruz

SECOFI
Zaragoza 106
96400 Coatzacoalcos, VER
(921) 200-28

SECOFI
Clavjero 1 Esq. Ávila Camacho
91000 Jalapa, VER
(281) 788-39

SECOFI
Av. 6 Norte 21
53400 Poza Rica, VER
(782) 230-28

SECOFI
Av. Juarez 13
Piso 1
92800 Tuxpan, VER
(783) 401-59

SECOFI
Av. 5 de Mayo y Ocampo
91700 Veracruz, VER
(29) 324-513

Yucatán

SECOFI
Av. Colón 501
97000 Mérida, YUC
(992) 568-22

Zacatecas

SECOFI
Av. González Ortega 126
98000 Zacatecas, ZAC
(492) 212-14

Secretary of Energy, Mines, and Parastatal Industries (SEMIP)

Dirección de Negociaciones
   Internacionales
SEMIP
Francisco Marquez 160
Piso 5
06140 Mexico, DF
(5) 553-9029

Office of International Negotiations

Dirección de Catastro y Registro
SEMIP
Arcos de Belen 30 Mezzanine
06720 Mexico, DF
(5) 578-9084

Office of Claims and Registration

Dirección de Información
SEMIP
Av. Insurgentes Sur 552
Piso 1
06769 Mexico, DF
(5) 564-9749

Office of Information

Dirección de Estudios y Proyectos
   Internacionales
SEMIP
Francisco Marquez 160
Piso 5
06140 Mexico, DF
(5) 553-9044

Office of Research and International Projects

Dirección General de Asuntos
   Internacionales
SEMIP
Francisco Marquez 160
Piso 5
06140 Mexico, DF
(5) 553-3815

General Office of International Affairs

Secretario de Pesca
SEMIP
Av. Álvaro Obregón 269
Piso 1

06709 Mexico, DF
(5) 208-9970

Secretary of Fisheries

Secretary of Fisheries
Embassy of Mexico
1911 Pennsylvania Ave., NW
2nd Floor
Washington, DC 20006
(202) 728-1607

U.S. office

Director General de Acuacultura
Priv de Trini 10
10200 Mexico, DF
(5) 683-0541

Director General of Aquaculture

Comisión Nacional del Agua
Av. Pimentel No. 1
Piso 2
Col. San Angel
01070 Mexico, DF
(5) 660-7079

National Water Commission

Secretariat of Foreign Relations

Embassy of Mexico in the U.S.
1911 Pennsylvania Ave., NW
Washington, DC 20006
(202) 728-1600

Dirección de Asuntos Migratorios y
　Derechos Humanos
SRE
Ricardo Flores Magón 1
Piso 17
06995 Mexico, DF
(5) 782-4080

*Office of Migratory Affairs and Human
Rights*

Dirección de Cooperación Técnica y
　Cientifica
SRE
Ricardo Flores Magon 1
Piso 9
06995 Mexico, DF
(5) 593-5318

*Office of Scientific and Technical
Cooperation*

Dirección General de Información
SRE
Ricardo Flores Magon 1
Piso 1
06995 Mexico, DF
(5) 782-3765

Office of Information

Dirección General de Asuntos Consulares
SRE
Ricardo Flores Magon 1
Piso 9
06995 Mexico, DF
(5) 782-4724

Office of Consular Affairs

See also Mexican Consulates in the United
States

Secretary of Communication and Transportation

Secretario de Communicaciones y
　Transportes
SCT
Av. Universidad esq. Xola Centro, Piso 1
03028 Mexico, DF
(5) 519-7456

Secretary's office

Dirección General de Normas de Sistemas
　de Comunicación
SCT
Av. Universidad esq. Xola Centro
Piso 1
03028 Mexico, DF
(5) 530-4315

Office of Broadcasting Standards

Dirección General de Aeronautica Civil
SCT
Providencia 807
Piso 6
03100 Mexico, DF
(5) 687-7660

Office of Civil Aviation

Dirección General de Carreteras Federales
SCT
Altadena 23
Piso 1

03810 Mexico, DF
(5) 687-1990

Office of Federal Highways

Dirección General de Transporte Terrestre
SCT
Calz de las Bombas 411
Piso 11
04920 Mexico, DF
(5) 684-0757

Office of Land Transportation

Dirección General de la Policía
Federal de Caminos y Puertos
SCT
Calz de las Bombas 411
Edif. Anexo
04920 Mexico, DF
(5) 684-0682

Office of Federal Port and Highway Police

Dirección General de Puertos y Marina
Mercante
SCT
Municipio Libre 377 Ala A
Piso 6
03310 Mexico, DF
(5) 688-8920

Office of Ports and Merchant Marine

Dirección General de Construcción y
Conservación de Obra Pública
SCT
Av. Cuauhtémoc 614
Piso 5
03020 Mexico, DF
(5) 530-6970

*Office of Construction and Conservation of
Public Works*

Dirección General de Proyectos Servicios
Técnicos y Concesiones
SCT
Av. Coyoacán 1895
03240 Mexico, DF
(5) 524-3481

*Office of Technical Service Projects and
Concessions*

Dirección General de Tarifas
SCT
Eugenia 197
Piso 10

03020 Mexico, DF
(5) 687-5920

Office of Tariffs

Dirección General de Fomento de las
Telecomunicaciones e Información
SCT
Av. San Francisco 1626
Piso 7
03100 Mexico, DF
(5) 534-1979

*Office of Telecommunications and
Information*

Dirección General de la Unidad de
Inspección de Obra y Operación
SCT
Av. Universidad esq. Xola Centro
SCOP, Cuerpo B
03028 Mexico, DF
(5) 519-9103

Office of Public Works Inspection

Subsecretario de Infraestructura
SCT
Av. Universidad esq. Xola Centro
SCOP, Cuerpo C
03028 Mexico, DF
(5) 519-8266

Undersecretary of Infrastructure

Subsecretario de Transporte
SCT
Av. Universidad esq. Xola Centro
SCOP, Cuerpo C
03028 Mexico, DF
(5) 559-5165

Undersecretary of Transportation

Secretary of the Comptroller General (SCGF)

Dirección de Información
SCGF
Insurgentes Sur 1735 Ala Norte-12 PB
01028 Mexico, DF
(5) 534-6804

Director of Information

Dirección de Auditorías a Adquisiciones
SCGF
Insurgentes Sur 1735 Ala Norte-208

01028 Mexico, DF
(5) 682-5340

Office of Acquisitions Auditing

Dirección General de Auditoria
  Gubernamental
SCGF
Insurgentes Sur 1735 Ala Norte-826
01028 Mexico, DF
(5) 524-9038

Office of Government Auditing

Dirección de Auditoría a Obras Públicas
SCGF
Insurgentes Sur 1735 Ala Norte-202A
01028 Mexico, DF
(5) 682-6869

Office of Public Works Auditing

Dirección del Centro de Información y
  Documentación
SCGF
Barranca del Muerto 234
01020 Mexico, DF
(5) 524-2885

Documents and Information Center

Secretary of Education (SEP)

Secretario de Educación Pública
SEP
República de Argentina 28
Piso 2-310
06029 Mexico, DF
(5) 521-9574

Secretary's office

Dirección General de Relaciones
  Internacionales
SEP
República de Argentina 28
Piso 1-241
06029 Mexico, DF
(5) 512-6647

Office of International Relations

Dirección General de Planeación,
  Programación y Presupuesto
SEP
Francisco Petrarca 321
Piso 11

11570 Mexico, DF
(5) 203-1680

*Office of Planning, Programming and
Budget*

Dirección de Derechos de Autor
SEP
Mariano Escobedo 438
Piso 7
Col. Nueva Ansuras
11590 Mexico, DF
(5) 250-0380, 250-0291

Office of Copyright Registration

Dirección General de Profesionales
SEP
Insurgentes Sur No. 2367
Piso 2
Col. San Angel
01000 Mexico, DF
(5) 550-0401

*Authorization and Registration of Foreign
Professionals*

Secretary of Health (SS)

Secretario de Salud
Lieja 7
Piso 1
Col. Juárez
06696 Mexico, DF
(5) 553-6967

Secretary's office

Dirección General de Salud Ambiental
SS
San Luis Potosí 192
Piso 4
06700 Mexico, DF
(5) 584-6745

Office of Environmental Health

Dirección General de Asuntos Sectoriales
  e Internacionales
SS
Lieja 8
Piso 11
06696 Mexico, DF
(5) 553-7656

Office of Sectoral and International Affairs

Subsecretario de Regulación y Fomento
  Sanitario

SS
Lieja 7
Piso 1
06696 Mexico, DF
(5) 553-6979

*Undersecretary of Regulation and Health
Promotion*

Dirección General de Control Sanitario de
   Bienes y Servicios
SS
Donceles 39
Piso 1
Col. Centro
06000 Mexico, DF
(5) 581-9717

*Office of Sanitation Control
(Issues SSA number)*

Dirección General de Control de Insumos
   para la Salud
SS
Insurgentes Sur 1397
Piso 3
Col. Guadalupe Inn
06500 Mexico, DF
(5) 553-2977, 553-9481

*Office of Medical Device, Pharmaceutical,
Food and Beverage Registration*

Laboratorio Nacional de Salud Pública
Tlalpán 4492
Col. Toriello Guerra
14050 Mexico, DF
(5) 573-3720

National Health Laboratory

Secretary of Government (SG)

Secretario de Gobernación
Bucareli 99
Piso 1
06699 Mexico, DF
(5) 566-0262

Secretary's office

Dirección del Diario Oficial
General Prim 43
Piso 1
06699 Mexico, DF
(5) 566-5342

Office of the Official Journal

Secretary of Labor and Social Welfare (STPS)

Dirección General de Inspección
STPS
Carr al Ajusco Km. 1.5-174
14209 Mexico, DF
(5) 652-5962

Office of Inspection

Dirección General de Registro de
   Asociaciones
STPS
Carr al Ajusco Km 1.5-174
14209 Mexico, DF
(5) 652-3735

Office of Association Registration

Secretary of Finance and Public Credit (SHCP)

Secretario de Hacienda y Crédito Público
SHCP
Palacio Nacional Primer Patio
Piso 3-3045
06066 Mexico, DF
(5) 518-5420

Secretary's office

Dirección General de Aduanas
SHCP
Av. 20 de Noviembre 195
Piso 8
06090 Mexico, DF
(5) 709-6185

Office of Customs

Dirección General de Seguros y Valores
SHCP
Av. Hidalgo 77
Edif. M-3 Ala Sur PB
06020 Mexico, DF
(5) 521-3938

Office of Securities and Insurance

Coordinator General de la Unidad de
   Desincorporación
SHCP
Palacio Nacional Patio Central
Piso 3-3012

06066 Mexico, DF
(5) 510-1994

Office of Privatization

Subsecretario de Asuntos Financieros
  Internacionales
SHCP
Palacio Nacional Primer Patio Mariano
Piso 4-403
06066 Mexico, DF
(5) 542-1300

Undersecretary for International Fianncial Affairs

Budget and Planning Office

Jefe del Departmento de Registro de
  Proveedores de la Administración
  Pública
Secretaría de Programación y Presupuesto
San Antonio Abad No. 124
Piso 1
Col. Tránsito
06820 Mexico, DF
(5) 740-7840, ext. 519 and 532, or 740-
  2431

Registration for doing business with the government

Programación y Presupuesto (SPP)
SHCP
Palacio Nacional Patio de Honor
Piso 4
06066 Mexico, DF
(5) 512-1616

Budget and Planning Office

Dirección General de Desarrollo
  Agropecuario Pesquero y de Abasto
SHCP
Paseo Reforma 350
Piso 9
06600 Mexico, DF
(5) 286-3205

Office of Agriculture, Fisheries and Supplies

Dirección General de Salud, Educación y
  Trabajo
SHCP
Paseo Reforma 350
Piso 13

06600 Mexico, DF
(5) 286-3286

Office of Health, Education and Labor

Dirección General de Energetico e
  Industrial
SHCP
Paseo Reforma 350
Piso 11
06600 Mexico, DF
(5) 286-3894

Office of Industry and Energy

Dirección General de Infraestructura y
  Desarrollo Humano
SHCP
Paseo Reforma 350
Piso 6
06600 Mexico, DF
(5) 286-3994

Office of Infrastructure and Human Development

Dirección General de Servicios
SHCP
Paseo Reforma 350
Piso 15
06600 Mexico, DF
(5) 286-3791

Office of Services

Dirección General de Información
SHCP
Palacio Nacional Patio Central-Anexo
Piso 4
06099 Mexico, DF
(5) 522-7508

Office of Information

Subsecretario de Desarrollo Regional
SHCP
Palacio Nacional Patio Central
Piso 4
06099 Mexico, DF
(5) 542-9008

Undersecretary of Regional Development

Secretary of Social Development (SEDESOL)

U.S. Office
Embassy of Mexico

1911 Pennsylvania Ave., NW
Washington, DC 20006
(202) 728-1770

Dirección de Asuntos Internacionales
SEDESOL
Constituyentes 947, Edif. B
Planta Alta
Col. Belen de las Flores
01110 Mexico, DF
(5) 271-4510
Office of International Affairs

Dirección de Protección del Ambiente
SEDESOL
Blvd. del Pipila No. 1
Tecamachalco
53950 Naucalpan, Edo. de Mex.
(5) 294-5950

Secretary of Tourism (SECTUR)

Subsecretario de Promoción y Fomento
SECTUR
Mariano Escobedo 726
Edif. Principal
Piso 2
Col. Anzures
11590 Mexico, DF
(5) 525-6175
*Undersecretary of Promotion and
Development*

Subsecretario de Operación
SECTUR
Presidente Masaryk 172
Piso 7
Col. Polanco
11587 Mexico, DF
(5) 250-8800
Undersecretary for Operations

Dirección Información y Difusión
SECTUR
Presidente Masaryk 172
Piso 1
Col. Polanco
11587 Mexico, DF
(5) 250-8948
Office of Information and Publicity

Dirección de Asuntos Internacionales
SECTUR

Mariano Escobedo 726
Edif. Anexo
Piso 1
Col. Anzures
11590 Mexico, DF
(5) 511-8704
Office of International Affairs

Dirección de Promoción Internacional
SECTUR
Mariano Escobedo 726
Edif. Anexo
Piso 1
Col. Anzures
11590 Mexico, DF
(5) 254-1960
Office of International Promotion

Dirección General de Promoción
SECTUR
Mariano Escobedo 726
Edif. Principal-PB
Col. Anzures
11590 Mexico, DF
(5) 511-4056
Office of Promotion

Dirección de Estadistica y Estudios de
    Mercado
SECTUR
Presidente Masaryk 172
Piso 10
Col. Ploanco
11587 Mexico, DF
(5) 250-0027
Office of Statistics and Market Studies

Coordinator del Sector Paraestatal
SECTUR
Presidente Masaryk 172
Piso 7
Col. Polanco
11587 Mexico, DF
(5) 254-0845
Coordinator of the Parastatal Sector

Mexican Government Tourism Office
70 Lake St., Ste. 1413
Chicago, IL 60601
(312) 565-2778

Mexican Government Tourism Office
128 Aragon Ave.

Coral Gables, FL 33134
(305) 443-9160

Mexican Government Tourism Office
2707 North Loop West, Ste. 450
Houston, TX 77008
(713) 880-5153

Mexican Government Tourism Office
10100 Santa Monica Blvd., Ste. 224
Los Angeles, CA 90067
(213) 203-8191

Mexican Government Tourism Office
405 Park Ave., Ste. 1402
New York, NY 10022
(212) 755-7261

Mexican Government Tourism Office
1911 Pennsylvania Ave.
Washington, DC 20006
(202) 728-1750

Fondo Nacional de Fomento al Turismo
(FONATUR)
Av. Insurgentes Sur 800
Col. del Valle
03100 Mexico, DF
(5) 660-4222

*National Fund for the Development of
Tourism*

Presidency of the Republic

Presidencia de la República
Presidente Constitucional de los Estados
Unidos Mexicanos Palacio Nacional
Patio de Honor
Piso 1
06067 Mexico, DF
(5) 522-2002

*The Constitutional President of
the United Mexican States*

Dirección de Comunicación Social
Palacio Nacional Patio Central
Piso 3
06067 Mexico, DF
(5) 522-8782

Public Relations Information Office

Dirección de Información Internacional de
Comunicación Social
Palacio Nacional Patio Central

Piso 3
06067 Mexico, DF
(5) 521-8921

*Public Relations International Information
Office*

Secretary of Defense

Secretaría de la Defensa Nacional (SDN)
Lomas de Sotelo No. 10
Lomas Hipodromo
11640 Mexico, DF
(5) 575-4500

Federal Registry of Firearms and Explosives

National Development Agency

Nacional Finaciera (NAFIN)
Insurgentes Sur 1971
Torre Sur
Piso 10
01020 Mexico, DF
(5) 325-6000

Government-Owned Companies

Compañía Nacional de Subsistencias
Populares (CONASUPO)
Av. Insurgentes Sur No. 489
Piso 6
Guadalupe Inn
06100 Mexico, DF
(5) 264-0360

Food Distribution

Comisión Federal de Electricidad (CFE)
Rib Rodano No. 14
Piso 7
06598 Mexico, DF
(5) 553-6617

PEMEX International (PMI)
Av. Marina Nacional No. 329
Piso 2
Torre Ejecutiva
Col. Anahuac
11311 Mexico, DF
(5) 250-2611

PEMEX International
3600 S. Gessner, Ste. 100

Houston, TX 77063
(713) 978-7974

Government, U.S.

Agency for International Development (AID)

Washington, DC 20523
(202) 647-4000

Export-Import Bank of the U.S. (Eximbank)

811 Vermont Ave., NW
Washington, DC 20571
(202) 566-4490
Export Financing Hotline,
(800) 424-5201

Eximbank (West Coast Office)
11000 Wilshire Blvd., Ste. 9103
Los Angeles, CA 90024
(213) 575-7425

Small Business Administration (SBA)

409 Third St., SW
Washington, DC 20416
(202) 205-6500

U.S. Department of Agriculture (USDA)

14th and Independence Ave., SW
Washington, DC 20250
(202) 720-8732

Trade Assistance and Promoting Office
(TAPO)
FAS
USDA
14th and Independence Ave., SW
Rm. 4939-S
Washington, DC 20250
(202) 720-7420, Fax: (202) 690-4374

Foreign Agricultural Service
American Embassy
Paseo de la Reforma 305
Col. Cuauhtémoc

06500 Mexico, DF
(5) 211-0042, Fax: (5) 533-6194

U.S. Mailing Address:
Foreign Agricultural Service
P.O. Box 3087
Laredo, TX 78044

Agricultural Cooperative Service
USDA
P.O. Box 96576
Washington, DC 20090
(202) 720-2556, Fax: (202) 720-4641

Animal & Plant Health Inspection (APHIS)
USDA
Import-Export Products Staff
Federal Bldg., Rm. 756
6505 Belcrest Rd.
Hyattsville, MD 20782
(301) 436-7885, Fax: (301) 436-8226

U.S. Department of Commerce (DOC)

14th and Constitution Ave., NW
Rm. 3026
Washington, DC 20230
(202) 482-2000

Foreign Commercial Service
U.S. Department of Commerce
American Embassy
Paseo de la Reforma 305
Col. Cuauhtémoc
06500 Mexico DF
(5) 211-0042, Fax: (5) 511-9980

U.S. Mailing Address:
Foreign Commercial Service
U.S. Department of Commerce
P.O. Box 3087
Laredo, TX 78044

U.S. Trade Center
Liverpool No. 31
Col. Juárez
06600 Mexico, DF
(5) 591-0155, Fax: (5) 566-1115
Trade shows

U.S. Mailing Address:
U.S. Trade Center
P.O. Box 3087
Laredo, TX 78044
Trade shows

U.S. Travel and Tourism Administration
U.S. Department of Commerce
Plaza Comermex 402
Boulevard M. Ávila Camacho No. 1
Col. Polanco Chapultepec
11560 Mexico DF
(5) 520-1194

Office of Trade Services
National Marine and Fisheries Service
U.S. Department of Commerce
1335 East-West Highway, Rm. 6490
Silver Spring, MD 20910
(301) 713-2379, Fax: (301) 588-4853

National Center for Standards and
  Certification Information
National Institute of Standards and
  Technology (NIST)
U.S. Department of Commerce
Technology Administration
Physics Building, Rm. A363
Gaithersburg, MD 20899
(301) 975-4040, Fax: (301) 963-2871
Gatt Hotline: (301) 975-4041

Office of Patent and Trademark Affairs
U.S. Department of Commerce
2121 Crystal Dr., Ste. 902
Arlington, VA 22202
(703) 305-9300

U.S. Department of Energy (DOE)

1000 Independence Ave., SW
Washington, DC 20585
(202) 586-5000

U.S. Environmental Protection Agency (EPA)

Office of International Activities
401 M St., SW
Washington, DC 20460
(202) 382-4880

U.S. Trade and Development Program

SA-16, Rm. 309
Washington, DC 20523
(703) 875-4357

U.S. Trade Representative (USTR)

600 17th St., NW, Rm. 400
Washington, DC 20506
(202) 395-7320

Grocery Store Chains

Dirección de Planeación Adjunto a la
  Presidencia
Aurrera Grupo Cifra, S.A. de C.V.
Av. Presidente Masarik No. 111
Piso 7
Col. Polanco
11560 Mexico, DF
(5) 522-0657

Jefe de Importaciones Gigante, S.A.
Ejercito Nacional No. 769-A
Col. Nueva Granada
11560 Mexico, DF
(5) 250-3011

Gerente de Compras Comercial Mexicana,
  S.A.
Calzada Chabacano No. 43
Col. Asturias
Mexico, DF
(5) 538-1145

Gerente de Compras
Centro Comercial de Todo
San Francisco No. 1621
Col. del Valle
03100 Mexico, DF
(5) 234-8100

Insurance Companies

Agentes Profesionales de Seguros
Eucken 20
06400 Mexico, DF
(5) 545-7445

Aseguradora Mexicana, S.A.
Paseo de la Reforma No. 175
Col. Cuauhtémoc
06500 Mexico, DF
(5) 703-1312

Asociación Mexicana de Agentes
Florencia 18-101

Mexico, DF
(5) 525-2975

Seguros la Comercial
Av. Insurgentes Sur No. 3900
Col. Tlalpán
14000 Mexico, DF
(5) 573-1100

Seguras Monterrey, SA
Diagonal Santa Engracía No. 221
Lomas de San Francisco
64710 Monterrey, NL
(83) 448-800

Leasing Companies

Arrendadora Hemolsa
Norte 170 No. 467
Pensador Mexicano
15510 Mexico, DF
(5) 751-1740

Arrendadora Her
Bahía de la Ascención No. 31-A
Veronica Anzures
01300 Mexico, DF
(5) 203-3552

Arrendadora Nimex
Providencia No. 503-Bis
Del Valle
03100 Mexico, DF
(5) 543-1747

Arrendadora Prime
Paseo de la Reforma No. 243
Piso 9
Col. Cuauhtémoc
06500 Mexico, DF
(5) 207-0020

Arrendadora Rama
Municipio Libre No. 161
Portales
03300 Mexico, DF
(5) 605-5707

Arrendadora Somex
Paseo de la Reforma No. 213
Piso 9
Col. Cuauhtémoc
06500 Mexico, DF
(5) 703-3257

Corporación Arrendadora
Miguel Laurent No. 615 esq. Sanchez
   Azcona
Del Valle
03100 Mexico, DF
(5) 605-9644

General Electric Capital
5400 LBJ Freeway, Ste. 1280
Dallas, TX 75240
(214) 419-3200

Grupo Promotor de Arrendamientos
San Lorenzo No. 153
Piso 1
Del Valle
03100 Mexico, DF
(5) 559-1809

Impulsora Mexicana de Arrendamientos
Paseo de la Reforma No. 136
Piso 13
Juárez
06600 Mexico, DF
(5) 592-2999, 566-9144

Multiarrendadora Mercantil
Paseo de la Reforma No. 115
Lomas de Chapultepec
11000 Mexico, DF
(5) 202-9507, 202-9573

Servicios y Arrendamientos Diversificados
Blvd. Miguel Avila Camacho No. 1994-
   702 y 703
Piso 7
San Lucas Tepetlalco
54055 Tlalnepantla, Edo. de Mex.
(5) 397-5141, 397-5152

Maquiladora/Border Commercial Assistance

Association of Mexican Industrial Parks
   (AMPIP)
P.O. Box 12245
El Paso, TX 79913
(16) 177-603, 177-979

Border Research Institute
P.O. Box 3001/3BRI
Las Cruces, NM 88003
(505) 646-3524

Border Trade Alliance
P.O. Box 220
McAllen, TX 78501
(512) 686-5536

Brownsville Chamber of Commerce
P.O. Box 752
Brownsville, TX 78520
(210) 542-4341

Brownsville Economic Development
   Council
1600 East Elizabeth
Brownsville, TX 78520
(210) 541-1183

Ciudad Juárez Economic Development
   Corp.
Adolfo de la Huerta No. 742-3
32340 Cd. Juárez, CHIH
(161) 632-68, 656-33

Ciudad Juárez Maquiladora Association
Río Nilo 4049-10, esq. López Mateos
32310 Cd. Juárez, CHIH
(161) 342-57, 614-61

Chihuahua Industrial Promotion
   Organization
Don Quijote de la Mancha No. 1
31109 Chihuahua, CHIH
(14) 175-888

Corpus Christi Area Economic
   Development Corp.
P.O. Box 640
Corpus Christi, TX 78403
(512) 883-5571

Del Rio Chamber of Commerce
1915 Ave. F
Del Rio, TX 78840
(512) 775-3551

Douglas Chamber of Commerce
1125 Pan American Ave.
P.O. Drawer F
Douglas, AZ 85607
(602) 364-2477

El Paso Industrial Development Corp.
9 Civic Center Plaza
El Paso, TX 79901
(915) 534-0523

Gallagher Enterprises
P.O. Box 3540

El Paso, TX 79923
(915) 566-6171

Greater Las Cruces Economic
   Development Council
400 S. Main St.
Las Cruces, NM 88001
(505) 524-1745

Iberman and DeForest
208 S. LeSalle
Chicago, IL 60604
(312) 263-0422
Maquila consultant

Imperial County Regional Economic
   Development, Inc.
1411 State St.
El Centro, CA 92243
(619) 353-5050

In-Bond Central, Inc.
4150 Rio Bravo, Suite 221
El Paso, TX 79902
(915) 533-9191
Recruiting services

International Gateway Insurance Brokers
3450 Bonita Rd., Ste. 101
Chula Vista, CA 92010-3209
(800) 423-2646
In CA: (619) 422-3028

Laredo Development Foundation
P.O. Box 2682
Laredo, TX 78044
(210) 722-0563

Laredo Manufacturers Association
Delmar Industrial Park
Rt. 4, Box 278W
Laredo, TX 78041
(210) 727-7200

Maquila Services Group
7661 N. Mesa
El Paso, TX 79912
(800) 992-7356

Maquilmex, Inc.
First City Bank Tower, Ste. 1111
McAllen, TX 78501
(512) 687-2464
Maquila consultant

MaquilaSoft Corp.
4190 Bonita Rd., Ste. 203

Bonita, CA 92002
(619) 470-6484

Maquila software

Maverick County Development Corp.
P.O. Box 1188
Eagle Pass, TX 78853
(512) 773-6116

McAllen Economic Development Corp.
1 Park Pl., Ste. 100
McAllen, TX 78503
(512) 682-2875

Mexicali Industrial Development
   Commission
P.O. Box No. 6343
Calexico, CA 92231
In Mex.: (655) 267-80, 257-30

Middle Rio Grande Development Council
209 N. Getty
Uvalde, TX 78801
(512) 278-2527

Nogales/Santa Cruz County
   Chamber of Commerce
Kino Park
Nogales, AZ 85621
(602) 287-3685

Port of Brownsville Directors of
   Development
P.O. Box 3070
Brownsville, TX 78523-3070
(210) 831-4592

San Diego Economic Development
   Corporation
701 B St., Ste. 1850
San Diego, CA 92101
(619) 234-8484

Servimaq
Insurgentes 5022-17
Cd. Juárez, CHIH
(161) 648-82, 348-61
In U.S.: (915) 581-3649

Maquila consultant

South Texas Development Council
P.O. Box 2187
Laredo, TX 78044
(210) 722-3995

State of Nuevo León—Proexport
Apartado Postal No. 3165
64000 Monterrey, NL
(83) 457-353

State of Tamaulipas—Office of Industrial
   Development
713 North Main St.
McAllen, TX 78501
(512) 631-2482

San Antonio World Trade Center
P.O. Box 899
San Antonio, TX 78293
(512) 225-5888

Solunet
4416 N. Mesa
El Paso, TX 79902
(915) 532-1166

Texas Department of Commerce
P.O. Box 12728
Austin, TX 78711
(512) 472-5059

Western Maquila Trade Association
P.O. Box 3746
Chula Vista, CA 91901
(619) 286-8865

Yuma Economic Development Corp.
P.O. Box 1750
Yuma, AZ 85364
(602) 783-0193

Publications

Agriculture

AgExporter
Trade Assistance and Promoting Office
   (TAPO)
FAS
U.S. Department of Agriculture
14th and Independence Ave., SW
Rm. 4939-S
Washington, DC 20250
(202) 720-7103

*Monthly publication on exporting
agriculture.
$14 per yr.*

Buyer Alert
Trade Assistance and Promoting Office
  (TAPO)
FAS
U.S. Department of Agriculture
14th and Independence Ave., SW
Rm. 4939-S
Washington, DC 20250
(202) 720-7103

A weekly newsletter that is electronically distributed to FAS officers in Mexico City who then distribute it. U.S. companies may advertise for free.

Dictionary of International Agricultural Trade
FAS
USDA
S. Bldg., Rm. 5920
Washington, DC 20250-1000
(202) 720-7937

Border Region

BorderBase
University of Texas at El Paso Institute for Manufacturing and Materials Management
El Paso, TX 79968
(915) 747-5336

Profiles of states along U.S.-Mexican border. Database.
$200.

BorderTrax
P.O. Box 251
El Paso, TX 79943
(915) 532-6212, (800) 284-4645

Monthly magazine and audio cassette on business issues along the border.
$29.95 per issue, $3.75 per cassette.

Business

Boletin Commercial
U.S. Embassy
Commercial Section
Reforma 305
06500 Mexico DF
(5) 211-0042, ext. 3739

Published quarterly. Targeted at Mexicans interested in representing U.S. firms.

Business America
Superintendent of Documents
Box 371954
Pittsburgh, PA 15250

Biweekly business magazine produced by the U.S. government. Topics include exporting highlights and calendar of events.
$53 per yr.

Business Latin America
Business Int'l Corp.
215 Park Ave., South
New York, NY 10003
(212) 460-0600

Weekly periodical on economic, political and commercial issues in Latin America.
$945 per yr.

Business Mexico
American Chamber of Commerce of
  Mexico
Lucerna 78
Col. Juárez
06600 México, DF
(5) 705-0995

Monthly publication on Mexico's investment and trade opportunities.
$114 per yr. plus $14 for delivery charges.

Commercial News USA
U.S. Dept. of Commerce
14th and Constitution Ave., NW
Rm. 1310
Washington, DC 20230
(202) 482-2000

Monthly publication that describes U.S. products that are available for export. Reaches 110,000 foreign businesses. Available in print and via electronic bulletin board.
Free.

Expansion
Sinaloa No. 149
Piso 9
524 Col. Roma Sur
06700 Mexico, DF
(5) 207-2176

Mexico's most important business magazine.
$333 per yr.

Global Glimpses
Assist International
475 Park Ave., South
26th Floor
New York, NY 10016
(212) 725-3311

Biweekly publication with information on seminars, conferences, newsletters and other resources on international trade.
$60 per yr.

Incoterms
ICC Publishing Corp., Inc.
156 Fifth Ave., Ste. 820
New York, NY 10010
(212) 206-1150

Trade terms.

A Guide to Incoterms
ICC Publishing Corp., Inc.
156 Fifth Ave., Ste. 820
New York, NY 10010
(212) 206-1150

This is a companion guide to Incoterms.

International Business
American International Publishing Co.
500 Mamaroneck Ave., Ste. 314
Harrison, NY 10528
(914) 381-7700

$59.97 per yr.

LA/C Business Bulletin
U.S. Dept. of Commerce
14th and Constitution Ave., NW
Rm. 1310
Washington, DC 20230
(202) 482-2000

Monthly publication on trade in the Latin American and Caribbean region. Also includes calendar of events.
Free.

Mexico Business Monthly
Dept. G, 52 Maplewood Ave.
Maplewood, NJ 07040
(800) 766-3949

Monthly update on business opportunities and issues.
$150 per yr.

Mexico Trade and Law Reporter
International Reports

114 E. 32nd St., Ste. 602
New York, NY 10016
(212) 685-6900

Monthly periodical on trade in Mexico with attention given to legal issues.
$475 per yr.

OECE Trade With Mexico and Central
America
National Technical Information Service
5285 Port Royal Rd.
Springfield, VA 22161
(703) 487-4650

Trade statistics produced by the Central Intelligence Agency.

U.S.-Mexico Chamber of Commerce
Newsletter
555 S. Flower St., 25th Fl.
Los Angeles, CA 90071-2326
(213) 623-7725

Monthly trade publication.

World Trade
4199 Campus Drive, Ste. 230
Irvine, CA 92715
(714) 725-0233

Monthly publication that includes information on Mexican trade and maquiladoras.

Company Directories

American Export Register
Thomas International Publishing Co., Inc.
One Penn Plaza
New York, NY 10119
(212) 290-7343

Two-volume directory of 38,000 exporters and their products.
$120.

Directory of American Companies
Operating in Mexico
American Chamber of Commerce
Lucerna No. 78, Piso 3
Col. Juárez
06600 Mexico, DF
(5) 705-0995

$155 for members, $310 for nonmembers.

Directory of American Firms Operating in
Mexico

World Trade Academy Press, Inc.
50 E. 42nd St., Ste. 509
New York, NY 10017-5480
(212) 697-4999

*Directory of Foreign Firms Operating in the
    United States*
World Trade Academy Press, Inc.
50 East 42nd St., Ste. 509
New York, NY 10017-5480
(212) 697-4999

Mexico Exporters Directory
Market Entry, Inc.
2351 Harwood, Ste. 400
Dallas, TX 75201
(214) 871-3184

*Directory of Mexican exporters. Produced
by Bancomext, Mexico's Bank for Foreign
Trade.
$50.*

Exporters Directory of Mexico
ALPC, Inc.
1762 Westwood Blvd., Ste. 400
Los Angeles, CA 90024
(800) 735-2572

Marketing in Mexico
Superintendent of Documents
U.S. Government Printing Office
Washington, DC 20402
(202) 783-3238

*Produced by the U.S. Dept. of Commerce.
$10.*

*Membership Directory of the American
    Chamber of Commerce of Mexico*
American Chamber of Commerce
Lucerna No. 78, Piso 3
Col. Juárez
06600 Mexico, DF
(5) 705-0995

*American Companies in Mexico.
$130 for members, $260 for nonmembers.*

*Mexico Export—Business to Business
    Directory*
Directorios Internacionales, S.A. de C.V.
Avenida Nuevo León 96
Piso 2
Col. Condesa

06100 Mexico, DF
(5) 553-7391, 286-7184

*Yellow pages directory of exporters.
Free of charge except shipping.*

Documentation

*U.S. International Trade Documentation
    Standardization*
National Council on International Trade
    Documentation (NCITD)
350 Broadway, Ste. 1200
New York, NY 10013
(212) 925-1400
$35.

Environmental

Ambiente
Río Lerma 277-401
Col. Cuauhtémoc
06500 Mexico, DF
(5) 211-2638
Environmental magazine.

Exporting

Export Administration Regulations
Superintendent of Documents
U.S. Government Printing Office
Washington, DC 20402
(202) 783-3238

*Annual subscriptions begin each October.
$87.*

*The Exporter's Guide to Foreign Sources
    for Credit Information*
Trade Data Reports, Inc.
6 W. 37th St.
New York, NY 10018

Export Shipping Manual
Bureau of National Affairs, Inc.
Distribution Center
Keywest Ave.
Rockville, MD 20850
(800) 372-1033

*Three-volume manual published annually
and updated weekly. All shipping and
market research info.
$524 per yr.*

Export Trading Company Guidebook
Superintendent of Documents
U.S. Government Printing Office
Washington, DC 20402
(202) 783-3238

Insider
Bureau of Export Administration
Att: OEL Insider
P.O. Box 273
U.S. Department of Commerce
Washington, DC 20044
(202) 482-4881

Regulatory updates of export licensing and controls.

Finance

Access Mexico
Cambridge Data and Development, Ltd.
307 N. Bryan St.
Arlington, VA 22201
(703) 525-3282

Book and directory. Excellent resource on Mexico's financial market.

Bolsa Mexicana de Valores
Centro de Información
Paseo de la Reforma 225 PB
Col. Cuauhtémoc
06500 México, DF
(5) 208-8174

The bolsa *provides information (often in English) through publications, faxes, and an on-line database. Highlights include:*

- *Stock exchange daily bulletins.* In Spanish only.
  $760 per yr.
- *Market indicators.* Monthly. In English. Includes investment fund performances.
  $207 per yr.
- *Trading report.* Monthly. In English. Surveys Mexican securities market.
  $190 per yr.

El Economista
Av. Coyoacán 515
Col. del Valle

03100 Mexico, DF
(5) 521-9342
Daily financial and business newspaper.

El Financiero
Lago Bolsena No. 176
Col. Anahuac
11590 Mexico, DF
Largest financial daily paper.

El Financiero Int'l
2300 S. Broadway
Los Angeles, CA 90007
(213) 747-7547
English weekly paper with highlights from El Financiero.
$140 per yr.

El Inversionista Mexicano
Felix Cuevas, 301-204
Col. del Valle
03100 Mexico, DF
(5) 534-9297
Biweekly newsletter on the stock exchange and capital markets. In Spanish only.
$260 per yr.

El Mercado de Valores
Apartado Postal 20-800
01020 Mexico, DF
(5) 510-4439
Biweekly newsletter on business issues published by Nacional Financiera. Free.

The Mexico Company Handbook
International Company Handbook
1280 S.W. 36th Ave., Ste. 3201
Pompano Beach, FL 33069
(305) 978-0553
Lists top 50 Mexican companies.

Mexico Service
International Reports
114 E. 32nd St., Ste. 602
New York, NY 10016
(212) 685-6900
Biweekly publication on Mexico's domestic and foreign investment.
$575 per yr.

Mexletter
Aptdo. Postal 10-711

11000 Mexico, DF
(5) 540-0795

*Monthly newsletter on leading financial
indicators.*
$45 per yr.

Franchises

Franchise Opportunities Handbook
Superintendent of Documents
U.S. Government Printing Office
Washington, DC 20402
(202) 783-3238
Stock No. 003-009-0096-5

$16.

Franquicias: La Revolución de los 90s
Asociación Mexicana de Franquicias
Insurgentes Sur No. 1783-303
Col. Guadalupe Inn
01020 Mexico, DF
(5) 524-8043

Notifranquicias
Asociación Mexicana de Franquicias
Insurgentes Sur No. 1783-303
Col. Guadalupe Inn
01020 Mexico, DF
(5) 524-8043

Monthly newsletter.

Free Trade Zones

Tax Free Trade Zones of the World
Matthew Bender and Co.
International Division
1275 Broadway
New York, NY 12204
(800) 424-4200

*Publication with information and listings of
zones and ports.*

General Information

Country Profile Report: Mexico
Dun's Marketing Services
2 Sylvan Way
Parsippany, NJ 07054
(800) 526-0651

Book with general information on Mexico.
$149.

Country Report: Mexico
Business International Corp.
215 Park Ave., South
New York, NY 10003
(212) 460-0600

Quarterly.
$295 per yr.

Country Risk Service: Mexico
Business International Corp.
215 Park Ave. South
New York, NY 10003
(212) 460-0600

*Quarterly report on the political and
economic situation.*

Databank
American Chamber of Commerce of
    Mexico
Lucerna 78
Col. Juárez
06600 Mexico, DF
(5) 705-0995

Bilingual databank of economic indicators.
$100.

*Latin American Regional Reports: Central
    America and Mexico*
Latin American Newsletters, Ltd.
91 Charterhouse St.
London EC1, England
(1) 251-0012

*Ten issues on political, economic and
financial information.*
$90 per yr.

Mexican Agenda
Dirección de Publicaciones
Palma 40, Piso 7
06000 Mexico, DF

*A yearly publication of the Mexican
presidency discussing the government's
reforms.*
Free.

Mexico Country Report
International Reports
114 E. 32nd St., Ste. 602
New York, NY 10016
(212) 685-6900

Annual economic report.
$390.

Mexico Watch
The Heritage Foundation
214 Massachusetts Ave., NE
Washington, DC 20002
(202) 546-4400

A monthly publication on political and economic issues involving the United States and Mexico.

The Times of the Americas
1001 Connecticut Ave., NW, Ste. 710
Washington, DC 20036
(202) 293-2849

Newspaper printed bimonthly. Covers political, economic and social issues in Latin America and the Caribbean. $25 per yr.

Industry/Manufacturing

Boletín Industrial
Editorial Nova, S.A.
Goldsmith No. 37-403
11550 Mexico DF
(5) 540-1642

Mexican industrial bulletin.

Mexico Product Guide
DePaula Publishing
421 7th Ave., Ste. 1206
New York, NY 10001
(212) 629-4541

Lists Mexican products, from raw materials to technology.

Transformación
Cámara Nacional de la Industria de la
   Transformación (CANACINTRA)
Av. San Antonio 256
Piso 2
Col. Ampliación Napoles
03849 Mexico, DF
(5) 563-3400

Labor

Survey of Salaries
American Chamber of Commerce
Lucerna No. 78
Piso 3
Col. Juárez

06600 Mexico, DF
(5) 705-0995

*Provides information on salaries at all levels of business.
$112 for members, $225 for nonmembers.*

Legal Issues

Mexican Legal Databank
Instituto Mexicano de Estrategicas, S.C.
Costado Atrio de San Francisco 28
Col. Coyoacán
04320 Mexico, DF
(5) 544-5792

Databank on Mexican legislation.

Maquiladoras

The Complete Twin Plant Guide
Solunet
4416 North Mesa
El Paso, TX 79902
(915) 532-1166

*A three-volume directory of maquiladoras with product descriptions.
$69.95 per volume, $195 for 3 volumes.*

*Location Decisions Regarding the
   Maquiladora In-Bond Plants Operating
   in Baja California, Mexico*
Institute for Regional Studies
San Diego State University
San Diego, CA 92182
(619) 594-5423

*Report.
$20.*

Maquiladora Handbook
American Chamber of Commerce of
   Mexico, S.A.
Lucerna 78
Pisos 3 y 4
Col. Juárez
06600 Mexico, DF
(5) 705-0995

*Handbook for establishing a maquiladora.
$130 for members, $260 for nonmembers.*

*Maquiladora Resource Guide: Exploring
   the Mexican In-Bond/Maquiladora
   Option in Baja California, Mexico*

Institute for Regional Studies
San Diego, CA 92182
(619) 549-5423

Information on maquiladoras and how to establish one. Directory.
$30.

Maquila Magazine
114 S. Oregon St.
El Paso, TX 79901
(915) 542-0103

Maquila Newsletter
American Chamber of Commerce of
  Mexico, S.A.
Lucerna 78
Pisos 3 y 4
06040 Mexico, DF
(5) 705-0995

The Source Book
P.O. Box 120182
San Antonio, TX 78212
(800) 274-3639

An excellent reference book.

Twin Plant News
Nibbe, Hernandez and Associates, Inc.
4110 Rio Bravo Dr., Ste. 108
El Paso, TX 79902
(915) 532-1567

Monthly magazine on maquiladora issues.
$65 per yr.

Who's Where in Mexico: A Roster of
  Maquiladora Management
Maquilla Magazine
114 S. Oregon
El Paso, TX 79901
(915) 542-0103

Lists names and positions within maquiladora management.

North American Free Trade Agreement

Free Trade Advisory
International Reports
114 E. 32nd St., Ste. 602

New York, NY 10016
(212) 685-6900

Biweekly publication on NAFTA and its effects.
$475 per yr.

How the North American Free Trade
  Agreement Creates Jobs.
The Heritage Foundation
214 Massachusetts Ave., NE
Washington, DC 20002
(202) 546-4400

Report.

Moving Toward Free Trade
International Reports
114 E. 32nd St., Ste. 602
New York, NY 10016
(212) 685-6900

Report on NAFTA.
$175.

NAFTA Review
U.S. Trade Representative
600 17th St., NW
Washington, DC 20206
(202) 395-3350

Describes details and steps in the NAFTA negotiations.
Free.

The North American Free Trade Agreement
Superintendent of Documents
U.S. Government Printing Office
Washington, DC 20402
(202) 783-3238

An actual copy of the agreement with tariff phaseout schedules.
$106.08.

North American Free Trade Association
  Newsletter
1130 Connecticut Ave., NW, Ste. 500
Washington, DC 20036
(202) 296-3019

Monthly newsletter on issues relating to NAFTA.

Trade Talks with Mexico: A Time for
  Realism
National Planning Association
1424 16th St., NW

Washington, DC 20009
(202) 265-7685

Book on NAFTA negotiations.
$15.

U.S.-Mexican Industrial Integration: The
   Road to Free Trade
Westview Press
5500 Central Ave.
Boulder, CO 80301
(303) 449-3541

Essays on NAFTA issues.

U.S.-Mexico Free Trade Issues for
   Agriculture
Texas Agricultural Market
Research Center
Texas A&M University
College Station, TX 77813
(409) 845-5911

A collection of studies.

Taxes

Doing Business in Mexico
Price Waterhouse
1251 Ave. of the Americas
New York, NY 10020
(212) 819-5000

Free.

Mexico Tax Letter
Touche Ross Int'l
1633 Broadway
New York, NY 10019

(212) 489-1600

Tax Guide to the Americas
Arthur Andersen and Co.
1330 43rd St.
Distribution Center
Chicago, IL 60609
(312) 523-5960

Free.

Tourism

Tourism Investment in Mexico
Institute for Regional Studies
San Diego State University

San Diego, CA 92182
(619) 594-5423

Report.
$45.

Real Estate Companies

Administraciones Polanco
Homero 1804-203
11510 Mexico, DF
(5) 580-0854

Arrendadora Sipco
Carr Saltillo Km. 339-117
66100 Monterrey, NL
(83) 363-245

Commercial

Asesores en Inversiones
Av. Lázaro Cárdenas 2400
66220 Garza García, NL
(83) 634-335

Bienes Raíces de Chihuahua
Independencia 2232
31000 Chihuahua, CHIH
(14) 123-537

Bienes Raíces La Urbana
Paseo Reforma 171
Piso 4
06500 Mexico, DF
(5) 592-7135

Bosques de Las Lomas
Paseo Reforma 2165
11000 Mexico, DF
(5) 596-0278

Century 21
Marsella 570-303
44150 Guadalajara, JAL
(36) 151-552

Century 21 Navarro
Matamoros 1538 Pte.
Piso 1
64010 Monterrey, NL
(83) 332-555

Consultar Profesional
R. Sandoval 57-301

53100 Mexico, DF
(5) 572-1726

Commercial

Despacho Heredia y Ortiz
Juárez 97, Edif. A 302
06700 Mexico, DF
(5) 512-6206

Inmobiliaria Humboldt
Libertad 1413
31000 Chihuahua, CHIH
(14) 152-356

Proveedora de Servicios
Ramal Ferrocarril 501-A
44900 Guadalajara, JAL
(36) 120-838

Commercial

Técnica Inmobiliaria
Bajio 167-BIS
06700 Mexico, DF
(5) 264-5821

Commercial

Stock Exchange and Securities Commission

Bolsa Mexicana de Valores
Paseo de la Reforma No. 255
Col. Cuauhtémoc
06500 Mexico, DF
(5) 208-8174

Mexican Stock Exchange

Comisión Nacional de Valores
Barranca del Muerto No. 255
Mexico, DF
(5) 593-9855

National Securities Commission

Telecommunications

AT&T International Mexico
Campos Eliseos 345-PH 2
11570 Mexico, DF
(5) 202-7097

Digital Sistemas Telefónicos
Lázaro Cárdenas 2400-A-12

66220 Monterrey, NL
(83) 633-458

NEC de Mexico
Jaime Balmes 11, Torre A
11510 Mexico, DF
(5) 395-7740

Cellular

Norcel Telefónia Celular del Norte
Av. Independencia 1401
31000 Chihuahua, CHIH
(14) 154-444

Cellular

Radio Movil DIPSA, S.A. de C.V.
Av. Nuevo León No. 202
Piso 9
Col. Hiprodromo Condesa
06140 Mexico DF
(5) 273-0754

TELCEL, Cellular Regions 1–9)

Radiomovil Dipsa
Calle 12 No. 606
31000 Chihuahua, CHIH
(14) 123-890

TELCEL (Telefónos de México)
Río Panuco 55
Piso 5
06500 Mexico, DF
(5) 703-3775

Cellular

Teleindustrias Ericsson
Av. Colón 1505 Pte.
64000 Monterrey, NL
(83) 311-111

Video Com Internacional
Moras 738
03100 Mexico, DF
(5) 534-3701

Transportation

Maritime Transport

Central de Fletes Monterrey, S.A. de C.V.
Av. Uranio No. 275
Unidad Industrial Vallejo
07700 Mexico, DF
(5) 754-2400

Coordinadores Maritimos Internacionales,
S.A. de C.V. (COMAR)
Manzanillo 83-401
Col. Roma
06700 Mexico, DF
(5) 564-6940

Grupo Maritimo Tolteca, S.A. de C.V.
Paseo de las Palmas No. 755
Piso 2
Col. Lomas
11000 Mexico, DF
(5) 202-7589, 202-0609

Nautomar, S.A. de C.V.
Tuxpan 2-504
Col. Roma Sur
06760 Mexico, DF
(5) 564-4802

Representaciones Transpacificas
Paseo Palmas 751
Piso 5
11010 Mexico, DF
(5) 520-2887

Representaciones Transpacificas
Aduana 203 Sur-102 Edif. Philco
89000 Tampico, TAM
(12) 140-830

Transportación Maritima Mexicana, S.A. de
C.V. (TMM)
Av. de la Cuspide No. 4755
Col. Parques del Pedregal
14010, Mexico, DF
(5) 606-0139, 606-0444

Transportación Maritima Mexicana, S.A. de
C.V. (TMM)
Zaragosa Sur 1300
64000 Monterrey, NL
(83) 427-505

Railroads

Atchison Topeka & Santa Fe Railway Co.
Amberes 4-5
06600 Mexico, DF
(5) 514-9564

Ferrocarril Chihuahua al Pacifico
Mendez y Calle 24
31000 Chihuahua, CHIH

(14) 122-284

Ferrocarriles del Pacifico, S.A. de C.V.
Enrique Díaz de León 336
44171 Guadalajara, JAL
(36) 256-823

Ferrocarriles Nacionales de México
Estación Central
06358 Mexico, DF
(5) 541-5060

Ferrocarriles Nacionales de México
Washington y 16 de Septiembre
Sector Hidalgo
44100 Guadalajara, JAL
(36) 125-291

Ferrocarriles Nacionales de México
Manuel L. Barragán 4859 Nte.
64000 Monterrey, NL
(83) 510-532, 516-262

Southern Pacific Transportation Co.
Napoles No. 36-401
06600 Mexico, DF
(5) 511-9283, 208-9966

Southern Pacific Transportation Co.
Chapultepec Sur No. 223-18
44100 Guadalajara, JAL
(36) 255-109

Southern Pacific Transportation Co.
Edif. la Nacional 315
64000 Monterrey, NL
(83) 405-545

The Texas Mexican Railways Co.
Av. de la Cuspide No. 4755
Piso 8
Col. Pedregal
14010 Mexico, DF
(5) 652-4111

The Texas Mexican Railways Co.
Tolsa No. 336
44100 Guadalajara, JAL
(36) 256-823

The Texas Mexican Railways Co.
Edif. la Nacional No. 204
64000 Monterrey, NL
(83) 433-305

Union Pacific Railroad Co.
Homero No. 1804-802

Col. Polanco
11560 Mexico, DF
(5) 557-4894, 395-7662

Union Pacific Railroad Co.
Juárez Sur No. 800-608
64000 Monterrey, NL
(83) 430-184

Shipping Lines

Agencia de Buques Internacional Barranca
del Muerto 525
Piso 3
01660 Mexico, DF
(5) 660-7673

Agencias Generales Maritimas
Amberes 38-A 201
06600 Mexico, DF
(5) 533-5888

Agencias Generales Maritimas
Hidalgo 922-A-Pte.
64000 Monterrey, NL
(83) 408-481

Nevemar
Homero 425-501
11510 Mexico, DF
(5) 395-9550

Representaciones Transpacificas
Paseo Palmas 751
Piso 5
11010 Mexico, DF
(5) 520-2887

Representaciones Transpacificas
Aduana 203 Sur, 102 Edif. Philco
89000 Tampico, TAM
(12) 140-830

Trafimar
Emilio Carranza 732 Sur
64000 Monterrey, NL
(83) 438-341

Trucking Companies

Autolineas Mexicanas, S.A. de C.V.
Calzado Vallejo 296
Mexico, DF
(5) 355-0300

Autolineas Mexicanas, S.A. de C.V.
Dr. R. Mechel 2154
Entre Río Totolán y Atotonilco
Guadalajara, JAL
(36) 575-761

Autolineas Mexicanas, S.A. de C.V.
Guerero Nte. 3530
64500 Monterrey, NL:
(83) 513-260

Camionera Regional
Lincoln y Napoles
Monterrey, NL: (83) 711-260
Tlalnepantla, MEX: (5) 369-0395
Nuevo Laredo, TAM: (87) 955-12

Carolina Freight Carriers
P.O. Box 697
Cherryville, NC 28021
(800) 532-0091
Mexico, DF: (5) 264-8709
Monterrey, NL: (83) 733-041
Guadalajara, JAL: (36) 159-044

Consolidated Freightways
3240 Hillview Ave.
Palo Alto, CA 94304
(415) 494-2900
Mexico Division: (905) 514-8127
Monterrey, NL: (83) 711-843
Guadalajara, JAL: 120-567

Hub City Rio Grande Terminals
8209 Roughrider, Ste. 200
San Antonio, TX 78239
(512) 656-5520
Mexico, DF: (5) 754-6571
Monterrey, NL: (83) 382-194

Lineas Unidas de Sur, S.A. de C.V.
Torno 89
15840 Mexico, DF
(5) 768-0022

Lineas Unidas de Sur, S.A. de C.V.
Carr. Constitución de 1917, No. 305
Nuevo Laredo, TAM
(871) 206-74

Lineas Unidas de Sur, S.A. de C.V.
Cuauhtémoc No. 213
Acapulco, GRO
(748) 501-22

Roadway Express
1077 Gorge Blvd.
P.O. Box 471
Akron, OH 44309
(216) 384-1717
Mexico, DF: (5) 536-9155
Monterrey, NL: (83) 353-166
Guadalajara, JAL: (36) 159-251

Transportes Aguila de Oro, S.A. de C.V.
Poniente 108 Bi. 559
Industrial Vallejo
Mexico, DF
(5) 567-8260
Guadalajara, JAL: (36) 576-082
Monterrey, NL: (83) 591-020
Nuevo Laredo, TAM: (871) 469-71

Tansportes Nuevo Laredo
Eje Central Lazáro Cárdenas 733
Unidad Industrial Vallejo
07700 Mexico, DF
(5) 586-6500
Guadalajara, JAL: (36) 451-274
Monterrey, NL: (83) 523-540
Nuevo Laredo, TAM: (871) 225-26

Warehousing

Almacenadora de Banpais
Paras Sur 860
64000 Monterrey, NL
(83) 401-944

Almacenadora Banpacifico
Calle 14 No. 730-112
44200 Guadalajara, JAL
(36) 145-549

Almacenadora de Hermosillo, S.A.
Blvd. Luis Encinas y Monteverde
Col. San Benito
83190 Hermosillo, SON
(621) 407-30

Almacenadora Monterrey, S.A. de C.V.
Virginia Fabregas 74
Col. San Rafael
06470 Mexico, DF
(5) 705-5150

Almacenadora del Nordeste, S.A.
Av. Manuel L. Barragón y Prol.

Lerdo de Tejeda No. 777
Col. Centro
San Nicolas de los Garza, NL
(83) 760-505

Almacenadora del Norte
Río Mixcoac 25
Piso 11
03940 Mexico, DF
(5) 524-2558

Almacenadora del Norte
5ta Av. 123
66480 Monterrey, NL
(83) 510-123

Almacenadora Monterrey
Calz. Azc La Villa 867
02300 Mexico, DF
(5) 587-0940

Almacenadora Monterrey
M. González 321
06920 Mexico, DF
(5) 583-3848

Almacenadora Monterrey
Vasconcelos 209 Ote.
Piso 2
66260 Monterrey, NL
(83) 781-813

Almacenadora Tijuana, S.A. (ALTISA)
Av. Ferrocarril No. 319
20 de Noviembre
22430 Tijuana, BCN
(66) 812-985

Almacenes del Pais, S.A. de C.V.
Blvd. Centro Industrial No. 1023-1025
Industrial Puente de Vigas
54070 Tlalnepantla, Edo. Mex.
(5) 390-4843

Fideicomiso del Limon NAFINSA
Emperadores 35-A
03300 Mexico, DF
(5) 539-9348

Frigoríficos y Almacenes, S.A.
San Juan de Aragón No. 214
Constitución de la República
07460 Mexico, DF
(5) 577-0041

Index